Essays on Law, Morality, and Religion

More Titles of Interest from St. Augustine's Press

Charles E. Rice, *What Happened to Notre Dame*

Charles E. Rice, *Right or Wrong?: Forty Years Inside Notre Dame*

Kenneth Baker, s.j., *Jesus Christ – True God and True Man*

Robert Hugh Benson, *Lord of the World*

Rémi Brague, *On the God of the Christians
(and on one or two others)*

Albert Camus, *Christian Metaphysics and Neoplatonism*

Edward Feser, *The Last Superstition:
A Reflection on the New Atheism*

Ernest Fortin, a.a., *Christianity and Philosophical Culture
in the Fifth Century*

H.S. Gerdil, *The Anti-Emile: Reflections on the Theory
and Practice of Education against the Principles of Rousseau*

Peter Geach, *God and the Soul*

Marc D. Guerra, ed., *Jerusalem, Athens, and Rome:
Essays in Honor of James V. Schall, s.j.*

Leszek Kolakowski, *Religion: If There Is No God . . .*

C.S. Lewis and Don Giovanni Calabria, *The Latin Letters of C.S. Lewis*

Gerhart Niemeyer, *The Loss and Recovery of Truth*

Gabriel Marcel, *Man against Mass Society*

George J. Marlin, *The American Catholic Voter*

Josef Pieper, *The Christian Idea of Man*

Josef Pieper, *Happiness and Contemplation*

Josef Pieper, *In Tune with the World: A Theory of Festivity*

Josef Pieper and Heinz Raskop, *What Catholics Believe*

Servais Pinckaers, o.p., *Morality: The Catholic View*

George William Rutler, *Principalities and Powers: Spiritual Combat*

James V. Schall, *The Regensburg Lecture*

James V. Schall, *The Modern Age*

Dietrich von Hildebrand, *The Heart*

J. David Woodard, *The Politics of Morality*

Essays on Law, Morality, and Religion

by Gerard V. Bradley

ST. AUGUSTINE'S PRESS
South Bend, Indiana

Manufactured in the United States of America

1 2 3 4 5 6   20 19 18 17 16 15 14

Library of Congress Cataloging in Publication Data
Bradley, Gerard V., 1954–
Essays on law, morality, and religion / by Gerard V. Bradley.
p. cm.
Includes index.
ISBN 978-1-58731-230-4 (paperbound: alk. paper)
1. Law – Moral and ethical aspects – United States. 2. Criminal justice, Administration of – Moral and ethical aspects – United States.
3. Same-sex marriage – Law and legislation – United States.
4. Same-sex marriage – Moral and ethical aspects – United States.
5. Freedom of religion – United States. I. Title.
KF384.B73 2013
174'.30973 – dc23   2012039824

∞ The paper used in this publication meets the minimum requirements of the American National Standard for Information Sciences Permanence of Paper for Printed Materials, ANSI Z39.481984.

ST. AUGUSTINE'S PRESS
www.staugustine.net

CONTENTS

INTRODUCTION

Public discourse in America (and in much of the West) about what the law *ought* to be is remarkably reticent about the discourse of *ought, par excellence,* that of genuine morality. It is not that our public disputation lacks turgid rhetoric or appeals to high-minded goals. There is plenty of both, just as there is much talk about different moralities. Our discourse is suffused with talk about how people have diverse views about justice and human well-being, and about norms of public argument which pay homage to abiding moral and religious pluralism. In these precincts of discourse there is plenty said, too, about what counts as a "reasonable" moral position, and about whether even absurd moral views are sincerely held. We hear, in other words, a lot about conventional morality, or what it is in fact that some people actually hold about morality.

What's missing from this picture is the vocabulary and grammar of moral *truth,* of what *really* is the case of human flourishing and about justice. There is too little about critical morality, about norms of right conduct which are supported, not (necessarily, or only) by tradition or the fact that someone believes them to be true, but by their truth. Even in our constitutional law, which is the realm of the moral values which most sharply define Americans as a distinctive people, there is scarcely an unguarded reference to critical morality. Our constitutional law is unfortunately almost monopolized by judicial modes of reasoning which are either about "original" values or about a moral vision which is somehow neither "original" nor critically justified, but simply "ours."

I do not suggest that our constitutional law or our public discourse more generally is actually innocent of affirmations (and denials) of what is really morally true. There is no such possibility. I do suggest, however, that we are carrying on a public discourse (and a constitutional jurisprudence) as if shadow boxing, as if looking through a glass darkly, or at least through public codes which conceal important premises from public view and which therefore shield those premises from the critical challenges which the stakes make imperative.

The essays in this book are offered as a corrective to the prevailing modes of discourse. In our public square, the truth about the three topics investigated in these pages—criminal justice, marriage law, and religious liberty—fit into this pattern of obscurity and incomprehension. It is not quite right to say that the public and constitutional discourse about these matters has altogether rejected moral truth claims (mine or anyone else's). It is that our manner of speaking obscures, elides, or rules out of order such claims. The central aim of this book is to show that we cannot intelligibly or justly proceed further along this path. The aim is to show in some detail just what the relevant moral foundations are and how grasping tight these roots illumines, justifies, and makes coherent our practices and thoughts about these crucially important matters.

I
CRIME AND PUNISHMENT

CHAPTER 1:

Retribution and the Morality of Punishment

INTRODUCTION

Punishing a criminal involves the deliberate imposition by the political community's administrative arm ("the state") of some harm upon an unwilling member of the society. Whether punishment takes the form of the rack or a fine or time in jail, the question arises just the same: how is such a grave imposition upon someone to be morally justified? Legal philosopher John Finnis asks "why a man's criminal guilt entitles certain persons [namely, public authorities] to do actions which would otherwise amount to direct attacks on basic human goods in the person of the criminal."[1] The question requires an answer. Oxford's John Gardner refers to the *prima facie* barbarity and the extraordinary abomination of deliberately "damaging … people's lives" by punishing them. Gardner says that this apparatus of privation "patently needs all the justificatory help it can get."[2]

In this chapter I try to answer the question: what justifies punishing criminals?

I

This question is usually treated in law school as an inquiry into the *point* or *purpose* or *rationale* of punishment. The question is typically the first topic in the introductory criminal law class. The laundry list of punishment's "purposes" on offer in the casebooks includes deterrence, rehabilitation, and incapacitation. These words refer to sanctioning a convicted criminal with a view to: providing a disincentive to others to commit similar crimes; making the criminal well; and isolating the wrongdoer from law-abiding people. The problem is that none of these "rationales" provides an adequate moral justification for punishing anyone. Retribution does. But it is secondary in the textbook discussions, and its meaning is mangled there, anyway.

Confusion about retribution and the moral justification of punishment is not limited to the classroom. Scholarly literature is only occasionally more lucid. Legislators rarely understand retribution and (to my knowledge) never accord it the central place which it should occupy if the institution of punishment is to be adequately morally justified. Political rhetoric about crime and punishment oscillates between "get-tough-by-locking-them-up" to second thoughts about the budget strains of locking up what is—by far—the world's largest prison population.

Judges are little more clued in. Supreme Court Justice Anthony Kennedy waxed high-minded about punishment at the 2003 meeting of the American Bar Association. His pointed comments about punishment brought forth a major review of sentencing philosophy by the ABA (the *Report of the Kennedy Commission*). Kennedy's speech was widely hailed as insightful. It was received as a clarion call to collective action. Kennedy struck a responsive chord; his speech hit the sweet spot of contemporary reflection about the morality of punishment.

Justice Kennedy said nothing about retribution, and what he did say about punishment's justification was tragically misguided. The Justice's central message was that punishment is needed to vindicate the law, to acknowledge the suffering of the victim, and to deter future crimes. Still, the prisoner is a person; he or she is still part of the family of humankind. A little later in his talk Justice Kennedy acknowledged that the debate over the goals of sentencing is a difficult one. Then he added:

> Prevention and incapacitation are often legitimate goals. Some classes of criminals commit scores of offenses before they are caught, so one conviction may reflect years of criminal activity. There are realistic limits to efforts at rehabilitation. We must try, however, to bridge the gap between proper skepticism about rehabilitation on the one hand and improper refusal to acknowledge that the more than two million inmates in the United States are human beings . . . .[3]

In these few sentences Kennedy succinctly articulates the central defect in how American society understands punishment: that "we" are simply *using* two million people at a time, just so many "human beings" that we have given up on, whose well-being and dignity no longer count. It is us or them. Kennedy juxtaposes two kinds of goals for punishment: prevention and incapacitation on the one hand, and rehabilitation on the other. Then he implicitly asserts that rehabilitation acknowledge[s] the prisoner's humanity, while prevention and incapacitation do not. Kennedy nowhere mentions retribution.

America's Catholic bishops stand within a long tradition of fruitful reflection upon retributive accounts of punishment. This tradition includes ample testimony to retribution as the central moral justification of punishment. In his address to the Sixth International Congress of Penal Law (in 1954) Pope Pius XII said that "punishment is the reaction, required by law and justice, to crime: they are like a blow and a counter-blow. The order violated by the criminal act demands the restoration and reestablishment of the equilibrium which has been disturbed." Pius XII calls this the "ultimate meaning" and "most important function" of punishment. The Catechism of the Catholic Church expresses the same conviction, when it says that the "primary aim" of punishment is "redressing the disorder introduced by the offense." Pope John Paul II said the same thing in his 1995 encyclical letter on life issues, *Evangelium vitae*. He asserted that the point of criminals' punishment is to redress the disorder caused by the offense. As the *Catechism* plainly states: "Punishment has the primary aim of redressing the disorder introduced by the offense."[4] All of these comments point to retribution, and reflect a basically sound understanding of it.

In their most recent collective statement about criminal justice, however, America's bishops appear to be wholly innocent of this tradition. By an overwhelmingly vote at their November 2000 meeting the bishops adopted a document titled *Responsibility, Rehabilitation, and Restoration: A Catholic Perspective on Crime and Criminal Justice*. There is some talk in it of "protecting society." The document makes clear that this "protection" is comprised of two things: reducing the incidence of crime through deterrence, and helping victims get themselves back in order. Indeed, "restoring" victims and rehabilitating criminals are clearly, according to the bishops, the good—that is, the upright and morally valuable—aims of punishment. Even "redress[ing]" the disorder caused by the criminal offense is largely reduced to "allow[ing] victims to move from a place of pain and anger to one of healing and retribution." The closest the document comes to expressing the view that retribution morally justifies punishment is probably this jumbled sentence: "In our tradition, restoring the balance of rights through restitution is an important element of justice." But even this sentence seems to be another reference to (somehow) making the particular crime victim whole.

When all was said and done, the bishops end up with Justice Kennedy and all those many for whom Kennedy spoke: punishment aims to make *us* safer by doing bad things to *them*. It is a regrettable necessity, and there is an end to it. The distinctively *humane* (good, morally worthwhile, edifying) aims of punishment have strictly to do with helping both the individual victim and the criminal get better. Imprisonment as such—which is to say, *punishment* in its predominant form and thus the phenomenon which most needs to be morally justified—serves neither of these purposes.

II

One reason why retribution is so neglected by today's scholars, lawmakers, jurists, and bishops is that it is badly understood. If retribution means what these people seem to think it means, then it *ought* to be eclipsed in serious discussion of punishment's moral justification. But retribution is not *lex talionis*, the law of retaliation—"an eye for an eye."[5] It is true that "eye for an eye" is found in the Bible, and that it was apparently meant to actually guide the ancient Israelites' practical affairs (and was not allegorical or parabolic). *Lex talionis* does express one truth about punishment: its measure should be proportionate to the offense. But that is not any sort of moral justification *for* punishment, for *lex talionis* does not tell us anything about *why* gouging another's eye is the right thing to do. Scripture scholars give us good reason to believe, moreover, that "eye-for-an-eye" was not originally meant to be an authorization of punishment, much less was it a divine command to exact a like penalty upon wrongdoers, whatever the wrong done. *Lex talionis* was instead a directive to limit retaliatory acts by victims' kin and friends to no more than the loss incurred. Besides, to apply the "eye for an eye" norm non-metaphorically, a community would have to be willing to do whatever its most depraved members might do. Probably no human society has so completely abandoned moral constraint in its handling of malefactors, though a few might have come close.

The historical prevalence and perennial allure of retaliatory excess—vendettas, blood feuds, honor killings, and the like—surely contributed to the emergence of public systems of criminal justice. According to the legal philosopher John Gardner, it was "for the elimination of these modes of retaliation, more than anything else, [that] the criminal law as we know it today came into existence."[6] Even so, we must distinguish between what

Gardner calls the "displacement" function of organized, state-imposed punishment and its critical moral justification. One has to do with historical facts, albeit with facts about what certain people in the past thought they were morally justified in doing. The other concerns what it is right for us to do. The former has to do with conventional (past) morality. The latter is solely about critical morality, and there is no necessary connection, either logically or practically, between a practice's origins and its critical moral worth. It is easy to see, too, that the "displacement function" cannot morally justify punishing anyone. Just because a crowd of people means to hurt someone does not justify a more organized attack upon that person's well-being.

Retribution's historical kinship with retaliation (whatever that connection is alleged to have been) does not change the fact that, understood as a critical moral proposition, retribution is not about domesticating popular hatred for a known criminal. It is not about channeling repugnance towards a particularly heinous crime into safer channels. An organized constabulary might, in some sense, be the historical successor to mobs of angry townsfolk armed with scythes and pitchforks. But punishment is not, nor should it be understood as, revenge, and "retribution" has nothing to do with these errors. Retribution need not and should not be driven by anger, hatred, or any other emotion; it is completely distinct from community outrage. It is admissible to hold that pacific tendencies are one desired effect or function of punishment, that punishment contributes to keeping the peace. But that is not to say that these tendencies constitute a moral justification for punishment. They do not. They do not illumine the true meaning of retribution.

The truth about retribution has nothing to do with H.L.A. Hart's famous suggestion that retribution traffics in the "intrinsic value" of inflicting suffering on wrongdoers.[7] Hart's notion that suffering could have any "intrinsic value" is itself odd, and troubling. Suffering is necessarily a privation, a loss, a difficulty, a subtraction from the way things ought to be. Suffering so described is just plain bad. By definition, something bad does not have "intrinsic value"; if it did, it would be good. It seems likely that what Hart actually had in mind was the fact that many people feel relieved when they see the unjust "pay" for their crimes, that the punishment is such a terminal point of analysis that one reasonably views its infliction as (one might say) a self-contained good. Maybe so, and the feeling is not itself wrong. But no such feeling is capable of morally justifying the practice of punishment.

III

What, then, is retribution?

The best way to begin answering that question is to begin with the birth of political society and the initial emergence of law.

In the absence of any established political order, people would do whatever they thought they should or, perhaps, could do, without any authoritative guidance from law. Their choices would not necessarily turn their environs into the uncontrollably selfish state of nature anticipated by Hobbes.[8] Absent political order, many (perhaps most) people would act reasonably, maybe even altruistically, and seek cooperation with others to achieve common benefits. No doubt some people would exploit the absence of enforced norms of conduct to selfishly manipulate and subordinate others. In any event, without law there would be no public, authoritative pattern according to which all could structure their cooperation for the general good. Each person would have to exercise personal judgment about the appropriate way to collaborate with those in society for mutual advantage and common good.

When people come to organize themselves into a political society, they establish (among other necessities and amenities) a single, authoritative scheme for structuring everyone's cooperation. One reason why a political society comes into existence is the felt need for just such a scheme. The utility of any such pattern for collaboration depends, however, upon its *exclusivity*; that is, upon its monopoly over the direction of persons' choices and actions affecting the common good. Under such a system, individuals are obliged to accept restrictions on their freedom to act on their own personal judgments about successful cooperation, lest all the prospective benefits of such a scheme be lost and the dangers which the scheme promises to forestall be visited. That authoritative scheme is likely to be some form of what we call law.

The following simple example illustrates these features and capacities of law. Neither driving on the left side of the road nor on the right is in itself immoral; there is no moral norm of the sort: drive to this side, or to that. Either side of the road could easily be chosen as the rule of the road. *Both*, however, cannot be chosen without disastrous consequences. But how is any society of drivers to settle upon right (or left), make known to everyone that it is to be right (or left), and then make sure that drivers go right (or left) by penalizing nonconforming behavior? Establishing legal norms such as the rule of driving right (or left) is one effective way.

Establishing such norms is how a public authority can make it *possible* for people to drive safely.

Fairness to others requires individuals to accept the pattern of liberty and restraint specified by political authorities. It would be unfair as well as dangerous for drivers to continue to follow their own designs on the road, in derogation of legal directives. Accepting this apparatus of political society and observing its requirements form the path of just collaboration with others. An equal liberty of free personal judgment and action as well as a fair distribution of restraint can be brought into being by law.

The central and invariable wrong in crime, we can now begin to see, is that the criminal unfairly usurps liberty to pursue his own interests and plans in a manner contrary to the common boundaries delineated by the law. Or, when the crime involves negligence, the offender demonstrates that he is unwilling to make the requisite effort to stay within the legally required pattern of restraint. The criminal's usurpation reaps for him an undue advantage over those who remain inside the legally required pattern of restraint.

Depriving the criminal of this ill-gotten advantage is the central aim or purpose of punishment. Since that advantage primarily consists of a wrongful exercise of freedom of choice and action, the most appropriate means to restore order is to deprive the criminal of that sort of freedom. Sometimes, a society's method(s) of punishing criminals includes sensory deprivation, even the infliction of transient pain, which will likely be experienced by the criminal as "suffering." Nonetheless and Hart notwithstanding, the essence of punishment is to restrict a criminal's will by depriving him of the right to be the sole author of his own actions. The goal of punishment is just to undo the criminal's bold and unjust assertion of his own will; punishment restores the equilibrium of liberty and restraint across society by diminishing (as it were) the criminal's lot. The proportionate punishment of criminals assures everyone in society that crime does not pay and that observing the law does or, at least, that law-abiding folks are not unfairly disadvantaged by criminal activity, when the situation is viewed diachronically.

IV

In his *Prolegomenon to Punishment*, H.L.A. Hart suggested that society may impose punishment on an offender only where society has been harmed. So far so good. Hart identified two types of possible harm to society: where the authority of law is diminished, and where a member of society is injured.[9] Hart's first category sounds, perhaps, like an awkward description of the retributive view described in Part III of this chapter. In reality, Hart has something very different in mind. He exhibited a solid understanding of the excess-liberty phenomenon just described here, but only in the context of tort compensation. In *The Concept of Law*, Hart refers explicitly to the artificial equality that just law imposes upon the inequalities of nature by forbidding the strong and cunning from exploiting their natural advantages to cheat or harm weaker or guileless individuals. This legal equality is disrupted, Hart concluded, whenever a *tortfeasor*—someone who injures another person (or persons) by careless acts— is "indulging his wish to injure [another person] or not sacrificing his ease to the duty of taking adequate precautions."[10] Legal remedies for torts attempt to restore the "moral status quo" in which victim and wrongdoer are, once again, on equal footing.[11]

In his account of torts Hart nearly describes (in effect) how retribution could explain and justify punishment of criminals. But Hart was confident *a priori* that retribution was solely a matter of inflicting suffering in return for wickedness, a premise derived in part from his assumption that punishment was simply about inflicting pain. Perhaps it never occurred to Hart to extend his initial idea from tort to crime and from victim to law-abiding citizen, even when, as in his book *Punishment and Responsibility*, he seemed very close to such a result.

The second harm Hart mentioned—that a member of society is injured—is also problematic, considered as both an explanation and as a justification for punishing criminals. For one thing, this harm is the focus of private law and especially that of torts, where the basic aim is to make the aggrieved specific victim "whole" (by and through remedies underwritten by the tortfeasor). But mature legal systems maintain criminal justice systems to redress the "harm" of crimes *in addition to* the remedies available according to private law. This double redress (if you will) obtains even where the underlying act—say, rape—is the same in the criminal proceeding as in what amounts to a parallel tort claim. Presumably then the criminal "wrong" is different from the tort.

Hart is scarcely the only philosopher to seek the roots of criminal justice in the soil of private wrongs. Richard Swinburne, in his recommendation of retributive punishment, indicated that the state only has authority to impose punishment for criminal harm where it serves as a proxy for the individual harmed.[12] Swinburne imagined a state of nature similar to that described by John Locke, in which individuals hold an exclusive right to punish those who harm them.[13] The idea here is that when political society is born, its administrative apparatus (the state) receives, as if by transfer or delegation, everyone's natural right to correct wrongs.[14]

Hart, Swinburne, and Locke are all mistaken. Civil society does not punish as transferee or delegate of the individual victim(s). Civil society punishes in its own name for its own sake because civil society is the victim of crime in a way distinct from the way that wrongdoing may victimize a tort plaintiff. As we have seen, the emergence of civil society—with its authoritative direction for how to cooperate with others—makes punishment possible, and intelligible. Civil society (and its laws) is a necessary condition of punishment, conceptually inseparable from it.

The transfer theory of punishment cannot explain our current penal code. Criminal acts often do involve an injustice to one or more specific persons: the defrauded old lady, the black-eyed assault victim, the hapless involuntary pedestrian whose car was stolen. But there are also many "victimless" crimes, such as drug possession, gambling, and prostitution. Some spectacular offenses (including treason, espionage, and lying to the grand jury) victimize the whole community, yet no one in particular, and usually no one more than any other person. The whole community is similarly victimized, though less seriously, in pollution or "quality of life" street offenses like public intoxication. The definition—indeed, the intelligibility—of some crimes arises only after a distinct, political community comes into being. These offenses "against the state" (treason, perjury) or "public morals" (public intoxication, gambling) victimize no one in particular. Their victim is the undifferentiated community. The manner in which a community is victimized by these crimes complements the conception of crime outlined in Part II as a usurpation of liberty. Where there is no particular victim, who could possibly "transfer" his or her natural right to punish to the state. And, if it be supposed that the transferor is in these cases everyone, then the force of the whole natural-right-to-punish foundation of sentencing is vitiated.

There is good reason to deny that individuals have any natural right to punish others, even in a state-less precursor to modern society's criminal justice system. Apart from the special case of the *pater familias*, no one has a natural right to punish another. Wicked deeds are a necessary but not a sufficient condition of punishment. Assume that *A* misbehaves and that his misbehavior warrants the judgment: *A* deserves to be punished. But saying that *A* deserves to be punished does not imply that *B*, *C*, *D*, or anyone else has the right to punish A. Imposing some privation upon a malefactor is an act that requires its own moral justification. Even in advanced legal systems, violations of law do not automatically authorize anyone to punish the violator; only certain officials wielding designated powers according to the relevant positive law are designated competent to punish others. In fact, we regularly witness acts of injustice by others—lying spouses, cruel parents, disrespectful children, cheating colleagues. But it scarcely occurs to us that each, or any, of us is authorized to punish those bad actions. We are conditioned by custom, experience, and the law to suffer criminal harms without becoming a vigilante. We recognize that police have the right to arrest and courts the power to punish; we have neither.

Individuals *do* possess a natural right of self-defense. In certain social conditions, this genuine authority resembles a putative natural right to punish and is therefore sometimes conceptually confused with it. People are also sometimes required to make their own arrangements to be made whole where they have been victimized by others; call this a natural right to a remedy. Again and especially if conjoined to self-defensive measures, *ad hoc* remedial action can look a lot like punishment—and thus heighten conceptual confusion. In a frontier settlement beyond the reach of any government's writ, for example, individuals, families, and allied groups might have to drive off cattle rustlers and forcibly recover property unlawfully acquired by such offenders; to do otherwise might court starvation for all the law-abiding folks around. But even forcible recovery of stolen livestock need not and should not be seen as an exercise of any natural right to *punish*.

To further illustrate how the conceptual confusion can be unwound in even desperate social conditions, let us presume a "state of nature" in which predatory nomads raid Farouq's oasis reserve, threaten to injure his family, and then escape with his herd. Before the marauders return for a reprise, Farouq gathers friends to help him fend off or capture the invaders. He sets his plan. And he waits.

Around midnight, Farouq's crew subdues and restrains the raiders, injuring two of them quite badly in the course of rebuffing their attempts to keep what they had previously stolen. Farouq takes back his livestock. But has he *punished* anyone? No: recovering one's own from a wrongful possessor is not to *punish* anyone. Should the raiders—who are subdued but unrepentant and who firmly believe in vendettas—now be let go, with a stern admonition to be kinder to their neighbors? There is after all no "justice system" to which they could be transferred. Farouq is the Elder who is finally responsible for the safety and well-being of everyone living at the oasis. If Farouq drove the rustlers out into the desert, they might return again, angrier than before, after Farouq's proto-posse had disbanded, or gone to sleep.

Let us imagine then that Farouq eventually decides, after careful reflection, that the only way to defend his family and property from these determined raiders is drop them into a deep pit, from which escape is impossible. He does so not quite intending to kill them, but rather to effectively incapacitate them in the only available effective way. This decision resembles the decision to impose capital punishment. It seems rather that, in this limited case, Farouq is exercising his right of self-defense with the only effective means available to him. The only way for Farouq to restrain his enemies is to consign them to an almost certain though not quite intended death.

In this snapshot from the state of nature, the righteous (and, in this case, the stronger) may seem to be *malefactors*. The bad guys do get it in the end. But that does not mean that the concept of punishment is in this violent picture. Natural rights are indeed necessary to make any moral sense out of Farouq's behavior, but those rights can and should be limited to the rights of self-help and self-defense. Punishment does not really have anything to do with it.

V

We can now put to rest the canard that retribution is "backward-looking," and for that reason somehow counterproductive, or dogmatic, or both. The leading contrast in this mistaken evaluation is deterrence, which (it is said, truly enough) anticipates a beneficial societal result (namely, less crime). But if the goal of retribution is to reestablish the balance of political society, as I have argued throughout this chapter, it is not usefully described as "backward-looking" at all. Retribution is as forward-looking as is deterrence. The difference lies rather in the accounts' particular vision of the future.

Hart relied upon the notion that retribution is "backward"-looking to discredit it. He considered the question: if, on the last day of civilization, only the hangman and the condemned remained on the town square, should the hangman execute the lawfully-imposed sentence? Kant famously concluded that such an execution not only may proceed but also must do so,[15] a position that Hart erroneously assumed was necessarily held by all retributivists.[16]

Hart's assumption is mistaken for two reasons. First, as discussed previously, the purpose of punishment in the retributive view of it is not to make the wicked "suffer," much less to do so for its own sake ("intrinsic value"). The purpose of punishment is to restore social balance. Second, that a person is capable of inflicting suffering on an offender does not indicate that he is morally authorized to do so. The hangman's authority to punish (as the presumably faithful remnant of public authority) may be taken as established. Yet his authority exists solely to preserve the common good of society, an institution long gone by the time only the hangman and the condemned remain. In my view, no one—not even a hangman—may act for the alleged common good of a nonexistent society. Thus, on the last day of civilization, the condemned would receive a stay of execution, and he and the hangman would be left to "work things out" as best they can.

VI

I said in Part I of this opening chapter that retribution is out of vogue these days, and that it is misunderstood where it is not completely neglected. But arguing that retribution should drive the moral justification of punishment is not like advocating that we dust off an outmoded or impractical moralism, as if retribution were somehow a "justification-in-exile." Retribution not only performs the invaluable service of helping us to understand and to then morally justify an essential but morally challenging social practice, namely, the deliberate and widespread imposition by society of serious harms upon its own (often enough) least able and most underprivileged members. Retribution also provides morally satisfying explanations for some anchor commitments within that social practice, commitments which cannot be easily explained by other so-called "aims" of punishment (deterrence and the like).

One such commitment is the now nearly universal practice of naming the entire community as plaintiff in a criminal case. Why are the "People" (or the "State" or the "Commonwealth") the complaining party in every criminal case? If the individual victim's loss is the moral lodestar of criminal justice, why not name that person, perhaps represented (for contingent reasons) by some public employee? In legal terms, why not then *The State ex rel. John Q. Victim*? If the whole point of the action is to rehabilitate the accused, why is it an adversarial ("versus") action at all? Why not (in legal terms again) style the matter *In re John Q. Criminal* (that is, *In the matter of John Q. Criminal*)? Retribution explains and justifies our invariable practice of naming criminal lawsuits as *The People* (or *State* or *Commonwealth* or some other public authority) *v. John Criminal* by showing how society *as a whole* is victimized by every criminal act. In addition to any harms to specific individuals, each criminal act victimizes the whole community.

Retribution also underwrites the whole moralistic framework and language of criminal justice in a way that no other account of punishment can do: "praise and blame"; "freedom and responsibility"; "guilt and innocence"; "crime and punishment." This whole panoply of concepts and terms is part and parcel of our criminal justice experience. It is well supported by retributive theory, which identifies the constant element of each crime as an unjust choice to exploit the entire community. Equally well explained and justified too is the overwhelmingly act- and choice- specific focus of the criminal law. No one's uncharitable attitudes, character defects, or personality disorders (all of which might trigger intervention in a rehabilitative or reformative regime of punishment) are fit occasions of punishment. The reason they are not predicates for punishment in our system owes to the fact that they are not *acts* carrying out *free choices* to treat everyone else *unfairly*. Proponents of rehabilitation and paternalistic moral reformers are hardly able to explain why their particular ministrations must always await—by dint of an unyielding moral imperative—the performance of some prohibited act and subsequent conviction.[17]

Another indication of how retribution explains and justifies punishment has to do with a perennial chestnut of first-year criminal law classes. What if a public authority could stave off riots and mayhem only by hanging an innocent person popularly believed to be guilty? The commonplace statement of moral priorities in our society has long been "better that a hundred guilty persons go free than that one innocent suffer."[18] Perhaps a hundred is hyperbole. Blackstone put the number at ten. The reader might say ten, or twenty. No matter: any such number (greater than one, I suppose) expresses an important truth: a just society never wittingly convicts an innocent. In fact, a just society does everything reasonably possible to avoid unwittingly doing so.

Why? What are the moral underpinnings of this commitment, which is deeply embedded in our law and institutions?

Where retribution forms the moral justification for punishment, the problem of punishing the innocent can be solved. The aim of retribution is always frustrated and never served by punishing the innocent. Punishing someone who has committed no offense is counterproductive: if someone has not distorted society's equilibrium by committing a criminal act, harming him cannot restore that equilibrium, especially while the truly deserving party escapes retribution. Making an innocent disgorge his bold act of will is simply impossible, for there is nothing to be disgorged. Punishing the innocent is easily seen by retributive light for what it is: scapegoating which, even if it could be somehow morally justified, is surely not *punishment* at all.

I do not suggest that, in cases of extreme need, it is morally impermissible for *one* to pay the ultimate price for the welfare of many. We have all heard of individuals who stepped into harm's way, of persons who sacrificed themselves for others. Heroic soldiers draw fire in battle while others run for cover, and some even more heroic fall on grenades to save a buddy or two. Saint Maximillian Kolbe chose the place of another destined for a Nazi gas chamber. Dickens's Sidney Carton and the passengers on the United Airlines flight that crashed in Pennsylvania on September 11, 2001, are civilian examples of people who chose to accept certain death in order to prevent harm to others.

Sometimes, the multitudes benefit by conscripting a reluctant heroine. "Typhoid Mary" spent decades in quarantine on the East River to protect the rest of her community from infection. Her selection was obviously reasonable: as the source of infection, it would make no sense (logically or morally) to have quarantined anyone but Mary. Yet it cannot be said that she "volunteered" in the traditional sense of the word.[19] Sometimes, too, a stranger is authoritatively selected to make the ultimate sacrifice, perhaps the lone passerby who is sent on a dangerous but necessary assignment. This apparent disproportion, morally palatable so long as the selection is fair, may bear an uncanny resemblance to the regrettable execution of a scapegoat for deterrent purposes.

But the two circumstances are not, in moral truth, nearly the same. Scapegoating the innocent cannot be understood by those doing the scapegoating as punishment. Passing off the oppression of an innocent as "punishment"—a necessity if the goal of scapegoating is to be attained—necessarily involves deception: the scapegoat would have to be declared "guilty" of the heinous act about which the citizenry is enraged. The scapegoat is no volunteer. His selection is neither fair nor reasonable. He is chosen usually for his membership in some despised class or for his resemblance to the villains of popular imagination.

Non-retributive "aims" of punishment stumble over the innocents. A utilitarian concern for tranquility, for example, may be served as well or better by the sacrifice of innocents. If we consider rehabilitation in either its therapeutic or moral sense, one can scarcely argue that the law's ministrations must be limited only to those justly convicted of a crime. Some people need moral or psychological help, quite apart from any criminal misbehavior. In all these perspectives the line between guilt and innocence is not simply blurred; it seems to be an arbitrary impediment to getting the job done.

Retribution also makes good sense of some important recent developments in our criminal justice system. It points, for example, towards the "determinate" sentencing which is (happily, I should say) much favored today. "Determinate" sentencing laws stipulate a specific, narrow range of penalties for each specific crime. A typical "determinate" sentencing statute might stipulate that anyone convicted of, say, armed robbery receive a prison sentence of between six and eight years, whereas an "indeterminate" sentencing law might leave judges free to impose any term of years up to eight, with even a possibility of an entirely non-custodial sentence. These more fluid sentencing schemes were in vogue from around 1960 to 1980; vestiges remain. They were fueled by two mistakes. One had to do with our main focus here, the "point" or "goal" of punishment. Enthusiasts for "rehabilitating" criminals thought that the key to sentencing was to hold someone until mental health professionals advising the parole board judged that he (or she) exhibited adequate signs of adjusting to the social demands. This mistaken basis for "indeterminate" sentences was compounded by another misunderstanding, this one about the "causes" of crime. The view was that, just to the extent that crimes were not the symptoms of mental problems, they were the inevitable and understandable response of the underprivileged to their surroundings. Anyone caught in the maws of this complex explanation of crime—and many who should have known better, were—could scarcely see crime as anything like a free wrongful choice which victimizes ordinary people. In the era of criminal as victim, retribution was invisible.

When retribution is brought back into view, however, and accompanied by a sound understanding of the unvarying wrong in each criminal act, the "causes" of crime recede from view, replaced by a focus on wrongful choices. Sentencing is bound to be more "determinate" because the essential harm of any crime is cabined within a defined act performed on a particular occasion, and the measure of punishment required to redress it is both conceptually and morally tied tight around that discrete act and its particular harm. Punishment in this scheme of thinking is not—at least, not mainly or centrally—about getting the offender well, scaring others from a life of crime, or even about warehousing dangerous folks indefinitely ("general" and "specific" deterrence, respectively).

Retribution points straightaway to a negative judgment, however, on the growing movement today to institutionalize respect for "victim rights." The specific victim(s) of a criminal act surely deserve to be taken seriously. They should be treated well by all actors in the criminal justice system, from their first police encounter all the way through to trial and sentencing; in fact, they should be treated better than they generally are. But soliciting victims' opinions about the disposition of what some call "their" cases, and memorializing their input about appropriate penalties— as is more and more often the case—gives victims' opinions credence and weight which may be inappropriate. After all, *society* is the operative victim in each criminal case, and it is duly represented by a public authority, namely, the prosecutor. Reconciling victims with their victimizers is not a bad idea. But it is in most cases quixotic, and in no case should it be a priority of those public officials who are in charge of criminal justice matters.

VII

Retribution does not provide a calculus or map from which one can mechanically read off what a particular defendant's sentence ought to be. Legislative and judicial authorities necessarily (and rightly) make important choices in setting up sentencing schemes and in entering judgment in individual cases. Untutored moral reflection tells us that assault and theft should be treated as crimes. But such moral thinking cannot stipulate which specific privations should be imposed for those crimes. The sentence for an offender is not directly deducible from any single relevant factor. It necessarily involves decisions guided, but not dictated, by reason. Retribution nonetheless supplies a guiding norm: *proportionality.* There are two relevant senses of it. One is that the measure of punishment— whatever it exactly is—be on par with the crime. There should be proportionality between usurpation and suppression. Sentencing should also be guided by a sense of where the instant crime (the usurpation of liberty) fits coherently within the global pattern of sentences authorized in a particular legal system. So, the intentional infliction of bodily injury should be treated more gravely than the negligent infliction of it. And murder should be treated more seriously than assault.

Retribution is not a theory of crimes. It does not tell us much about which acts are so unfair to others and which so harm the common good that they ought to be denominated as "crimes"—and *punished* accordingly. But retribution nonetheless supplies important *limits* upon the nature of conduct which may properly be made a crime. One example of this limitation in action pertains to the growing phenomenon most often called "overcriminalization." The laws embraced by the term criminalize conduct which is not only morally innocuous. They often capture conduct which would otherwise be natural and even desirable in business, commercial, accounting, or everyday life. The worry about "overcriminalization" is, centrally, about strict liability regulatory offenses. "Overcriminalization" is mainly a worry about federal, and state, criminal law.

A focal case of "overcriminalization" might be a law which makes a business executive criminally liable whenever a subordinate fails to file a certain form required by regulatory authorities. Full stop. No actual knowledge of the failure (by the executive) is required to make the criminal case. No more schematic dereliction is required, either. That is, there need be no systemic laxity or failure of oversight. Let's call this our "central case" of overcriminalization.

I offer below five distinct criticisms of this phenomenon. Each is based upon moral principle. Each cuts deeply. Together (that is, cumulatively) they support the conclusion that the central case of "over-criminalization" is a case of unjust punishment; which is to say that it should not be done. To say that plainly: if *punishment* would be unjust (unsupported, even scarcely intelligible) according to the basic moral justification for punishing *anyone,* then the conduct nominated for criminal status is not a suitable candidate at all. I do not consider whether any one of the criticisms, or some combination of them short of five, supports this strong conclusion.

The first criticism of the central case is perhaps the most basic: "overcriminalization" is the product of a deterrent driver. As the Manhattan Institute's Marie Gryphon writes: "[O]ften the overriding reason for enacting a piece of legislation is to produce an overall social benefit, and the criminal sanctions attached to certain forms of conduct . . . are chiefly aimed at conducing to that benefit by deterring that conduct rather than stigmatizing it and punishing the person who carried it out. . . ."[20]

It is not altogether misleading to say that the goal of any criminal justice system is that certain conduct become rarer than it otherwise would be. It is often said that retribution looks backward while deterrence, for example, looks forward and anticipates a beneficial societal result (specifically, less crime). In this construal, retribution may also be said to inflict socially useless suffering upon people, and so be beyond the pale of worthy social policy. But we have seen already that the goal of retribution is to re-establish the balance of political society. Retribution is at least as forward-looking as deterrence, in that both theories of punishment attempt to positively affect society *after* the incidence of criminal activity, albeit in different ways. Deterrent aims may be integrated (up to a point) with retributive moral underpinnings in a functioning criminal justice system, such as our own.[21]

The sole goal of deterrence is to reduce future incidence of crime. Deterrence thinking is suffused with utilitarian theories of value, and tends towards social engineering. Retribution aims to restore a lost balance of fairness and equality, for its own sake—and not (as utilitarians would probably insist) because it is an overall state of affairs which includes proportionally more of whatever goods or values or preferences than it does of corresponding negations, however these matters are determined.

The second criticism is pretty basic too: "over-criminalization" confuses the whole moralistic aspect of criminal law and its enforcement, in two very different ways. The first boggle arises from the fact that for the foreseeable future conviction of a crime will continue to stigmatize the offender as morally deficient, as the possessor of tainted if not just plain bad character. But someone convicted in our central case does not deserve this obloquy. Nor is he rightly made to suffer the many collateral consequences—all the legal and informal social disabilities and handicaps—that come with a criminal conviction.

The second confusion stems from the first. Precisely because our central case defendant is not a moral reprobate, the moral obloquy of criminal conviction is liable to be watered down by its improvident extension to him by "over-criminalization." This sullying effect is not limited to the precise offense at issue or to a class of similar offenses. It is, rather, the general social identification of criminal conviction with serious moral fault that is diffused across the board. Because there are very good reasons to retain and to preserve this connection and to preserve it as a common good, "over-criminalization" portends a potentially serious social harm.

The third criticism is basic, too. It hearkens back to the retributive understanding of the defining harm of criminal conduct: the malefactor's unilateral grab of more liberty than he is due. It is the morally reprehensible preference for one's own will over against the prescribed legal course and at the expense of the common good. Our central-case offender, however, had no opportunity to choose to comply with the law (or not). Or, he might have chosen to (try to) comply but non-negligently failed to do so. In either event, he ought not to be punished.

This criticism is complicated by our criminal justice system's nearly dogmatic commitment to the proposition *ignorantia legis neminem excusat*—"ignorance of the law is no excuse." This maxim may be an impregnable—and largely sound—element of our criminal litigation system; at least any alternative maxim could present intractable problems of proof, and might portend too much lawbreaking license. But "overcriminlization" is not a courtroom issue. It is a policy question for legislators. In that arena, the anticipation that many people who could be prosecuted in our central cases would not have chosen to ignore the established pattern of restraint and forbearance—and so would not have chosen to selfishly and unfairly preferred their own will and freedom of judgment—is a very good reason *not* to enact the proposed criminal legislation.

The fourth criticism grows partly out the third. This fourth criticism depends also upon a moral imperative: punishment of criminals is necessary to avoid the injustice which would otherwise fester in the wake of any criminal's unfair usurpation of liberty. Punishment assures all of those who adhere to the law that they are not, for that reason, hapless losers, suckers, or chums.

John Finnis explains this important point more fully:

> There is a need to give the law-abiding the encouragement of knowing that they are not being abandoned to the mercies of criminals, that the lawless are not being left to the peaceful enjoyment of ill-gotten gains, and that to comply with the law is not to be a mere sucker: for without this support and assurance the indispensable co-operation of the law-abiding is not likely to be continued.[22]

Just as our central case defendant can scarcely be accused of choosing to usurp liberty which society's members deny to themselves, society's members can scarcely be described as "suckers" for not doing likewise.

The fifth criticism depends upon recognizing how retribution guides the competent lawmaker towards a schedule of actual sentences. There are two very different facets to this picture. Moral principles can tell the lawmaker that assault and theft, for example, should be treated as crimes and that those who commit these crimes should be punished. But moral principles—including those supplied by the retributive justification of punishment—do not by themselves tell the lawmaker which privations should be imposed for those crimes. Nor does moral principle tell the lawmaker how much of any specific privation—confinement, a fine, community service, civil disabilities—is just right. There is, in truth, a very substantial range of free choice here for the lawmaker.

The retributive understanding of punishment implies that any sentence be doubly proportional—first to the harm caused by the crime, and second among the various crimes, so that the more egregious crimes be subject to proportionally greater sanction. Retribution also provides a common metric of harm according to which the appropriate sanction may be gauged.

How so? The essential harm of a crime is not mainly the tangible loss to a specific victim. If that were the case, then we would not have (for example) the many gradations of homicide that we do have, ranging from murder in the first degree all the way down to negligent homicide, and then off the criminal chart entirely to actionable civil homicides and then to cases those in which one person causes the death of another without acting unlawfully at all (the cases of accidents or justified killings). If that were the case, it would be hard to justify punishing attempts at all, much less at just a shade less than the punishment for consummated offenses.[23] Clearly, our criminal justice system is predicated upon an understanding of crime as—in some very basic way—a matter of bad choices.

By fleshing out those bad choices as unfair grabs of liberty retribution supplies a common measure of the harm done in every crime. This is not to say that the more tangible damage done by a criminal's bad choice does not matter at all. Someone who chooses to intentionally kill another human being has obviously demonstrated an extraordinary preference for his own freedom of choice, in gross derogation of any serious regard for the equal liberty and equal dignity of other people. This murderer's usurpation is much greater and more flamboyant than that of the petty thief—and they should each be sentenced accordingly.

The fifth criticism may therefore be stated this way: by eliminating *mens rea* and stipulating punishment for a morally innocuous act which the "wrongdoer" may never have chosen in conscious derogation of the legally specified pattern of mutual restraint, our central case defies intelligent sentencing. Sentencing for such an offense is either arbitrary or crudely (and therefore unjustly) tied to the raw tangible damage wrought by the putatively criminal act.

CONCLUSION

I do not maintain in this chapter that we entirely abandon other traditional justifications for punishment which may serve as valuable secondary aims. For example, a retributive system able to effectively detect crimes and apprehend criminals would also include considerable deterrence in the traditional sense, namely, the threat of bad consequences to motivate compliance among those tempted to commit crimes. Retribution also includes a second type of deterrence, which provides reassurance to the law-abiding that those who voluntarily obey the laws will not be sacrificed to those who would not. The main point of this chapter is that retribution is indispensable to any moral justification of punishment.

CHAPTER 2:

The Morality of Plea Bargaining

One widespread criticism of plea bargaining has been succinctly stated by Thomas Church: "So long as defendants routinely expect to receive some form of sentencing consideration in exchange for an admission of guilt, the essence of a system of bargain justice is present."[1] The idea is that "bargain justice" is defective justice. The view is that the state "cuts a deal" to get a case off its calendar, and that the defendant escapes some portion of that punishment which he, in truth, deserves. The implication is that the "routine" upon which plea bargaining depends should be significantly modified, if not eliminated. In short: plea bargaining is a morally dubious regimen, a regrettable necessity at best.

This is all quite mistaken. Most of those persons accused of crimes by prosecutors are really guilty and most of them should plead guilty. Any really guilty defendant who pleads guilty should receive a lighter sentence than he would have received upon conviction after trial. The "should" here is not the instrumental "will have to" of, on the one hand, the defendant seeking to minimize his losses or, on the other hand, the "system" keen to meet its quota of dispositions. The "should" here is the moral ought. Most really guilty defendants have a moral obligation to plead guilty. Those who discharge this duty *should* receive leniency.[2]

I begin the argument in support of this nest of conclusions by taking stock—in Part I of this chapter—of the manifold good effects brought into being by the pleading defendant. The criminally accused person has a singular opportunity to provide valuable benefits to other people precisely by pleading guilty and aborting a trial. Unless he has compelling reason not to do this good which only he can do, most guilty defendants should plead.

In Part II I bring these salutary effects into contact with the moral bases of punishing criminals—centrally, retribution and, secondarily, the moral reform and specific deterrence of the offender. In this Part we shall see how plea bargaining makes such moral sense as a transaction upon which punishment is predicated that the moral principles which justify and shape punishment *require* a reduced sentence for the pleading defendant.

Part III anticipates and meets some objection to the argument of Parts I and II.

In Part IV I identify some cases where the common good calls for a trial, even where the defendant is really guilty. Defendants in these cases should receive the same concessions that pleading defendants do, because (like the pleading defendant) these defendants do what they can to promote the well-being of others.

In Part V I identify some implications of the conclusions of previous parts for the conduct of criminal defense attorneys.

I

All criminally accused persons—no matter how guilty they in fact are and no matter how overwhelming the evidence against them happens to be— have the legal power to force the political community to prove its case against them. No defendant is obliged by the law to state, or even to have, any reason(s) for pleading "not guilty." It is as close to an unreviewable discretionary power as one is likely to encounter in the legal system. His "not guilty" plea is not an assertion (explicit or implicit) of innocence. "Not guilty" means, simply, "not admitting guilt." The guilty can therefore plead otherwise without deception. Our constitutional law stipulates, moreover, that the defendant need prove nothing at trial. The entire burden of proof rests upon the prosecution, and the law declares that no inference of guilt may be validly drawn from a defendant's decision to do, and to say, nothing at trial.

In our system of justice, then, the criminal defendant possesses a unilateral, and perhaps perfect (in the sense suggested in the preceding paragraph), freedom to go to trial. He unilaterally summons the "resources" needed to prove him guilty—or leaves them to be consumed by others. The court transcript of any plea colloquy reflects faithfully this command. The pleading defendant must be heard to understand that he freely relinquishes a set of personal prerogatives (rights to trial, compulsory process, to testify or not on his own behalf) established by the community for several reasons. Among these reasons is, to be sure, protecting accused persons against being railroaded into being convicted. But the civil liberties of the criminally accused are valuable to everyone else, too, for the community has no legitimate interest in punishing anyone undeserving of it, or in reducing someone in trouble to the status of a beast. Nonetheless, the typical plea allocution chiefly portrays the defendant as standing outside the community, arrayed over against it, with scarcely a moral obligation to anyone in it. It is all about the power "we" have over "him" and the concessions (usually, some dropped charges and an agreed-upon sentence) made in consideration of his waiving certain valuable rights.

There is no mention in most of these courtroom exchanges of the pleading defendant's contributions to the community, not a word about the benefits which he would bestow on sundry individuals by pleading guilty. There is usually no suggestion that the accused is doing anyone else any good at all, much less that he is discharging any moral obligation that he already possesses.

Now, there are sufficient reasons why the defendant has a perfect legal liberty to plead or not. There are also good reasons to not speak of any moral duty to plead guilty. One reason is that discussing moral duty might confuse the defendant about his legal prerogatives, and so produce a coerced plea. Even so, the positive contributions of the defendant's plea—its moral worth, if you will—could be, and should be, emphasized more than they presently are, especially by defense counsel.[3]

There are two basic sorts of positive contributions. Each is considerable. One has to do with communal goods preserved. The other involves individual burdens removed. The pleading defendant releases the community's resources provisionally dedicated to proving him guilty, and permits them to be directed to other worthwhile uses. In addition, the defendant who waives his right to trial releases various individual participants from their duties.

Let me explain.

The criminal justice system—the vast institutional apparatus located around the courthouse, populated by lawyers, judges, probation officers, attended by police officers, lab technicians, coroners, and civilian witnesses—is an indispensable and expensive community resource. This complex is maintained for the limited but important purpose of fairly and accurately adjudicating accusations of criminal misconduct. Since it is a resource of (at any given time) fixed dimensions, duties of fairness in its utilization arise for everyone with a say about how the resource is to be expended. The criminal defendant is one such person.

It makes no practical difference either to the existence of this duty or to its scope whether one thinks that the system is understaffed or underfunded, or even dysfunctional. The relevant duties of fairness do not depend upon opinions such as these. The duties arise from the law of supply and demand; there is a fixed quantity of common resources available to a number of users with legitimate claims upon them. Even if it is true (as this or that defendant thinks) that the stingy county council ought to spend more than it does on criminal justice, everyone must still use what is on offer fairly—just as one must *fairly* use the parks, roads, schools, and other public amenities that happen to exist, regardless of one's personal opinion about the measure of each that is, in fact, available.

When first we attempt an inventory of the good effects wrought by a guilty plea, we are tempted to focus upon these wholesale stock goods—dollars, man-hours, utilities, costs and benefits; the stuff of accountancy and human resources. Such calculations are useful in their way. But it is more perspicuous to gauge the pertinent effects by retail reckoning. Who gains most immediately by the pleading defendant's choice to turn back to the community scarce resources which he could have consumed? In which specific ways are these beneficiaries helped?

These prime receivers are not taxpayers or courthouse personnel. The chief beneficiaries of a plea are other criminal defendants, especially those for whom trials really are needed. *They* gain access to resources which they deserve and which become available as cases which should plead out, do. The gains are also enjoyed by defendants who are inclined to plead guilty, but whose cases require comparatively more time from defense counsel, prosecutors, judges, and other court workers. Perhaps one such plea-ready defendant needs a careful psychological work-up before sentencing. Maybe another has a complicated restitution agreement in his pending bargain. The resources needed to work out these pleas could dwarf those of another defendant who could commandeer the system for a two-week, felony jury trial. In the time it takes to try that one felony to verdict, perhaps hundreds of plea negotiations could be conscientiously conducted, or maybe dozens of misdemeanor trials (some to juries) completed. So, it is not "The Man" or the taxpayer who chiefly benefit by the pleading defendant's choice. It is rather his companions in difficulty.

The pleading defendant also acts for the benefit of many specific persons who are *not* in trouble. He relieves witnesses of their duty to testify. A few such witnesses might lament their lost opportunity to take the spotlight downtown. Most experience testifying as a burden, as a net subtraction from their appointed set of tasks. Most nonetheless testify willingly; it is their duty. But testifying in court is rarely fun. It is often a time-consuming diversion from other important duties at work or at home (or both). The pleading defendant gives all these folks what amounts to a gift.

Some witnesses discover that testifying in court, especially when they are cross-examined, can be quite harrowing. Defense counsel might humiliate some prosecution witnesses (victims of sexual misconduct, say, whose own conduct was not morally upright where prevalent "shield" laws permit such inquiry), abuse others (a robbery victim whose identification of the defendant is shaky but decisive to the trial's outcome), and portend danger to still others (someone testifying against the mob chieftain or another well-connected violent offender). Witnesses clued into these prospects do not have an opt-out option. If the prosecutor (or the defendant) subpoenas them, they have to go, on pain of imprisonment for contempt of the summons. There is no sure way for any savvy witness to get a head-start out of town, either. Either party to a criminal case may seek a Material Witness Order to hold a prospective witness in custody, just in case there is reasonable ground to believe that the witness would flee if served with an ordinary subpoena.

The defendant's guilty plea also extinguishes a host of moral hazards, because trials present numerous temptations to many persons to act unethically. Where the defendant pleads out the defense lawyer faces no dilemmas about putting on perjured testimony (not least often, that of his client). No other witness, perhaps especially including those would provide "alibis" for the defendant, is tempted to perjure himself. The hankering to at least massage the truth is as great for police and civilian witnesses against the defendant as it is for his own witnesses. Lawyers and judges are also tempted to act immorally during trial, by culpably misleading jurors, by (occasionally) lying to them or to each other, or by treating each other unfairly.

Jurors face distinct ethical challenges, too. From the get-go, and repeatedly throughout a trial, they receive solemn cautions from the trial judge which they are likely to be tempted to ignore. Often they do. Among these cautions are such counter-intuitive rules as the admonition not to talk among themselves (or to anyone else) about the case until deliberations begin; to keep an open mind until the conclusion of the trial; not to speculate about all sorts of things; and to refrain from drawing any adverse inference whatsoever about a non-testifying trial defendant. Judges tell jurors that the justice of the trial depends in part upon their fulfillment of these legal obligations. Jurors are required to swear that they will abide by them. All too frequently, they break their oaths. In my judgment, these (and other) moral hazards of trials are greatly under-valued by almost everyone involved in the criminal justice system. It is not that participants underestimate their presence, even their ubiquity. It is that perfidy and faithlessness are routinely *expected* during any trial. The pleading defendant nonetheless does all these folks a great, if underappreciated, favor.

II

How do the benefits of pleading guilty earn the defendant more than our hearty thanks, or the satisfaction of doing the right thing, or perhaps a modest bounty? How does giving back to the community establish that he deserves reduced punishment; indeed, that it would be wrong to not to lighten his load?

Let us start to answer that question by considering some secondary goals of sentencing which legitimately play a small role in determining appropriate punishment.[4] One of them is the moral reform of the criminal. This traditional point of punishment has unfortunately been obscured in our therapeutic culture by what is commonly called "rehabilitation." This modern notion resembles somewhat the traditional idea of reform, for "rehabilitation" refers to shaping the convicted person into a law-abiding citizen, just as does moral reform. But "rehabilitation" today refers mainly to the project of eliminating (through treatments meant to alter behavior) the psychological pathologies which are thought to "cause" someone to commit crime, where those pathologies are attributed to social causes, such as poverty, or to deep-seated personality disorders over which the defendant exercises little conscious control.

The criminally accused comes to court laden with gifts. He is master of his plea—guilty or not. The law requires that he plead voluntarily, of his own free will, for reasons sufficient to himself. He is sovereign. Morally, things are quite different. A defendant who is guilty, who has no real defense and so is almost certain to be convicted after trial, and who has no special reason to go to trial, chooses badly by refusing to plead guilty. The defendant who goes to trial out of spite, vanity, sheer cussedness, or just to "screw" the system and everybody in it, treats others unfairly, and thus unjustly. This defendant's choice is selfish; it is wrong, and it compounds the wrong of the criminal act of which he stands accused.

The pleading defendant is clearly on the path to genuine moral reform. By accepting responsibility for his actions and by doing right by others, he manifests (already, before sentencing) improved responsiveness to the demands of justice. He shows that he is willing to act to enhance the well-being of others. He acts unselfishly. He makes amends. The pleading defendant exhibits improved, if not yet good, character.

Another secondary aim of punishment is specific deterrence. The idea here is that sentencing authorities should be conscious of imposing upon convicted offenders enough unpleasantness so as to dissuade—deter—them from committing additional crimes. General deterrence shifts the focus to other potential lawbreakers. The question then is which measure of punishment suffices to persuade them against committing the crimes committed by the convicted person being sentenced, now serving as a warning example to them.

General deterrence has little to do with the morality of plea bargaining; it does not in any straightforward way justify leniency for the pleading defendant. Specific deterrence is a different matter. It is not so much that the pleading defendant signals his acceptance of the personalized stern message, of the threat to him of renewed unpleasantness in case he becomes a repeat offender. It is rather that the message is gratuitous. The pleading defendant shows that he need not (anymore) be dealt with on such crude terms. The pleading defendant exhibits incipient moral reform. He demonstrates a readiness to cooperate freely in the project of living with others in peace and justice. Sentencing authorities should treat him like it.

A sentencing judge should take both moral reform and specific deterrence into account when he sentences any convicted criminal. Working within a determinate range of options established by statutes drafted (hopefully) in light of retributive considerations, the judge consulting these two secondary goals should treat the pleading defendant better than a defendant convicted after trial. That is, within limits, these ancillary aims rightly influence a sentencing determination, and by their lights the pleading defendant is entitled to a concession.

What about that main channel of the morality of punishment, retribution? Does the pleading defendant deserve favorable consideration by its lights?

Yes. We saw in Chapter One that the essential (but not exclusive) moral wrong in criminal behavior is the selfish grab of more freedom than is one's due. "One's due" here is measured by the law which establishes the pattern of restriction and liberty incumbent upon everyone in the community. We saw too in the first chapter how the entire population is victimized by the criminal's unilateral usurpation of a liberty which others more or less freely deny to themselves.

The central aim of punishment is to restore the equilibrium of restraint within a society bounded by law, a balance which the criminal's act disrupted. In suffering punishment criminals are made to disgorge their undeserved advantage over law-abiding citizens. To set things right, the defendant must endure an imposition upon his will.

John Finnis further explains the retributive point of view:

> [T]he defining and essential (though not necessarily the exclusive) point of punishment is to restore an order of fairness which was disrupted by the criminal's criminal act. That order was a fairly (it is supposed) distributed set of advantages and disadvantages, the system of benefits and burdens of life in human community. The disruption consisted in a choice to take the advantage of following one's own preferences rather than restraining oneself to remain within that fair order (or, where the crime is one of negligence, an unwillingness to make the effort required to remain within the legally or morally required pattern of actions and restraints). Since freedom to follow one's preferences is in itself an important human good, the criminal's act of self-preference was itself the gaining of an advantage over those who restrain themselves to remain within that legally and/or morally required pattern. So the essential point of punishment is to restore the disrupted order of fairness by depriving the criminal of his ill-gotten advantage. And since that advantage consisted at least primarily in (wrongful) freedom of choice and action, the appropriate means of restoring the order of fairness is by depriving the criminal of his freedom of choice and action.[5]

The pleading defendant freely declines to exercise his legal liberty to consume scarce resources, which resources he gives back to that community which he mistreated by committing a crime. The pleading defendant takes ownership (if you will), insofar as he can, of the project of restoring justice. He anticipates (if you will) some portion of his punishment. Retributive justice thus calls for a certain relief in sentencing after a plea.

Part I of this chapter established that the pleading defendant confers a great benefit upon the community and many particular persons within it. Part II has established that leniency is a natural consequence of such a plea. When the moral rationales of punishment are brought into view, we can now see that the pleader stands in a favorable position at sentencing, better not only in relation to his non-pleading peers, but (more important) in relation to the whole set of rationales or criteria of his punishment. The moral *ought* of leniency for the pleading defendant arises from the internal sense of punishment. It would be unreasonable, and even arbitrary, not to reduce the pleader's sentence.

The pleading defendant's comparatively lesser sentence is therefore not an unrelated incentive or reward, tied to his plea by dint of another person's (the prosecutor's or the judge's) choice. A plea bargain is not like the deals which parents commonly make with their children, such as when Mom promises Junior that if he eats his broccoli she will let him play X-Box for an extra hour. There is no logical or moral tie between vegetables and video games. Mom brings them together to prod Junior into doing what she wants him to do. It would not be unreasonable for Mom to offer a different incentive, or to simply insist that Junior eat his greens, full stop.

III

The most obvious objection to reducing the pleading defendant's sentence gains loft from the central moral justification of punishment. Retribution (we saw in Chapter One) leads straightaway to determinate sentencing. This direction is set by retribution's treatment of the specific criminal act as the controlling relevant consideration at sentencing. The basic norm is that two people convicted of robbery should receive the same sentence, because their unjustified usurpation of liberty and hence their disturbance of society's pattern of equal restraint and forbearance under law are the same. The same counter-force upon the defendant's will is required to restore society's equilibrium.

In reply: we just saw in the latter stages of Part II how the logic of retribution as well as that of some secondary aims of punishment leads straightaway to concessions for the pleading defendant. We saw how the pleading defendant already begins to disgorge his unfair advantage over the rest of the community, precisely by relinquishing his legal prerogatives for the benefit of the community. This decision constitutes partial restoration of the equilibrium he disturbed.

In addition: the description of retribution at the top of this Part III leaves out some relevant considerations which would require somewhat different sentences for persons convicted of precisely the same offense. For example: three persons convicted for acting in concert to pull off the same armed robbery come up for sentencing. Upon a careful look at the papers, the sentencing judge sees that the youngest defendant did no more than stand as a lookout while the other two went inside the store and pointed pistols at the clerk. One of those two is, however, illiterate and scarcely a functioning adult. This addled gunman has also long been under the dominating influence of the third robber, who conceived the instant heist and ran the whole thing. Established principles of accomplice liability make all three guilty of the same offense. But it is easy to see that these criminals' choices varied considerably. These variances could (and most often would as well as should) lead the sentencing judge to impose different terms of imprisonment, within (perhaps) the five-to-nine year range set by statute.

This distribution pattern is a commonplace of criminal activity and sentencing. People convicted of the same crime of pickpocketing, prostitution, robbery, rape, or murder may all exhibit varying degrees of malice, planning, indifference to the victim's distress, and willingness to flout the demands of justice. Within the limited parameters of a sentencing scheme basically determined (as it should be) by retributive ends, they deserve different sentences. Retribution does not lead to a one-size-fits-all approach to sentencing.

The foregoing reply to the "obvious" objection raises another objection: is it not a trick to say that the defendant's plea constitutes (or brings into being) partial restoration? After all, that is tantamount to saying that the defendant has chosen his own punishment, or that he has punished himself. But—our next objector might assert—that is absurd. Punishment consists of being made to suffer some unwelcome privation, some suppression of one's liberty. It will scarcely do to be author of one's own sentence.

The objection seems sound enough. One should not be at liberty to choose one's own punishment, right? The danger is that the person might choose something which appears to be a privation to outsiders, but which actually pleases him. The misbehaving child given a choice by an inattentive parent, might choose (at his parent's invitation) to give up Nintendo for a week as "punishment" for missing curfew. If, unknown to Mom and Dad, the child is sick of Nintendo anyway, it would indeed hardly be a fit punishment at all.

But this hardly describes our pleading defendant. He is not vouchsafed a choice between Nintendo or not. He has no capacity whatsoever to determine the *nature* of his punishment. That is settled by lawmakers who establish terms of imprisonment, fines, and unattractive community service as authorized forms of punishment. The pleading defendant is not given final say over how much punishment he is to endure. That is securely within the court's portfolio. All that the pleading defendant can do to affect his punishment is to make a choice between two options shaped by others, by circumstances, and (up to a point) negotiated with him or his lawyer. But then the "deal" is presented to the accused "as is." This then is his situation. Option A is to proceed to trial, there to expect (should he be convicted) a sentence greater than that promised in Option B, the plea offer. It is fanciful to suggest that this dilemma empowers the defendant to choose his own punishment. No one need wonder if the defendant secretly welcomes prison, as our miscreant juvenile might when giving up the Nintendo.

Consider next this objection. Someone might say that the defendant who positively embraces his imprisonment, in the limited sense of seeing its moral appropriateness, could be said to "approve" of it, and occasionally even to "accept" or "welcome" it. Some prisoners might truly embrace the chance to "pay" their "debts back to society." Is this not, one might say, a perversion of punishment?

No. Everyone in the community should wish that more prisoners would so "embrace" their punishment. One ligament holding together the retributive understanding of punishment is exactly to re-invite (if you will) the accused back into the web of moral responsibilities of living in a law-respecting political society. If it were somehow an inalienable feature of genuine punishment that the guilty party *resist* and even *reject* this invitation and maintain his selfish attitude towards the due requirements of others, then we would have to say that The Bird Man of Alcatraz, or a jail-house lawyer or inmate minister or any other prisoner who makes a good life behind bars, would never be able to pay his debt to society. That would indeed be absurd.

Finally, someone might object that plea bargaining gives the prosecutor too much power. This objection is comprised of two different claims, and one of them has two related aspects. To take the complex claim first, the charge seems to be that prosecutors have, in a system characterized by guilty pleas, too much to say about the defendant's eventual sentence and, for that reason, the prosecutor invades the province of other institutional branches, foremost the judiciary.

In reply: it is certainly the case that, in a regime of developed classifications of crimes accompanied by determinate sentencing, prosecutors have a great deal of power. By offering to reduce a top count of murder, for instance, which might carry a mandatory minimum of fifteen years, to manslaughter, which carries a minimum of five years, a prosecutor constrains a sentencing judge's options and offers a defendant a powerful incentive to plead. Another prosecutor might charge a felony with a view to obtaining a misdemeanor plea or a plea to a lower-grade felony which carries no mandatory prison time. Is this to say that the prosecutor possesses too much power, or that he is a usurper, or both?

With important ethical side-constraints which I state below, the answer is no. For one thing, the argument may prove too much. The prosecutor's discretion to charge (or not) and what to charge is an ineradicable aspect of executive authority as it is generally understood in our constitutional system. There are other important discretionary executive functions; among them the power of clemency, pardons, and the decision to immunize a witness. No way to significantly limit all this discretion is at hand. A statute to command prosecution of "all offenses without exception" is unworkable. A directive to charge the highest provable crime does not avoid prosecutorial judgment calls: what is the highest provable crime? Constraints with more modest ambitions, such as those requiring a plea to, say, a felony no more than one classification lower than that charged, may blunt much of the force of the "prosecutors-have-too-much-power" criticism. But that would not confirm the objection's soundness. It would instead vacate the grounds for it.

Is the prosecutor a usurper? The legislature invests great authority (and, yes, great leverage) in the prosecutor by setting up a classification scheme in which the sentencing differences between adjacent classes of crimes are great. There may be a usurpation argument here, though I doubt it. But if there is an argument, it is an argument against the legislative branch. By granting a host of debatable assumptions, it might be argued that some proper discretion of judges has been legislatively transferred to prosecutors. Again, I do not think so. In any event, much of the prosecutor's leverage over sentencing is a function of judicial eagerness to impose sentences which the prosecutor is not heard to oppose.

The proper limitations upon the prosecutor's power must, it seems to me, be ethical. The first constraint is familiar to anyone who has seen a standard code of professional responsibility: a prosecutor should not accept a plea from a defendant whom the prosecutor does not believe is really guilty. The second constraint arises from the set of ethical considerations we have been examining, and I can only give a general expression to it here: plea offers ought to be consistent with viewing the guilty plea as an opportunity for the defendant to act for the good of others. Nothing the prosecutor can do could make it sure that defendants accept plea offers only for good reasons. The prosecutor can, however, give defendants a chance to be good.

IV

It is always wrong to seek to convict an innocent person. Doing so would necessarily involve some, and perhaps a great deal of, lying along the way (perjured testimony and the like). More important, the conviction itself would be a profound lie; the judgment of "guilty" would be false—and grossly unjust, for it would be the predicate for "punishing" one who is not only undeserving of it, but (in a sense) *ineligible.* "Punishing" an innocent would be empty and thus oppressive: no unjustified self-assertion can be redressed by imposing upon one who has not unjustifiably asserted himself. No one known to be innocent should ever be brought to trial. Great care should be taken by prosecutors to ascertain that everyone they bring to trial is, in truth, guilty.

There are no exceptions to this rule of justice. The career criminal who has escaped many times from just punishment but who is not guilty of the instant offense, should not be falsely accused to settle his accumulated debts to society. Even a guiltless accomplice who could be turned into the state's witness against those truly culpable for serious crimes by leveraging a plea should not be falsely accused, even if the authorities are bluffing and never intend to follow through to conviction. In this case there is no appreciable risk of punishing an innocent. But the bluff would be a lie.

Most persons accused by prosecutors of criminal offenses are really guilty. Most of them should plead guilty and receive leniency when they do. But not all guilty defendants should plead guilty. Sometimes the common good calls for a trial, even where the defendant is guilty. When is the common good better served by a trial than by a guilty plea, where the defendant could plead guilty without speaking falsely, and where punishing him would not be unjust?

There are two kinds of what I call "common-good" trials, cases which require no specific defendant. In other words: there are some types of *cases* which should be tried by *some* guilty defendants. But it does not matter which ones.

First, some defendants do a public service by making it possible to carve a common law of convictions. A certain number of cases need to be tried in any given jurisdiction in order to flesh out just what constitutes a proved case, to show what counts, in this place at this time, as proof beyond a reasonable doubt. In what circumstances and by what quantum of proof is one liable to be punished? There is one sense in which this information is unedifying: a morally indifferent person might use it to gauge what he *should* or *may* do, where that norm is really to be found in the terms of criminal statutes. But there are more wholesome uses for this common law of convictions. Participants in the criminal justice process regularly, if not always consciously, have in mind the prospects of jury conviction when they make decisions about what to charge, how to defend a case, and whether to make or accept a plea offer.

Second, in many criminal trials, the jury reaches a decision that amounts to more than the termination of one lawsuit. Jury verdicts may also amount to interstitial lawmaking. "Reasonable force," "negligent infliction," and "unreasonable noise" are moral evaluative terms in the criminal law. They indicate in very broad terms what is not to be done. But they do not have more concrete meaning than that when read off the lawbook page. They are given concrete meaning by jurors applying common sense and contemporary community standards. The common good is plainly served by having these more exact standards about terms operative in criminal laws. Some trials are needed. Since innocent defendants should not be accused and those that are nonetheless tried are liable to be poor candidates for intelligent jury lawmaking, some guilty defendants must take their cases to trial.

Here are several more specific examples of "common-good" trials.

The defendant is in fact guilty of selling drugs and is willing to plead guilty. He is convinced, however, that the pattern of police misconduct in his neighborhood, which includes harassment of African-American male youths, could be and should be put on trial along with him. This defendant's lawyer promises to litigate the matter fully. The defendant's own testimony and his lawyer's cross-examination of the police (an interrogation aided by subpoenaed police records) may provoke the serious review of police operations in the defendant's neighborhood that is needed.

The defendant is in fact guilty of operating a livery without a proper hack license. But due to prevalent stereotypes, government corruption, bureaucratic inertia, and the greed of others, there is no available taxi service in his minority neighborhood. The defendant is convinced that nonenforcement of this ordinance would serve the common good. He has reason to believe that a jury drawn from a true cross-section of the community will not convict him, no matter what the evidence of his violation of the positive law is. He hopes to help decriminalize this valuable service.

The defendant is in fact guilty of trespassing at an abortion clinic. Like the civil rights demonstrators of the preceding generation, he believes that the positive law that he has admittedly broken is unjust. He holds out little hope that he will be acquitted but believes that passive resistance to the unjust law, including a zealous defense of the charges against him, serves the common good.

There are probably many other types of cases where the defendant serves the common good by going to trial notwithstanding his actual, and even his provable, guilt. I do not imagine that all such defendants act out of concern for the common good. But the burden should be on the prosecution to rebut the presumption that they do.

V

If it is true (as I have here argued) that most guilty defendants should plead guilty and receive leniency for doing so, then criminal defense counsel acquire a new two-fold duty. The first new chore is that counsel should explain to his clients the opportunities to benefit others which pleading portends. Only then can the defendant do the right thing for the right reason, and thus truly earn the leniency he "bargains" for.

Defense counsel's second new task arises in "common-good" trial cases. It is to explain to a sentencing judge why a particular defendant, convicted after trial, might be deserving of favorable treatment even though it appears that the defendant acted selfishly in declining earlier plea offers.

The center of gravity of existing conversations between defendant and counsel is pretty much the courthouse market: what the state must offer to secure that large number of non-trial dispositions it needs to keep the system from collapsing. The conversation instead should be centered on the unique opportunity the defendant has to act uprightly. This does not make the defendant's attorney a paternalistic intermeddler; only the defendant can decide what to do. The attorney should make sure that the defendant is aware of the morally important quality of the decision to plead, a decision now treated all too often as a self-centered, prudential calculation.

Every defendant has a lot of motivation and some reasons to avoid imprisonment and, perhaps, to steer clear of lesser types of punishment. Punishment is a privation. Almost every defendant has some worthwhile friendships. Many are valuable members of families whose members will sorely miss them if they should be sent to prison. People accused of crimes have worthwhile projects, perhaps including an education in progress, employment of genuine value to others, or familial responsibilities of extraordinary urgency. All these goods may be collaterally affected by punishment, and the effect is rarely positive. Even so, if they are truly guilty they have a *prima facie* moral obligation to plead guilty, and counsel should do what he can to explain the nature of that obligation and the reasons for it.

CHAPTER 3:

Criminal Justice and the Family

INTRODUCTION

The authors of a comprehensive recent critique of how our criminal justice system treats the family pose two main questions. One question is descriptive and the other is morally evaluative. "First, how *does* the criminal justice system in this country approach the issue of family status? Second, "how *should* family status be recognized, if at all, in a criminal justice system situated within a liberal democracy committed to egalitarian principles of nondiscrimination?" [emphasis added].[1] These are important questions. In this chapter I shall take up chiefly the second question, the normative one, and take up these authors as conversation partners.

Privilege or Punish [*PoP*] divides the realm of "family status" into the "benefits" and "burdens" of "family ties."[2] The former include evidentiary privileges and domestic violence statutes, and some concessions predicated upon family status in pretrial release, sentencing, and prison administration. The latter are entirely substantive crimes. These "burdens" include sexual acts long understood to be subversive of the family (bigamy, incest, and adultery), and familial duties unrelated to sexual morality, such as supporting indigent parents and dependent children.[3] Another "burden" is the legal obligation to rescue family members from danger.[4]

The authors of *PoP* describe their work as "synthetic."[5] They see it as an effort to construct an analytical "framework" for critical evaluation, so that "policymakers" might better reflect upon their choices, which "have been insufficiently analyzed in a synthetic manner by academics before this project."[6] *PoP* is relentlessly philosophical. It is a sustained normative critique of "family ties" in criminal justice.

PoP's moral evaluations are bold. The authors judge that all the "family ties benefits" they examine should be modified or abolished. Some "can remain viable in a liberal criminal justice system so long as these benefits are extended more broadly on the basis of relationships of caregiving, rather than arbitrary familial status."[7] On the "burdens" side, the authors would decriminalize the sex crimes (though they remain "divided" on certain "sub-issues" involving incest).[8] They oppose most of the other family ties burdens they examine.[9] They also oppose the family itself, because it is "gendered, and otherwise unjustifiable."[10] In their view, the family is, morally speaking, very bad news.

I shall argue that these authors' normative claims are question-begging, vague, or simply mistaken. And I shall set out a more sound way to view the family, as it relates to the criminal law.

In Part I of this chapter I affirm the authors' understanding that liberty and equality are the moral pillars of the criminal justice system. But the authors mistakenly conclude that these foundations support a presumption against family predicates in that system. Their mistake is to overstate the role of coherence in reasoning about legal practices. This part also argues, dialectically, that granting the authors' presumption against family "status" would undermine countless other (that is, non-familial) criminal justice "status" predicates that no one seriously questions.

Part II is a first installment of my criticism of the authors' package of four "normative" criteria. These criteria include two "costs" specific to criminal justice. These "costs" ask two questions: first, whether family ties "undermine the pursuit of accuracy in the effective prosecution of the guilty and the exoneration of the innocent (thus, possibly leading to unwarranted harshness or leniency in the administration of justice)," and second, whether family ties "tend to incentivize more crime and more successful crime."[11] No one disputes the legitimacy of the latter of these criteria, which does not pull justificatory weight in *PoP* anyway. It is a redundant makeweight. The former is two-sided: "accurate" conviction of the guilty and "accurate" exoneration of the innocent. But this axiom about "accurate" convictions is seriously mistaken. It ignores the complex relationship between the moral norm of just deserts and the overall common good of political society, a relationship at the heart of any sound understanding of criminal justice.

Part III takes my investigation deeper into the authors' evaluative matrix. Here I try to describe and evaluate the distinctive contribution of political theory to the authors' overall argument—basically what they seek to accomplish by their frequent adjectival use of "liberal" (as in "liberal democracy" and a "liberal state").[12] My judgment is that these "liberal" usages are unsuccessful. They are vague, redundant, question-begging, or mistaken. This part also suggests that the authors assign greater moral value to individual "autonomous" choice in the family context than their evidence and arguments warrant.

Part IV is the second installment of my "package" critique. The remaining two "normative costs" are exogenous to criminal justice and support the authors' rejection of the family on broad—that is, not specific to criminal justice—moral grounds. The argument is that, first, family status has "historically facilitate[d] gender hierarchy" and, second, that family status "disrupt[s] our egalitarian political commitments to treat similarly situated persons with equal concern and discriminate[s] against those without families recognized by the state."[13] The family is, according to *PoP*, inegalitarian, sexist, and insufficiently inclusive of other personal ties that the authors consider to be "family." The authors do not so much establish as they assume the validity of these norms. They are apparently ignorant of the radical mutuality and equality upon which the family is, in truth, founded, and they do not take full account of how their radical interjection of a strong sense of autonomy into family life would affect personal well-being and, even, personal autonomy.

Finally, in Part V, I sketch how we could better analyze family status in the criminal justice system.

I

PoP often describes its normative foundations modestly, expressly limiting them to the moral implications and entailments of the criminal law and its just administration. The authors disclaim any "endorse[ment]" of incest: "[R]ather, we simply think the state should not be using the criminal law to tread upon the intimate associational rights of mature individuals."[14] The authors say that "prosecution is ordinarily unnecessary to prevent [incestuous] conduct," which "social stigma" will deter.[15] They do not suggest that this noncriminal moral disapproval is unjust. Again, "[i]t is one thing for the law to recognize how citizens organize themselves into close circles of affection; but it is another for the criminal law to take a stance on how citizens ought to organize themselves."[16] The authors say that their "focus" is "on whether currently criminal conduct should be decriminalized or reformed," and they "restrict [their] discussion to that subject."[17]

What are the moral bases within criminal justice for these judgments? The authors say that "the principle of equality should be a lodestar guiding our collective actions in the criminal justice system."[18] As discussed above, the authors also emphasize the central place of "voluntarism," "consent," "choice," and "autonomy"—collectively, what one might call "liberty"—in that system.

So far so good: Liberty and equality *are* the moral axes upon which the criminal law and it's just administration spin. A just criminal law system presupposes individual liberty. The essential condition of liability for any crime is that the accused could have done otherwise. No one is liable for the criminal acts of others, save where one has freely chosen to align oneself with the other's criminal undertaking. Crimes are all about an individual's free choices.

For a criminal law to be just, moreover, it must apply equally to all similarly situated persons. Consider that the *dramatis personae* of criminal statutes are mainly generic people with unidentified characteristics: "whoever," "a person," and "another person." These anonymous individuals are equal in life and in death. "Murder," for example, occurs whenever one "person" intentionally causes the death of "another person." Neither proper names nor social attachments have anything to do with it.

The criminal law is famously concerned with acts freely chosen, and not with one's character, personality, condition, or habits. No one may be criminally punished for being a bad boy all these years, for possessing mischievous character traits, or for holding unpopular opinions. Even in prosecutions for freely chosen criminal acts, evidence of character is strictly circumscribed, lest the trial become a referendum on the defendant's reputation or on the conduct of his life to date.[19]

The basic moral justification for punishing criminals depends upon these two leading values. The harm common to every criminal act, over and above that visited upon any particular victim, is the undue advantage that the criminal obtains compared to all others in the community. We have talked extensively about retribution in the first two chapters of this book. Little more need be said here. The central moral aim of punishment is to undo the criminal's bold and unjust self-assertion, which constitutes the criminal's "debt to society." Proportionate punishment restores the *ex ante* condition of equal liberty among society's members. The authors seem to acknowledge this moral justification of punishment when they say that "if a criminal derogates from the democratically derived codes of proper conduct, he indicates a superiority that claims he is not bound by the rules that bind others."[20]

The moral norms of equality and free choice that undergird the criminal justice system do not establish a moral presumption against family ties within the system. However, the authors go wrong with the presupposition that systemic principles shape every act within the system. This presupposition is a mistake. To say that A and B are the principles of a system is not to say or imply that they are the exclusive sources of justification or explanation within that system. It is not to say or imply that they must explain all of the concepts and definitions at work within the system.

One might well observe that religion, like the family, is rarely a legitimate criterion of treatment in the criminal justice system. One could also suppose that making what one believes about God a predicate for good or ill offends liberty and equality. Nonetheless, Muslim prisoners should probably be accorded special diets, permitted to congregate as a group for required prayer, and excused from court on Friday—all demands that other believers do not make and that unbelievers have no standing to make. Making unreasonable noise near a house of worship may be a crime, as may be selling liquor or drugs in the vicinity of a church. Negligent supervision of clergy by an ecclesiastical superior could be a special crime. There is the priest-penitent evidentiary privilege, shielding confessors from compulsory disclosure of relevant information obtained in the confessional. These allowances (and more) for religion are statistically unusual; they would take up little space on a shelf arrayed with all of our criminal laws and procedures. But that footprint creates no presumption at all against their justice, or their wisdom.

The authors nonetheless seem to be on sound footing in arguing that one's fate in the criminal justice system should not depend upon familial status. After all, criminal law is concerned with an individual's freely chosen acts and not with anyone's character or condition. One might then ask: Do not these commitments lead straightaway to the conclusion that "status" predicates should be jettisoned from our system of criminal justice?

The answer is yes and no, because the term "status" is multivocal. Yes, it would be unjust, for example, to make being poor a crime. Yes, it would be unjust to establish, say, the crime of assault with a deadly weapon, but then to exempt retirees and veterans from its scope. But no, it is not unjust to define crimes according to "status," insofar as we are talking about the law's strategic concern for the requirements of certain socially-important roles.

Many crimes pertain exclusively to specific roles, relationships, and positions. Among these specialized roles are those of bookkeeper, gun dealer, shop owner, union official, congressman, and lobbyist. It is true (as the authors might reply) that no one is born or forced into any one of these roles. People can and do choose to become a pilot, accountant, or school-teacher. So the authors might say that people should be bound, at least in the eyes of the criminal law, *only* by the rules of those roles that they freely choose.

The robustness of any such consent is often questionable, and even illusory. Roles and their accompanying forms of criminal liability are presented on an "as is," "take-it-or-leave-it" basis. No one may choose to be a lawyer who has not satisfied all the established entry requirements (obtaining a J.D. degree, passing the bar exam, and receiving certifica-tion from a state character committee). No lawyer enjoys the option of practicing according to a personal view of professional ethics, save where those views coincide with the enacted local rules of professional responsibility.

No one can predict upon becoming a lawyer in 2013, in any event, what the professional rules will be in 2043. It is a pretty hollow "choice" that one may have at that later point between either abandoning one's liveli-hood or "consenting" to the latest regime of professional criminal liability. Considering all the regulatory crimes at a given moment, and that any adult not-to-the-manor-born has to earn a living somehow, some role-based criminal liability may be inescapable.

Even those out of work may find role-based liability inescapable. Students, air travelers, and money-borrowers all have to put up with oner-ous regulations backed by criminal sanctions. Other roles are forced upon us, as anyone who has been subpoenaed or who has net income will read-ily attest. Witnesses and jurors and taxpayers are typically conscripted against their wishes; in some democracies (Israel is one), young men and women are still conscripted into the military. No one is free to ignore these summonses to serve the common welfare.

Public authority sometimes deems a particular role-relationship incompatible with sexual intimacy. Examples include the teacher-student (including adult students), lawyer-client, doctor-patient relationships. To some extent, these prohibitions are derived from concerns about the gen-uineness of any putative consent to sex between persons of unequal employment status. But they also owe to the judgment that these are valu-able relationships that would be undermined, in various ways, by truly con-sensual sexual relations. Even employees of equal stature in the one gov-ernment office may be forbidden to fraternize.

In more general terms, one could say that liberty and equality constitute the system's normative infrastructure, the moral preconditions of criminal liability, and the moral justifying aim of punishment. But the super-
structure built up around them and which they suffuse and animate—the
substantive criminal law—comes mainly from elsewhere. Criminal law
emerges out of a reflection upon the myriad truths that form the foundation of the common good of political society. Contrary to the authors'
claims, the axiomatic position of liberty and equality in criminal law does
not tend to show that "crimes against the family" is an oxymoron.

II

Among the "normative costs" of family ties in the criminal system, the
authors count "undermin[ing] the pursuit of accuracy in the effective prosecution of the guilty and the exoneration of the innocent."[21]

The authors of *PoP* contend that "[i]f innocent people mistakenly sit
in prison (or guilty people escape prosecution altogether) as a result of
these benefits, then our commitment to the accurate distribution of justice
is undermined at an intolerable cost."[22] They even go so far as to say that
"prosecuting the guilty fairly and protecting the innocent from crime and
prosecution" are the "primary criminal justice values."[23] A "cost" of recognizing family benefits is thus that they "tend to incentivize more crime
and more successful crime."[24] The authors have in mind the family exception to the crime of harboring a fugitive and spousal testimonial immunity.

But this "cost" is a redundant makeweight. It is anyone's guess how
much crime these "incentives" create (the authors provide no data). The
true extent of the putative crime wave is certainly limited to one side of the
"distribution of justice," for these impediments enable the occasional criminal to evade capture and exclude some probative testimony, much as the
warrant requirement and any evidentiary exclusionary rule do. So, the cost
is that some guilty people may go free. None of the family-ties benefits to
which the authors apply these norms create any risk of false conviction.
The innocent are not put at peril. Only the guilty are affected insofar as
some of them may get away with crimes.

Let us now look more closely at this normative "cost." The authors'
commitment to moral symmetry between convicting the guilty and exon-
erating the innocent is quite striking. The commonplace statement of moral
priorities in our society has long been (as we saw in Chapter Two) "better

that a hundred guilty persons go free than that one innocent suffer."[25] Perhaps twenty or five is a better balance of the relevant equities. No matter. All these numbers express an important truth: a just society stops at almost nothing to avoid convicting the innocent. But just societies—including ours—limit the "accurate" and "effective" prosecution of the guilty according to a host of competing moral and practical considerations. It is a grave injustice to punish an innocent person. It is not a grave injustice to forego the investigation, arrest, prosecution, or conviction of someone—or even of many people—clearly guilty of a crime. Any family-ties benefit that creates a risk of convicting an innocent person is wrong. Period. But not all benefits (or burdens) that increase unpunished criminal behavior are wrong.

Why? What supports this widespread belief that moral asymmetry in the "distribution of justice" is morally justified? The answer lies in the complex relationship between the principle of just deserts and the larger common good of political society. All societies have limited pools of common resources, and the common good places great demands upon them. Criminal justice is only one such demand. In any given set of social circumstances, the demands of public health, common defense, public education, and many others may be more pressing than the marginal needs for criminal law enforcement. Hard choices must be made, all having more or less predictable negative side-effects. Reduced "accuracy" in convicting the guilty is one. It is often a tolerable cost.

Many discrete aspects of the common good justify sacrificing convictions. Diplomacy (not equality or choice) explains diplomatic immunity from prosecution; national security explains non-prosecution of some terrorists; privacy explains the limits upon evidence gathering that hinder "accurate" prosecution; scarce resources explain the practical immunity of some trivial offenses from prosecution; family welfare explains the spousal testimonial privilege. The list could go to considerable length.

The authors might reply that unanswered wrongdoing threatens the fundamental equality of all persons in society.[26] But this is not true. The principle of moral desert establishes a presumption that punishing any guilty person is not unjust.[27] But the common good of political society—which includes but goes beyond justice, and which goes far beyond just deserts—is often better served by pursuing other objectives, even if doing so leads to fewer convictions. Even when society does not punish a criminal, however, crime victims usually retain their civil remedies; that aspect of their "equality" is preserved.[28] Because the common good requires that we tolerate some criminal behavior, the victim *qua* plaintiff in any foregone criminal action—one of the "People" or a citizen of the "Commonwealth"—receives treatment no different from that other members of society would receive were they in the same situation.

PoP emphasizes a great deal the distinctively "liberal" character of our criminal justice system and of criminal justice in a "liberal" state. But there is nothing distinctively "liberal" about the system so far described. The foundational moral principles of liberty and equality are no less conservative than they are liberal. Saint Thomas Aquinas clearly articulated the retributive justification for punishment[29] to which the authors point. Was Aquinas a "liberal" or a "conservative"? Are there contrasting "liberal" and "conservative" views about whether being a slob should be made a crime? Or on whether having an income above $100,000 annually should be a defense against murder charges? One has serious doubts.

The leading indicators today of "conservative" criminal justice opinions are probably preferences for long prison sentences and for aggressive police investigative techniques (searches, seizures, and confessions less encumbered by rules in favor of privacy). But the authors of *PoP* do not engage these issues. It therefore seems that this adjectival move either is misplaced, or simply shifts the justificatory burden to some wider doctrine of "liberalism."

To that displacement that I now turn.

III

The authors support their normative judgments by reference to a wider "liberal" body of thought: "[W]e think a liberal state may not use its criminal law to reinforce a very particular version . . . of the family."[30] They say that they rely upon "the institutional design of criminal justice practices in a liberal state."[31] Such burdens "run afoul of principles that should constrain the use of the criminal justice system in a liberal democracy."[32]

The authors of *PoP* make crucial use of the link between liberalism and a strong moral valuation of autonomous individual choice. They espouse a "liberal minimalist approach" to criminal justice, a framework by which any "family relationship that is an element of criminal liability must be one that is the product of freely chosen behavior."[33] "Family status" causes substantial problems for the "liberal state" because it "can burden relationships that persons have had no autonomy in creating or rejecting" and because it "risks infringing upon citizens' liberty."[34]

Here are five criticisms of the authors' liberal usage of "liberal," the last of which is particular to the autonomy link.

One. The authors' adjectival arguments are dense with morally-freighted terms. The combination of such terms in close proximity calls for subtle explanation. The authors do not provide it. The reader is left guessing about the distinctive contribution of "liberal" in any particular sentence.

Two. *PoP's* use of "liberal" is dependent for its meaning and cogency upon one of contemporary liberalism's characteristic arguments, namely, that the state must be "neutral" on controversial moral questions concerning the good life. But such "neutrality" remains an illusion, even when borrowed from a larger philosophical framework, be it Rawlsian or some other brand of modern political theory.

Three. The authors' position is implausible and counterintuitive. "Liberal[ism]," "democracy," and "egalitarianism" are all good things—in their proper frames of reference. But those frames are limited. Some institutions critical to our society do not conform to these norms of internal order. Neither the military nor the modern business corporation can be readily described as "liberal" or "democratic" or even "egalitarian." Neither can most churches. The contemporary university is "liberal" and possibly "egalitarian," but it is hardly "democratic." No one seriously proposes that, in our "liberal democratic state," the military, the corporation, and the university must, as a matter of justice, be rendered invisible to the criminal law, or somehow reconstituted by state power to mimic the state's "liberal," "democratic," and "egalitarian" ordering principles. There is no obvious reason why the family is a more deserving candidate for such a disappearing act or makeover.

Four. *PoP* adopts a contestable, partisan conception of liberalism without acknowledging the choice. Much less do the authors defend or justify their preference.

In truth, contemporary liberal thought is a house divided when it comes to questions about the family and the state's responsibilities.[35] The division runs along two analytical axes. The first axis is the division between perfectionist and anti-perfectionist liberals. John Rawls is the leading anti-perfectionist liberal of the last generation. Rawls and those who follow his lead (including, at times, *PoP's* authors) maintain that the state is obliged in justice to remain scrupulously neutral on controversial questions concerning the morally good life.[36] "Perfectionist" liberals, on the other hand, do not affirm any strong doctrine about the state's duty to refrain from acting on the perceived moral truth about the good. The leading "perfectionist" liberal is the legal-moral philosopher Joseph Raz.[37] Raz affirms, for example, the state's authority to protect traditional marriage if it represents the moral truth about marriage.[38]

The second axis divides what might be called "progressive" liberals from more "conservative" liberals. The subject matter of this disagreement is not so much political morality (as it is between Rawls and Raz), but rather political theory, or even political science. "Progressive" liberals characteristically consider the central political moral value to be a radical personal autonomy. One very prominent expression of this viewpoint is the so-called "Mystery Passage" from *Planned Parenthood of Southeastern Pennsylvania v. Casey*, the 1992 Supreme Court case affirming the basic holding of *Roe v. Wade*: "At the heart of liberty is the right to define one's own concept of existence, of meaning, of the universe, and of the mystery of human life. Beliefs about these matters could not define the attributes of personhood were they formed under compulsion of the State."[39]

More "conservative" liberals hold that a liberal society requires the people's possession of certain moral virtues. Chief among these virtues are a deep sense of personal moral responsibility, a strong ethic of self-restraint, and an abiding devotion to the well-being of others.[40] "Conservative" liberals recognize further that these virtues are threatened when government acts in such a way as to undermine the civil institutions—family, church, and school—that inculcate virtue. They recognize that one way that government threatens these nonpolitical "little platoons" is by imposing a progressive vision upon them. One of the state's most important functions is to protect and promote the nonpolitical institutions—the family perhaps above all others—that can and usually do directly inculcate the necessary virtues.

Five. The authors' "progressive" liberalism is problematic. They locate their endorsement of the caregiving function within a broader endorsement of a distinct moral value that they call variously "voluntariness," "autonomy," and "choice." They assert that the criminal sanction is only appropriate if "individuals have roughly consented to these extra obligations by their antecedent conduct to join or start particular relationships."[41] "It follows, we believe, that if voluntariness matters, then a family-ties burden should not be placed on someone who has had a familial status imposed upon him."[42] As a result, "[t]o our mind, the family relationship that is an element of criminal liability must be one that is the product of freely chosen behavior."[43] This need for free choice purportedly compels the conclusion that "we think a liberal state should . . . give people some autonomy about entering relationships before using the relationship status as an element of a crime."[44]

To some extent, the authors in these (and other similar) statements reiterate the same status-anxiety that I criticized in Part II as destructive of role-based liabilities that no one seriously questions. Additionally, the authors fail to address the paradoxical effects of trying to expand individual choice by legally unpacking the "traditional" family. They do not consider that, insofar as their proposed legal changes will change cultural practices, it will soon become the case that persons who wish freely to choose traditional marriage and family may be denied that choice. Individuals can only choose from among the marriage and family options offered in their society. It is really difficult in America today to really "choose" between polygamy and monogamy. The difficulty arises not from widespread ambivalence about these two versions of marriage. Quite the opposite: the difficulty owes instead to our overwhelming cultural and legal commitment to the latter as choice-worthy. As Raz has argued, "[m]onogamy, assuming that it is the only morally valuable form of marriage, cannot be practised by an individual. It requires a culture which recognizes it, and which supports it through the public's attitude and through its formal institutions."[45]

PoP considers only one major set of the effects from just one side: the perspective of the one who chooses to abandon a committed relationship. The relevant considerations, however, are bilateral and multilateral relations (consider the case of a father and husband who walks out to begin a new romance). For every person who exercises his freedom to choose, there may be several others who have been deprived of the relationship of his choice. Even assuming that individual autonomy is the sole relevant value, a full accounting of the net effects of the authors' proposals across the population must still be done if that relevant valuation is to be adequately defended. The authors attempt no such accounting.

IV

The authors of *PoP* are not shy about moral evaluation. Their book is awash in normative criteria and in decisive judgments based upon them. *PoP* is also all about the family. It is therefore curious that *PoP* contains no philosophy of the "traditional" family, not even as a suitable target for its critical exercises. *PoP* lacks an account of the family's moral constitution and its moral value. This vacuum is consistent with the authors' evident belief that the family is rooted in bias, all the way down.

The authors say a great deal about the family. They say that the family is "heterosexist," which refers to the fact that same-sex couples are in most places unable to legally marry.[46] They complain that the family evinces "repronormativity," meaning that the prevailing legal understanding of the family is still linked to having and raising children.[47] They say that persons in same-sex or polyamorous unions might feel "marginalized" by the state's restriction of marriage to opposite-sex couples.[48] They disapprove of all these realities. They also say that the family is "gendered" and "discriminatory."[49] All in all, the authors judge the family to be morally wrong.

These judgments express a limited set of criticisms. But they converge upon the argument that the traditional family is suffused with an indelible inequality. This defect forms the core of the authors' other two "normative costs," those concerned with gender hierarchy and discrimination.[50] To be sure, the authors also maintain that the prevailing notion of "family" is underinclusive; households that the authors believe should be counted as families—same-sex and polyamorous households—are not.[51] But the validity of this criticism depends in turn upon the truth of an underlying account of what the family represents. And so these two remaining "normative costs" collapse into one weight-bearing assertion: the "traditional" family itself is "heterosexist" and otherwise infected with inequality.

The authors recognize that only their two "normative costs" pertain to the "burdens" half of *PoP*.[52] Worries about "inaccurate" convictions and "incentivizing" crimes have no bearing upon whether making adultery a crime is morally justifiable. These criteria also influence the authors' "benefits" analysis. *PoP* thus has a lot riding on its broad moral rejection of the family.

Make no mistake about it: These non-neutral moral criteria for judging the family swing free of any specific argument about the moral foundations of criminal justice. If the authors are right that the "traditional" family is a structure of oppression, then their analysis of family-ties burdens in criminal justice succeeds for that reason alone. One does not need a theory of criminal justice to conclude that the state has no business criminalizing certain acts as assaults upon the "family," where they are, in moral truth, assaults only upon an unjust social practice calling itself the "family."[53]

The moral truth about the family has long supplied an essential, though not sufficient, condition for legal protection of the family. The law has long made the family morally-normative for sexual activity to protect and preserve the valuable relationships that constitute the family. Incest is forbidden to protect the sibling relationship from ruin by sexual attraction and activity. Adultery is forbidden to preserve the fidelity which defines spousal love.[54] Fornication has also historically been forbidden as a crime against marriage, on the grounds that marriage is morally normative for both sex and having children.[55]

The sublime and powerful equality at the family's root makes doubtful the authors' "inegalitarian" charges. The practice of family life in a given society may still be unjustly discriminatory, as it so often has been with regard to wives and mothers. Nonetheless, recovering the truth about the family is a much surer first step towards genuine reform. Erasing the family from the law or reducing it to a web of chosen contingent commitments, which is practically the same thing, is not a surer way to reform the family along more egalitarian lines. The authors' medicine is too strong. They would burn down the house to roast the pig.

V

It is scarcely the province of civil law to superintend family life. The law must tolerate a great deal of miserable behavior by family members towards each other. But the family's basic structure and the sexual morality that flows from it—and that in turn protects it—should always be respected by the civil law.

Protection of the family may, but need not, extend to the criminal law.[56] The argument for criminalizing bigamy, adultery, and incest is strong. Each is *malum in se*. Each is almost universally regarded as immoral and deserving of social reprobation. Each act attacks a defining feature of family life; in other words, each seriously subverts a socially important set of relationships.

At least with regard to bigamy and incest, the occurrence rate is so low that prosecuting all those who are provably guilty would not overly burden the criminal justice system. And juries are unlikely to acquit bigamists and those who practice incest. The incidence of adultery is considerably higher than that for bigamy or incest, however, and so potentially arbitrary selective enforcement of criminal laws against it is a genuine threat. Jurors may also be unwilling to convict adulterers because, unlike the situation with bigamy and incest, many will have been tempted to commit adultery and may think: "There but for the grace of God go I." They may also believe that many marriages can survive an adulterous affair. They will then see that putting the philandering party in jail eliminates that chance, to the detriment of children and, perhaps, the faithful spouse.

Adultery stands today in some danger of losing its social stigma. Defining it as criminal may stop its slide toward respectability. It is thus a critical question whether our society can preserve adultery's status as objectively immoral and socially harmful—a necessity, in my view—without making it a crime.

Criminal laws against incest, adultery, and bigamy occupy one polar region of "family ties" predicates. Here, the family (or a particular family relationship) is the terminal point of the law's solicitude. The family is not transparent or a proxy for some ulterior or accompanying value, policy goal, or relational quality. The family is the end of the line.

At the other pole are cases of pure proxy or perfect transparency. Here, the lawmaker pursues a non-familial good, a benefit marked or symbolized, but not constituted, by the family. The population of this polar region is both large and small. It is large insofar as the law commonly treats "family" as an indicator of other facts, such as relations of dependency, friendship, or support, or of common ethnic and racial identity. The population is small because the law usually proceeds directly to the targeted fact, and explicitly treats the family as one member of the designated class, or as a species within the valued genre. The census counts "households" and tax law cares about "dependents" because family relations are included in, but not exhaustive of, these categories.

Most explicit references to "family ties" reside somewhere between the poles. These references are ambiguous because they often contain both a descriptive and a normative component. They often signal didactically that the family as such is good, and prosaically that the "family" stands in close proximity to some other purpose. One law may both promote the family as morally normative and accomplish some non-familial business by using the "family" moniker. Of course, the descriptive component may be more or less accurate, because the correlation between the marker and the desired goal may be more or less tight.

What can we say of a general evaluative nature about these in-between cases? I do not think any general presumption of injustice (such as the authors') is warranted. One could better imagine two lines of analysis intersecting at right angles, one expressing the clarity and appropriateness of the lawmaker's didactic intent, and the other tracing the fit between the family marker and a targeted trait or goal. As that correlation becomes tighter and the didactic intent of the law more prominent—and we might here imagine ourselves staring at one quadrant—the overall justness of the law approaches a zenith.

And so on around the four corners. As the fit loosens, and especially as normative moral values recede from the lawmaker's mind, the family tie is morally suspect, and probably should be abandoned. At least, non-familial applicants ought to be freely permitted to make a case for the subject legal benefit. The relevant public authority may then argue that the possibility of abuse or opportunism (or both), in addition to the transaction costs of deciding all the non-familial applications, justifies limiting the benefit to family members.

The authors of *PoP* cleave to a more categorical and dogmatic approach to family ties. They conclude "that the family exemption" to criminal harboring is misguided, and that it should "be soundly rejected by state legislatures," partly because it is unjust to "close friends who provide assistance."[57] But this argument insists gratuitously that family relations are, or should be viewed by the law as, examples of "friendship" and not as *sui generis*.

A more nuanced analysis would go as follows. The family exemption for harboring a fugitive probably includes some normative ingredient; to some extent, the lawmaker is making a teaching point about the special nature of family ties. The exemption is also partly an application of excuse principles. The lawmaker might think it is just too much to ask a mother, for example, to choose between escaping her own liability for a crime and caring for her escaped son, who may be seeking no more than a meal or a bed or even a brief reunion with her. The exemption may also reflect difficulties of proof: The line between "harboring a fugitive" and innocently caring for one's own may be hard to draw (much as it could be for a homeless shelter or a church soup kitchen for an undocumented migrant). Or, the exemption may reflect the lawmaker's recognition that juries will not convict mothers for feeding and housing their fugitive sons.

The lawmaker could also believe that, lest there be a complete defeat of law enforcement efforts to apprehend fugitives or limit assistance to criminals after the fact (or both) only a small number of exemptions (if any) may be made. It is then a choice from among these options: Exempt mothers and fathers only, exempt the whole immediate family, or exempt no one. Extending the exemption to all "close friends"—which the authors suggest justice requires—is not a viable option. Society's likely choice may be made clear by applying the Golden Rule: would "close friends" allow that mothers and fathers should get the exemption, as opposed to exempting no one at all? My guess is that they would say yes.

CONCLUSION

The authors of *PoP* say that "the criminal justice system, with a few exceptions, is not generally an appropriate place to foster a particular vision of family life."[58] "Having a family . . . is typically morally unrelated to the offender's claim of superiority represented by the crime."[59] Just so: the benefits and burdens of family ties should indeed be few in the criminal justice system, because the family is indeed "typically" beside the point— but not always.

The authors also assert that "the family can sustain itself without special immunity from the criminal justice system."[60] "[A]t least right now," they state, it is "doubtful that the family needs systematic support through the use of criminal justice benefits in order to enable and ensure its flourishing."[61] The authors may be right. But they offer no data to support their claim. And nothing about the possibility that the family might get by with non-systematic support or ordinary immunity from the criminal justice system tends to prove that we should either render the family altogether invisible, or define it differently when it comes to the criminal law, as they argue unsuccessfully in *PoP*.

II
LAW and MARRIAGE

CHAPTER 4:

What's At Stake in the Marriage Debate?[1]

Many people who say that the law should recognize same-sex relationships as marriages say that all that is at stake is opening the membership rolls. They say that those uninterested in same-sex relationships can carry on just as before. They say that legal recognition of same-sex "marriage" would have no effect upon the vast majority of people who are, after all, heterosexual. These advocates suppose that the meaning of marriage in the law and in the culture would not be changed by making it the union of "spouses," instead of that between "man and woman." They say that it is just a matter of making some valuable benefits available to a slightly larger cohort of eligible people. Same club, more members.

Is this claim—that the meaning of marriage is *not* at stake—true? Or should we rather believe that, by eliminating any essential connection between marriage and procreation, the legal meaning of marriage would change? Should we believe, in other words, that the proposed legal change would affect the wider cultural understanding of marriage, so that before long very large numbers of people would think of marriage as a different sort of relationship than they, or their elders, previously thought it was? If so, would that change of meaning be good for people; that is, would it enhance rather than impede their access to the truth about marriage and thus to the genuine benefits it holds out?

In this chapter I answer each of these questions. I shall argue that recognizing same-sex "marriage" would change the legal and thus the cultural meaning of that relationship. The change would be from marriage as in some way essentially oriented to procreation to not. What's at stake in the marriage debate is whether the civil law is going to do what it can and should do to promote and protect marriage, so that people can truly understand and effectively enter into it as the procreative type union that it is.

I

Culture is a human artifact. But culture is not about tangible items like pottery or hula hoops or wood-pulp sheets like this page. Tangible artifacts can reflect truths about the human culture from which they hail. Scholars of ancient civilizations sift through the remnants of firepits and dwellings, and infer from them how long-gone people lived and, even, some of what they believed. These scholars tell us about Mayan or Aztec (or whatever) *culture*. But the artifacts themselves are not the "culture."

It is perfectly natural for people to create culture. But culture is not natural. It is not given to people by their environment. Culture is not the inevitable manifestation of mental hardwiring or biological drives. Culture is what people add to nature by their reflection, choices, and acts. It is a distinctively human reality.

Culture is about *meaning*. "Meaning" distinguishes human acts from occurrences in the physical world, from matters of cause and effect in which human choices play no role. Apples fall from trees due to atrophy in the branch; kids sitting in trees sometimes throw apples at passersby. One is an event, the other is an act. An apple falling from a tree is a mere occurrence. An apple being thrown by a child intending to startle or hurt somebody is an expression of choice—it is a meaningful (though wrongful) human act. A dog knows the difference between being kicked, and being tripped over.

Blessed John Paul II once told a UNESCO conference that "culture is the realm of the human as such."[2] One part of that "as such" is this: culture is constituted by the human person's capacity for conceptual thought, for abstraction. Culture has to do with people's purposive and expressive activities. It has most of all to do with their choices. Culture is shaped by what people consider valuable, choice-worthy, worthwhile, and good. Culture sorts out for us what is good, and what is bad.

The great cultural anthropologist Clifford Geertz wrote that "[u]ndirected by cultural patterns . . . man's behavior would be virtually ungovernable, a mere chaos of pointless acts and exploding emotions, his experience virtually shapeless."[3] Culture gives shape, provides order, supplies the cognitive map. Culture involves what Geertz and other scholars call "symbolism." They mean (again): how a people understands the world, how they account for things like life, death, suffering, joy, hunger, or pain.

Though woven out of abstraction and intention, culture is no gossamer tapestry. Studying culture, Geertz says, "is thus not to abandon social analysis for a Platonic shadow, to enter into a mentalistic world of introspective psychology or, worse, speculative philosophy"[4] (let the record show that I here emphasize Geertz's reticence about philosophy, not my own). Geertz rightly observes that culture is comprised of "social events . . . as public as marriage and as observable as agriculture."[5]

People produce culture. But they do not do so on purpose. One rarely hears another person say, "I was busy this morning establishing a culture." The world of meaning and value which surrounds us—our *culture*—is very largely the by-product of everyone's day-to-day lives. Ancients who roasted pigs or who built cliff-houses were not consciously scattering artifacts for Clifford Geertz to examine. People do what they do. They choose, they act, they speak, they join, they *live*. When they do so, they leave behind a culture. Culture is, in this important sense, a *residue*. We make it, more or less unwittingly. It makes us, more or less effectively.

The deposit of meaning we call culture confronts us, in season and out, as a given, as an objective reality which interprets the world for us and which, if society is insular, might be our whole mental horizon. Beyond it lies exotic possibilities which we understand but which we understand we cannot choose. The culture—out there, put in place by the many over the years, and beyond our fashioning—limits our choosing and acting. We cannot choose what we cannot see and bring to mind as a live option for choice. One's cultural milieu, for better or for worse, makes certain options unavailable, even unthinkable.

One's culture sorts out options for living, selecting some for the menu and eliminating others. The vast majority of us cannot believe in magic and astrology because we live in a scientific culture. Some of us do not believe in God for the same reason: some think that Darwin debunked Scripture and that science debunks miracles. We know about the *harem* and the *posse* and the arranged marriage. They are conceptually and physically possible in our social world. But they are unavailable for anyone's choice. These practices cannot be established by individuals; it takes a collective effort to make them available. Our culture does not endorse them, or sustain them, and our law basically forbids them.

In all too many cultures genuine friendship between persons of different races or clans, for example, has been impossible due to false cultural beliefs about the indelible inferiority of some group. Stories as diverse as *Romeo and Juliet* and *Driving Miss Daisy* compellingly explore the difficulties of friendship across cultural divides. In many cultures today parents can scarcely regard baby girls as they do baby boys.

Their culture tells them to value their children, not intrinsically, but for what the kids can do—for the nation, for the parents, for the clan. And what girls can do (compared to boys) is limited by the surrounding culture's sexist prejudices. If we lived in a culture which had neither need nor interest in a liberal education, then only the heroic among us could come to see the value of learning. If we lived in a culture which degraded women, then only the few could aspire to genuine mutuality with one's spouse. If we lived in a culture which treated religion as just another baneful superstition, then only the spiritually adventurous could still get right with God.

When we think of "culture" we think of arts, leisure, and entertainment, of what the *New York Times* covers in a separate section each day, and in a very large one on Sundays. But culture can be high-brow (like the Met or Matisse) or down-market, way beneath the *Times'* notice (NASCAR or nachos). The difference is both great and small. Things of beauty there truly are, and great artistic achievements, too. Most of us recognize, however, that culture in this sense involves legitimate differences in taste, and that a wide swath of arts, leisure, and entertainment choices do not have much to do with whether one's life is going well, morally speaking. We are prone, too, to identify distinctive cultures by morally indifferent matters: cuisine, costumes, architecture, pageantry, folkways. Or by a peoples' temperament: hot-blooded, melancholy, whimsical, artistic. This is the cultural diversity of National Geographic. In such venues, even morally corrupt cultural patterns, such as exploitative labor arrangements or vendettas or oppressive family relations, may be treated as curiosities.

Culture is much more than museums and art fairs and musicals. Culture is comprised, most importantly, of large social institutions and practices: the family, educational systems, public morality, the market, courtship. These have great purchase upon persons' hearts and minds. These things are intimately related to whether persons' lives go well or poorly. Persons' understanding of these great matters and decisions about God, marriage, the value of knowledge, and the like are central to their well-being. All these things come to us in cultural wrappings. The family or schooling or romance which we are able, here and now, to pursue is very largely that which our culture offers to us. Anyone's culture is, in other words, likely to mediate between certain important moral realities—such as religious observance, friendship, knowledge—and the deliberating and choosing individual. Marriage is among these culturally arbitrated matters.

II

In some places the civil law has little or no purchase upon the local culture. Sometimes the government is too weak to matter. Sometimes the government is too remote to matter. Sometimes the government has no moral authority. Sometimes folk customs, tribal ways, and religious norms of conduct are enough to keep a community on track. Civil law might then be an afterthought.

But in some places the civil law mightily influences culture. The United States is one such place. Francis George has argued that the "law has peculiar and unique cultural functions in American society."[6]

> The many components of our culture are largely united by law, not by blood, not by race, not by religion, not even by language, but by law. It's the one principal cultural component we all have in common. . . . [L]aw is more important in teaching or instructing us than it is in directing us . . . . [O]ne must therefore ask how it is that law functions as a cultural carrier in [this country], and what does that mean for cultural institutions that are universal [i.e., objective, natural] but that are qualified by law: marriage, family [and others].[7]

The mechanisms by which the law holds sway are many. Sometimes it is enough that the law simply re-direct our behavior, with no particular message (moral or otherwise) specifically intended. Each time our government mobilized the nation's human and material resources to fight a war, the collateral effects upon the culture (and thus upon us) have been enormous, and often unpredictable. The effects of the 2010 comprehensive health care overhaul—often termed "Obamacare"—are sure to include new understandings of "health," "equality" of access to medical treatment, and of the place and meaning of organic functioning in overall "well-being."

Flipping the switch of the criminal law can change a culture. Because criminal law pertains to the most serious offenses against the common good, because crimes are so often not just unlawful acts but acts which are in themselves gravely immoral, and because criminals are *punished* as moral wrongdoers, any act which counts as a crime is almost invariably *stigmatized*. People typically read off from the ambient roster of crimes a list of "thou shalt nots," with a strong moral sanction to it. Acts which were within recent memory decriminalized—abortion, gambling, extra-marital sex, some drug use—quickly became morally acceptable. In *Lawrence v.*

Texas the Supreme Court decriminalized consenting homosexual acts performed in private, and did so with the state goal of removing precisely the moral stigma which making any act a crime inevitably communicates.

Some acts which were not crimes but which were nonetheless penalized by the civil law—divorce, unwed motherhood, viewing pornographic videos—became culturally acceptable soon after the demise of their legal stigmatization. It works the other way around as well. Within recent memory many acts which had long had been culturally acceptable (and lawful) have been made crimes, or legally discouraged in other ways. Racist comments, all sorts of other "hate speech," "date rape," cigarette smoking, drinking-and-driving, and corporal punishment at school and at home, have been culturally marginalized, partly by being made illegal.

The United States Supreme Court has often spoken of the law's profound capacity to shape an entire culture. Even an authoritative gesture can, according to the Court, be enough. The Court's church-state jurisprudence, for example, is animated by a concept which the Justices have named "endorsement." "Endorsement" happens (according to the Court) when a hypothetical reasonable observer could conclude that the government has somehow shown favor to ("endorsed") religion. When that happens (again, per the Court's story) the observer may feel "stigmatized" as an "outsider" and as a "second-class" citizen—and the First Amendment's prohibition of "establishments" of religion is violated!

"Endorsement" doctrine is more than a little overwrought. But the civil law can and often does send authoritative signals about what is good, valuable, and how things are rightly ordered, all with considerable effect upon the ambient culture. The Supreme Court was on firm ground, for instance, in saying—as it did at the dawn of the modern era of civil rights, in the 1954 case of *Brown v. Board of Education*—that segregation conveyed to African-Americans that they were "inferior" to whites, that their abilities were less, and that their prospects in life were rightly limited. This powerful message could be conveyed by legal slights (a water fountain reserved for "coloreds only") or by monstrous wrongs (the toleration of lynchings).

Affirming the central holding of *Roe v. Wade*,[8] the Court wrote in *Planned Parenthood v. Casey* that "[a]n entire generation has come of age free to assume *Roe*'s concept of liberty in defining the capacity of women to act in society and to make reproductive decisions. . . ."[9] To what effect?

> [F]or two decades . . . people have organized intimate relationships
> and made choices that define their views of themselves and their

places in society, in reliance on the availability of abortion in the event that contraception should fail. The ability of women to participate equally in the economic and social life of the Nation has been facilitated by their ability to control their reproductive lives.[10]

Note well: *Casey* was not talking about just, or even mainly, the millions of women who have had abortions. The *Casey* Court was talking instead about how *Roe* altered the psychology and self-understanding, the dreams and potential achievements, of every woman. *All* women, according to the *Roe* Court, benefit from the reproductive control which abortion allegedly gives them. The abortion liberty is much like unemployment insurance or Medicaid, or any other strand in the social safety net: no matter what chances one takes with one's money or job, no matter how bad one's luck turns, one knows that one is not going to starve, or be left to die with no doctor to lend a hand. *Casey* effectively tells women (and men): no matter what chances you take with sex—even if contraception fails—abortion is your safety net. According to the Court, *Roe* would have transformed our world, even if no one had abortions.

There is no reason to doubt, and there is good reason to hold, that the civil law about *marriage* has shaped our cultural patterns and thus, in turn, what people believe about marriage in ways similar to the way that so many authoritative witnesses say the law has with abortion, segregation, and sexual morality. Testimony in favor of the proposition abounds in the struggle over same-sex "marriage." Proponents of it claim that denying same-sex couples the legal opportunity to marry stamps them as inferior. They seek the special "affirmation" and "endorsement" of their relationships which, they assert, only the law can give or withhold. Opponents of legalized same-sex "marriage" say that the meaning of marriage for *everyone* in society will be degraded if the law treats gender-complementarity as the preference of just so many couples, and not as an essential feature of marriage, just as monogamy is.

To that story I now turn.

III

Civil law often enters into creative partnerships with cultural institutions and practices it does not make. Public authority helps these practices and institutions in various ways—it recognizes, ratifies, regulates, promotes, supports, and protects. Law supervenes upon these institutions, and by so doing creates, within limits, a legal version or dimension of a particular social practice or institution. The state's partnership with marriage and family is the most important example. And the law's version of marriage (and family) is a powerful influence (as we have seen) on what marriage is for the people whose law it is.

This partnership is quite one-sided: law exists for these institutions because law is for the persons whose well-being and flourishing is dependent upon them. Marriage does not exist for law, or for the polity, or for the success of the nation-state as a world historical actor, or for the GNP.[11] Things are the other way round. Law supports certain institutions of civil society for the sake of the common good. The common good is that ensemble of social conditions which make it more or less easy for persons to perfect themselves, to live worthwhile lives. Law supports these institutions for the sake of genuine human flourishing. For the sake of genuine human flourishing, then, the law must shape its "version" of marriage around the truth about marriage. The civil law has always recognized that marriage possesses foundational features beyond human choosing.

The Supreme Court has often made grateful references to marriage as the precondition of American political institutions. This universal recognition is manifest in the Court's many declarations in favor of the choice, or opportunity, to marry as a natural right which the state must respect, and which it may never abridge.[12] All of this is ultimately an acknowledgment that marriage is a pre-political moral and cultural institution upon which the law supervenes. The law recognizes marriage, regulates it, promotes it, and protects it. But law does not create marriage. Even where our law refers to marriage as a "civil contract," it is mainly to emphasize that persons must freely consent to marriage for the marriage to be valid.

Public authority in America has traditionally protected all the constitutive features of marriage. The civil law has long maintained that marriage is monogamous, heterosexual, sexually exclusive, presumptively permanent, and the morally legitimate context for having children. William was not legally able to marry his male neighbor, or the two sisters next door, because neither same-sex marriage nor polygamy was lawful in the United States. No one in the United States is today legally free to marry anyone so long as one's spouse is alive. "Bigamists" and "polygamists" are not persons with more than one spouse, for no one can have more than one spouse. Marriage is, in reality, monogamous; it is for couples only. A "bigamist" is someone who, with a spouse still living, attempts to marry another.

About the relationship among law, culture and the moral truth concerning marriage, Oxford legal philosopher Joseph Raz has said: "[m]onogamy, assuming that it is the only morally valuable form of marriage, cannot be practiced by an individual. It requires a culture which recognizes it, and which supports it through the public's attitude and through its formal institutions."[13] Corrupt culture and law conspire to deprive people of the opportunity to choose (real) marriage where, for example, polygamy is the social norm, or where wives are treated as chattel, and not as equal spouses. In the latter situation, where true equality and mutuality between spouses is unimaginable due to false beliefs about the inferior nature of women, marriage as a two-in-one-flesh communion is simply not available for choice.

Raz does not suppose that, in a culture whose law and public morality do not support monogamy, someone who happens to believe in it will be unable to restrict himself to having one wife or will be required to take additional wives. The point, as expressed by Princeton's Robert George, is rather that even if monogamy is a key element of a sound understanding of marriage, large numbers of people will fail to understand that or understand why that is the case—and will therefore fail to grasp the value of monogamy and the intelligible point of practicing it—unless they are assisted by a culture which supports, formally and informally, monogamous marriage. Marriage is the type of good which can be participated in, or fully participated in, only by people who properly understand it and choose it with a proper understanding in mind; yet people's ability properly to understand it, and thus to choose it, depends upon institutions and cultural understandings that transcend individual choice.[14]

Someone who chooses to marry for life, to the exclusion of sex with all others, enters into a different relationship than someone who does not really choose fidelity unto death. Someone who enters into a marriage understanding it as procreative enters into a different relationship from one who does not. All these persons may, as far as our law is concerned, be married. But the relationships which these married couples participate in is different because—at least partly—of what the law about marriage is. So, what is at stake in the struggle over same-sex "marriage" is this: whether, to the very considerable extent (over time, and for the bulk of people) that civil law determines *what it is that people enter into when they marry,* the marriage on offer in our society shall have an essential relationship to procreation. Is "marriage" to be a reproductive communion of the spouses, or not?

IV

Activists seeking to redefine marriage hold that "excluding" same-sex partners from marriage violates a moral right possessed by every individual to marry a person of one's choice (with that person's consent). Their argument presupposes a false dichotomy regarding marriage: that it must be either (1) a mere means in relation to procreation as its extrinsic end, or (2) a partnership which, though perhaps more emotionally intense than most friendships and typically marked by the presence of sexual relations, is nonetheless like other forms of friendship inasmuch as it bears no intrinsic relationship to procreation.

This is the crucial weight-bearing claim in their argument, for same-sex "marriages" are necessarily sterile. Although same-sex couples often raise children together, none of those children is the offspring—fruit, issue—of the *couple*. None is the embodiment of that couple's two-in-one-flesh bodily union. Where the law abandons marriage as a union of man and woman in favor of that between two spouses, then marriage *in law* is sterile. Many if not most married couples would continue to have children of their own. But that contingent fact would not be constitutive of marriage, just as such.

Defenders of conjugal marriage reply (in part) that marriage is not malleable in the ways that their opponents suppose. It is by nature oriented to procreation, and so defining marriage as a male-female union is not unjust discrimination. On a sound understanding of marriage, they argue, it is no more unfair to "exclude" same-sex partners from marriage than it is to "exclude" three (or more) polyamorous sexual partners from marriage. Indeed, it is not accurately characterized as *exclusion* at all.

There is a better understanding of marriage—one that is in fact historically embodied in our law and in the philosophical traditions supporting it. On this understanding, marriage is a sexual union of the type that is specially apt for, and would naturally be fulfilled by, having and rearing children together, but whose value, precisely as such a relationship, is intrinsic (as an irreducible aspect of integral human fulfillment) and not merely instrumental (as it would be if marriage were properly understood as only a means to procreation and the rearing of children).

Those who support defining marriage in such a way as to include same-sex partnerships deny that marriage has any intrinsic relation to procreation. When striking down Proposition 8 (which re-established conjugal marriage under California law after it had been invalidated by that state's supreme court), Judge Vaughn Walker curtly argued: "Never has the state inquired into procreative capacity or intent before issuing a marriage license; indeed, a marriage license is more than a license to have procreative sexual intercourse."[15] The same argument was advanced earlier by Chief Justice Margaret Marshall in her majority opinion in *Goodridge v. Department of Public Health*, the ruling that struck down Massachusetts' conjugal marriage law. Replying to the contention that marriage's primary purpose is procreation, Marshall confidently said that:

> This is incorrect . . . [the marriage law] contains no requirement that the applicants for a marriage license attest to their ability or intention to conceive children by coitus. Fertility is not a condition of marriage, nor is it grounds for divorce. People who have never consummated their marriage, and never plan to, may be and stay married.[16]

This argument—that since infertile couples can marry, marriage is not oriented to procreation—is radically unsound.

The key is to understand the specific type of community marriage actually is—in particular, how it is bodily, sexual, and of a type that would naturally be fulfilled by procreation. In every society we find something like the following type of relationship: men and women committed to sharing their lives together, on the bodily, emotional, and spiritual levels of their being, in the kind of community that would be fulfilled by procreating and rearing children together. That such a distinctive type of community—marriage—does exist in every society is undeniable. There are, of course other relationships *similar* in some ways to marriage. Men and women may cohabit, regularly have sex together, and view the possibility of having children as a possibly attractive optional "extra," (or perhaps instead as a burden to be avoided). Or, two or more individuals may form an alliance for the sake of bringing up children—two sisters, for example, or several celibate religious men or women.

But these relationships are not marriages. Marriage is that type of community that is both a comprehensive unity (a unity on all levels of the human person, including the bodily-sexual) and a community that would be fulfilled by procreating and rearing children together. Moreover, there is an intrinsic link between these two aspects of the community; the comprehensive (and therefore intrinsically sexual) relationship is fulfilled by, and is not merely incidental to, the procreating and rearing of children.

These points can be clarified. First, the bodily, sexual aspect of the relationship is *part of* and is inherently linked to the other aspects of the marital union. The sexual communion of a man and a woman establishes a real, biological union—a one-flesh union is an accurate description of it— for in this act they are biologically a single agent of a single action. Just as an individual's different organs—heart, lungs, arteries, and so forth—perform not as isolated parts, but in a coordinated unity to carry out a single biological function of the whole individual (circulation of oxygenated blood), so too in coitus the sexual organs of the male and those of the female function in a coordinated way to carry out a biological function of the couple as a unit—mating. Hence coitus establishes a real biological union with respect to this function, although it is, of course, a limited biological union inasmuch as for various other functions (e.g., respiration, digestion, locomotion) the male and female remain fully distinct.

Now, the human body is part of the personal reality of the human being, and not an extrinsic instrument of the conscious and desiring aspect of the self. So the biological unity just described can be a truly personal unity and a part (indeed, the biological foundation) of the comprehensive, multi-leveled (biological, emotional, rational, volitional) union that marriage distinctively is. When a man and woman make a commitment to each other to share their lives on all levels of their being, in the type of community that would be fulfilled by cooperatively procreating and rearing children, then the biological unity established and renewed in sexual intercourse is the beginning or embodiment of that community we know as marriage. Unlike other forms of friendship, the marital community is structured by norms of monogamy, exclusivity, and the pledge of permanence, partly because of the intrinsic link between it and procreation. The sexual communion of spouses is the bodily component proportionate to, indeed part of, the kind of multi-leveled personal community they have consented to in marrying.

Second, such a community is extended and naturally fulfilled by procreating and rearing children together. The child is the concrete fruit and expression of their marital commitment and their love for one another; indeed, each child born of the marriage is the union of the spouses made concrete and prolonged in time. So the cooperative rearing of their children does not establish a new type of relationship, but rather deepens and naturally fulfills the relationship that they have established precisely in marrying. Rearing children is to tend to the marriage, to cultivate its fruit, to serve the good of the parents' marriage by and through each act of service to each child. As a form of human relationship, marriage is indeed, then, intrinsically oriented to procreation—but not as a mere means in relation to an extrinsic end. The union of the spouses to one another in a relationship whose distinctive structure is what it is because of its aptness for procreation and the rearing of children is no mere instrumental good, but is rather good in itself—an intrinsic fulfillment of those united in the relationship. And it is for this reason that a marriage is and remains a marriage—a true marriage—even if procreation does not result and even if the spouses know that it will not result. With or without children, spouses are in a relationship of the type that is especially apt for procreation and would naturally be fulfilled by their having and rearing children together—their children (if they were to have children) would be embodiments of their marital communion. The marital communion of the spouses is good in itself, and as such provides a non-instrumental reason for conjugal relations whether or not they are capable of conceiving children; but it is also naturally fulfilled when it becomes part of a larger community, the family.

Given these two points regarding the nature of marriage, it is clear why marriage is the union of sexually complementary spouses. Same-sex partners, whatever the character or intensity of their emotional bond, cannot form together the kind of union that marriage is. To marry, a couple must, in principle, be able to form a real bodily union—not just an emotional and spiritual union. Same-sex couples are unable to do this: the sexual acts that persons of the same sex can perform on each other do not make them biologically one, and so cannot establish the bodily foundation for the multileveled union that is marriage. And to marry, a couple must form the kind of communion that would be naturally fulfilled by conceiving and rearing children together. Same-sex couples cannot form this type of union: they (two or more) can form sexual arrangements, and can also form alliances for child-rearing, but the one relationship is distinct and not inherently linked to the other.

Also, given these points about marriage, it is easy to see that infertile opposite-sex couples *can* form a true marital union. They are able to fulfill the two essential conditions just mentioned for marrying. First, infertile opposite-sex couples can form a biological unit—they can mate (that is, they can perform the kind of act that results in procreation when conditions extrinsic to their conduct obtain). Second, infertile opposite-sex couples can form the kind of bodily, emotional, and spiritual union of precisely the sort that would be naturally fulfilled by procreation and rearing of children together—even though in their case that fulfillment is not reached.

It is sometimes objected that infertile couples cannot biologically unite, since their act is not in fact capable of procreating—they cannot (it is objected) perform an act that is procreative in kind, which is necessary for a biological union. However, no couple can directly or simply choose to procreate. The only thing any couple can directly do regarding procreation is to perform the kind of act that will lead to procreation, provided other conditions extrinsic to their conduct obtain. (Thus, children are not *products* of their parents' sexual acts: rather, parents should rightly view them as *gifts* that supervene upon their bodily expression of love in their sexual union.) So, opposite-sex couples who are infertile can perform precisely *the same kind of act* that fertile couples can perform. In both cases, they fulfill the behavioral conditions of procreation. And so the sexual intercourse of an infertile couple, no less than that of a fertile couple, unites them biologically: they *mate*, even though in the case of the infertile couple procreation will not result. In each case their sexual act can consummate or embody their marriage.

So, the state's granting marriage licenses only to opposite-sex couples is based on the nature of marriage and does not constitute unjust discrimination. The state grants a license to do X only to someone presumptively capable of doing X. It is no more unjust discrimination to deny marriage licenses to couples of the same sex than to twelve-year olds, to those already married, or to polyamorous groups of three or more sexual partners: in each case the license is denied simply because the individuals in question are unable to form with each other the kind of union that marriage *is*.

V

Marriage is a union of a man and a woman, committed to sharing their lives together on the bodily, emotional, and rational-volitional levels of their being, in the kind of community that would be naturally fulfilled by having and rearing children together. Since that kind of multi-leveled community cannot be formed by two persons of the same sex—such persons cannot unite biologically in the way that has always been understood to consummate marriage, and they cannot form the kind of community that would be fulfilled by conceiving, bearing, and raising children together— there cannot in reality be such a thing as same-sex marriage (any more than there can be such a thing as polyamorous marriage—that is marriage involving three or more partners). Since same-sex (and polyamorous) partners cannot form what are, in truth, marriages, the state's not granting them marriage licenses is not unjust discrimination.

This argument for marriage as necessarily a man-woman relationship is sometimes obscured even by proponents of conjugal marriage. It is sometimes argued that the state's interest in marriage is simply to ensure that as many children as possible are raised in "an optimal setting," and that this interest justifies "restricting" marriage to opposite-sex couples. But the fact that intact homes are the optimal setting for child-rearing does not *by itself* justify a policy of recognizing only opposite-sex partnerships as marriages. For a good end (ensuring optimal care for children) would not justify the means (excluding same-sex "marriage") if it could be shown that the means were unjust—and denying marriage to such couples, if they were able to form a true marital partnership, would be unjust.

If this argument is advanced as the central one—rather than as a secondary confirmation—then it is misleading. For in that case the impression is given that the state itself has created marriage for the extrinsic purpose of child-rearing. In fact, however, marriage is indeed naturally oriented to and fulfilled by conceiving, bearing, and raising children, but not as to an extrinsic end—and this orientation belongs to marriage independently of any action on the part of the state. In a profound sense, marriage is a "pre-political" institution, albeit one that law and the state rightly recognize, regulate, promote, and protect.

Moreover, if advanced as the main argument, the "optimal setting" argument locates the center of debate in the wrong place. For even if it could be shown that another type of alliance (for example, two men and a woman, religiously active families, or very wealthy families) would tend to produce better child-rearing outcomes, it would not follow that these alliances were also (or alone) real marriages; and the state's duty not to confuse true marriage with other arrangements would still obtain. Hence the real ground for the state's duty to restrict marriage licenses to opposite-sex couples—who are of the age of consent, and have other relevant qualifications—is, not an extrinsic goal of marriage, but the actual nature of marriage itself. While the optimal setting argument has a confirming evidential force, advancing it as the central argument diverts attention from how marriage is most centrally related to procreation: marriage is intrinsically (and not merely incidentally or instrumentally) related to procreation.

The state does have a legitimate interest in promoting and regulating marriage; indeed, it is obligated to do so. The state exists in order to promote ends that (a) serve all within that society, and (b) can effectively and appropriately be pursued by political society (unlike ends that can best be pursued only by individuals, families, or voluntary associations). Such ends constitute the *public good,* and clearly include defending against external attacks, preserving internal order, facilitating transportation, providing a judicial system for fair resolution of disputes, etc. But in virtually every political society, the promotion, protection, and regulation of marriage has been understood as part of the public good. This is partly because regulating marriage, and so distinguishing between who is and who is not married, is a task the state cannot escape. For, though marriage is more than a contract, it still is one (it is more, not less, than a contract). And so the state must adjudicate some disputes about marriage, inheritance issues, child custody, and property when spouses separate. For this reason among many others, privatization of marriage is a practical impossibility. Further, it is abundantly clear that healthy marriages provide social benefits to all.

But the most important reason that the state should protect and promote marriage is that it is itself an irreducible human good, a distinctive and irreplaceable way in which human persons (men, women, and children) can flourish. Hence the strength or weakness of marriage as a social institution profoundly affects the well-being of everyone in a political society.

The state can perhaps most effectively promote marriage by influencing the public understanding of marriage through its laws and regulations. The public understanding and appreciation of marriage—the marriage culture in a given society—greatly influences people's capacities to participate as fully and richly as possible in this intrinsic human good. By conveying a gravely distorted view of marriage, the state can weaken and even undermine its members' capacities for full and rich participation in this important aspect of human flourishing. So, it is not only appropriate but also morally obligatory that the state promote and protect marriage.

CONCLUSION

The state must promote *real* marriage, not any counterfeit of it. The state must not obscure the nature of marriage by equating it with other arrangements which differ essentially from marriage. By redefining marriage so as to include same-sex partnerships, the state would convey the message that marriage, instead of being an objective interpersonal union both good in itself and intrinsically linked to procreation, is a relationship principally defined by emotional connection, the exchange of sexual pleasure, and shared housekeeping—all important but nonetheless ancillary features or entailments of genuine marriage. This would undermine the public understanding of marriage and erode respect for the genuine human good of marriage. In a misguided effort to expand access to marriage, the state would instead make it more difficult for people to enter into and live out true marriages.

CHAPTER 5:

Three Mistaken Arguments for Same-Sex "Marriage"[1]

The main constitutional argument for legally recognizing same-sex relationships as "marriages" is a simple-looking non-discrimination claim: because there is no legally cognizable difference between the capacity of same-sex couples and opposite-sex couples for marriage, restrictive laws arbitrarily withhold the recognition and benefits which legal marriage entails. The notion is that the statutory category—in this case, the couple's gender composition—does not contribute to the realization of any legitimate state goal. For that reason traditional marriage laws lack a rational basis and, so the argument goes, therefore have their roots in outmoded prejudices or in esoteric religious beliefs, neither of which is a suitable basis for civil law in our constitutional system.

This has been the basic structure of the argument in every judicial decision which has required same-sex "marriage." As the Massachusetts Supreme Judicial Court concluded in *Goodridge v. Department of Public Health* (the first such decision), the state "failed to identify any constitutionally adequate reason for denying civil marriage to same-sex couples."[2] As a result, same-sex marriage debuted in Massachusetts. It is also the basic argument which the Obama Administration used in early 2011 to explain its decision to stop defending in court the Defense of Marriage Act. That statute stipulated wherever the term "marriage" appears in federal law, it means the union of "one man and one woman." DOMA also declared that wherever the word "spouse" appears, it means "only a person of the opposite sex who is a husband or a wife." The Administration declared that it could identify no "reasonable arguments" for the law, and that it could no longer ask courts to uphold it.

It is indeed settled constitutional doctrine that laws without a "rational basis" violate the Constitution. And *if* there really is no reason why same-sex couples cannot enter into marriages, then excluding them *would* be arbitrary, and thus unconstitutional. Correctly applying the "rational basis" test to marriage laws requires courts (and the Administration), however, to identify *why* the law defines marriage as the union of a man and a woman: what is the law up to, what is it trying to do, what is its interest in saying that marriage is just such a union? The correct answer to this question (as we saw in the preceding chapter) is that the law recognizes only the union of man and woman as marriage because that is what marriage *really* is, and the law should promote and protect only real marriage so that people may genuinely flourish. The law refuses to recognize the relationships of two men or two women because their relationships cannot be marriages. That is the "rational basis" of traditional marriage laws. Courts (and others) inclined towards same-sex "marriage" avoid it like the plague.

The three mistaken arguments for same-sex "marriage" examined here share one common defect: they are all attempts to avoid the unavoidable core question about what marriage is. Courts are sorely tempted to do this because judges in general, and those who favor same-sex "marriage" in particular, cleave to grounds of decision which steer clear of disputed philosophical premises (such as the nature of marriage). Doing so results in the desired, if illusory, appearance of "neutrality." As a general tendency or rebuttable presumption about how to decide cases, this philosophical reticence is understandable, and even correct. But sometimes the "deep" question is essential to a correct decision. This is one of those times.

Each of the three arguments criticized here puts aside the question of what marriage really is. These arguments ask instead about the "purpose" of our civil law of marriage, where the truth about marriage is deemed (at least implicitly) to be irrelevant or non-existent. Each mistaken argument is characteristically liberal, in an important (but different) sense. Each could go viral; that is, these mistaken views about the role of coherence in legal reasoning and about the relationship between critical morality and positive law could infect any judicial decision, and all sorts of arguments about what the law should be. That is: these mistakes could be used (wittingly or not) as avoidance techniques in situations having nothing to do with the marriage question.

Here are the three mistaken arguments.

First. Proponents of same-sex "marriage" argue that the law of marriage does not rest upon a view of marriage as, in some basic or essential way, "procreative."[3] It is easy to see why they do so: an unrebutted claim that the law cares for marriage as procreative would doom their position.

The sexual acts of two women or two men cannot be reproductive. There can never be children born of the same-sex union. If marriage is about (in some decisive way) procreation, then limiting it to opposite-sex couples easily passes the rational basis test.

Courts favoring same-sex "marriage" do *not* claim that the truth about marriage (as a procreative union) is not the basis for our laws. They do not say that this truth has never been the reason of the law. They do not say that no lawmaker today holds this truth as ground for today's laws. They say rather that this truth about marriage (as procreative) cannot *coherently* predict the manifold laws any jurisdiction happens to have, concerning not just marriage, but also about adoption, foster care, same-sex sexual acts, IVF, and other more distant matters. But this argument depends essentially upon a gross misunderstanding of the role of coherence in law, as I show in Part I.

Second. Opponents of same-sex marriage propose that marriage be limited to opposite-sex couples because the intact mother-father home is the "optimal" setting for successfully raising children.[4] Proponents of same-sex marriage have accepted debate on this ground. In Part II of this chapter I criticize "optimal setting" arguments, insofar as they are offered as premises in an argument about the legal meaning of marriage. I will show that optimal setting arguments do not succeed in excluding same-sex couples from marriage.

Third. Some people argue that the law must recognize same-sex relationships as marriages because equal respect for the self-constituting choices of homosexuals and lesbians requires it. To do otherwise, it is claimed, is to treat them as "second-class citizens." I offer three criticisms in Part III of this way of looking at the relationship among legal recognition, choice, and moral value, and conclude that this particular understanding of "equal respect" should be discarded.

I

The first step in the argument for legal recognition of same-sex marriage is often (and, I think, must be) to refute the claim that the law protects marriage as a procreative relationship.[5] That marriage is procreative is plausible enough: common moral sense and practical experience suggest to most people that marriage is, somehow, essentially about children. The law of marriage reflects this conviction, that marriage is the morally normative context for conceiving and having and raising children. This conviction is the genesis of the legal limitation of marriage to man and woman. Because there can never be issue from the sex acts of two men or two women, denying marital status to same-sex couples makes, at least *prima facie*, good sense.

Here are two statements by same-sex marriage advocates of this first move against the marriage-is-essentially-procreative target. The *Goodridge* court said that Massachusetts' legislative rationales for prohibiting same-sex couples from marrying include providing a "favorable setting for procreation."[6] The Vermont Supreme Court in *Baker v. State* said that Vermont's aim was to promote a "permanent commitment between couples who have children to ensure that their offspring are considered legitimate and receive ongoing parental support" and that there be a sustained public message that child rearing is "intertwined" with the procreative acts of a man and woman married to each other.[7]

Advocates of same-sex marriage do not really question that as a matter of historical fact our definition of marriage as heterosexual is rooted in convictions about procreation, along the lines described in *Baker* and *Goodridge*.[8] Advocates sometimes even concede that a restrictive definition may have once made sense, back when people did marry to have children, had lots of them, and could scarcely do (or think) otherwise, given the lack of effective birth control and the couples' need for supportive children in their old age.[9] Advocates say, however, that it is time for a change.[10] Or, that it is past time.[11]

Proponents of same-sex marriage pursue two rhetorical strategies in support of their proposed change. The first is frankly normative; it is an argument about what the law ought to understand marriage to be.[12] This argument centers upon what marriage really (philosophically and morally) is. Marriage is, they propose, about the adults' relationship and the many satisfactions which each partner derives from being the other's spouse.[13] It is true, the argument goes, that most married couples at some point have or obtain children.[14] But not nearly all, and in any event, our society has already accepted the divorce of children from marriage (as previously unimaginable rates of out-of-wedlock births attest).[15] So marriage is not in any essential way "procreative."

Children who happen to come along need not be seen, in this construal of marriage, merely as objects which satisfy adults' desires for a parental experience or as players in the parents' life dramas (though there would be a tendency towards doing so, and many couples would in fact see kids that way). In my judgment, however, the couple's marriage would have to be seen, at least initially, as a certain sort of childless bond (say, an intense sexual friendship), which later morphs into something else. Legal recognition of same-sex relationships as marriages implies just this view: children are not part of what defines marriage; marriage is not the type of union which is fulfilled by conceiving, having, and raising kids. Children do not perfect the union which the couple entered into on their wedding day. Kids change it. I think this (or something very close to it) is what it means to say, "Marriage is not a procreative relationship."

The legal descriptions of same-sex marriage and "civil unions" on offer in court opinions and in legislative definitions describe exclusively adult relationships of "mutual affection,"[16] "caring and commitment,"[17] and that are "stable and lasting."[18] Nothing is said of children or of procreation. Of course, nothing about kids is implicit in these accounts of same-sex relationships. Because all same-sex couples are (as a couple) sterile, even the highest praise and most intense descriptions of their coming together cannot include an intrinsic connection towards children.

This first strategy—which is (again) frankly normative—depends for its success upon the truth about marriage. We saw in the last two parts of chapter four that it is untrue. We saw how marriage is indeed so essentially oriented to procreation that neither two men nor two women can really marry. Same-sex "marriage" proponents have also adopted a second strategy, which would by-pass the frankly normative question of what marriage really is. By adding some information about recent legal changes affecting the family, advocates position themselves to offer a descriptive-sounding conclusion. This second claim is *not* that the law's interest in marriage may not be, or should not be, its procreative nature. The claim is instead that *the law has already rejected the procreative view.*

Same-sex "marriage" advocates maintain that the law has *already* severed its ties to children. It *is* now about adult commitments, experiences, and satisfactions, such that same-sex couples are as suited to marriage as are opposite-sex couples. These advocates say that it is just not true for Massachusetts or Vermont to say that they limit marriage to opposite-sex couples because they (the states) treat marriage as procreative.[19]

Here are two examples of this mode of argument.

In late 1999, the *Baker* court blazed the path towards legal recognition of same-sex marriage.[20] That court declared (to the surprise of many) that Vermont's 1777 Constitution required that same-sex couples be accorded "identical" marital benefits as those accorded to men and women.[21] The court permitted the legislature to withhold the name marriage and to call same-sex relationships civil unions.[22] That is what Vermont's legislators subsequently did.[23]

The *Baker* court responded to the state's assertions that marriage is, in some essential manner, procreative by saying that it is "undisputed that many opposite-sex couples marry for reasons unrelated to procreation, that some of these couples never intend to have children, and that others are incapable of having children."[24] "[I]f the purpose of the statutory exclusion of same-sex couples is to further "the link between procreation and child rearing," the court concluded, "it is significantly underinclusive."[25] "The law extends the benefits and protections of marriage to many persons with no logical connection to the stated governmental goal. . . . [T]he statutes plainly exclude many same-sex couples who are no different from opposite-sex couples with respect to these objectives."[26] The court's conclusion, then, was that the state does not, as a matter of fact, care for marriage as essentially oriented to procreation.[27]

Justice Scalia is no supporter of same-sex "marriage." He nonetheless supplied in *Lawrence v. Texas* (the 2003 decision striking down criminal laws against sodomy, an outcome from which Scalia dissented) a pristine example of the same-sex advocates' second mode of argument.[28] "[E]ncouragement of procreation," he said, could not possibly be a legitimate basis for denying marital status to same-sex couples because the "sterile and the elderly are allowed to marry."[29] Scalia previously argued that marriage laws are a constitutionally legitimate expression of a majority's moral disapproval of homosexual conduct,[30] a position which I have criticized elsewhere.[31]

Scalia's thinking about sterile couples embodies a startling naiveté about the normative role of coherence in law. The *Baker* court displayed a similar innocence. Scalia assumes that if marriage were procreative, then the civil law not only may, or should, but would prohibit "elderly" and "sterile" opposite-sex couples from marrying. The assumption is unwarranted. All that the civil law's asserted laxity may show is that the law is over-inclusive: some people who cannot really (morally speaking) participate (or fully participate) in marriage are legally permitted to marry anyway.

The apparent over-inclusiveness identified by Scalia may be the best that the law can do to mark out a bright and enforceable line for marital eligibility. The finer cuts suggested by antecedent moral or policy reflection are either impossible to make or the effort and intrusiveness of doing so would work comparatively greater mischief. Legal categories and criteria are often—and maybe characteristically—rough approximations of an underlying moral or policy position. Where unrestricted thinking about the common good results in the judgment that the state ought to meet a financial "need," or that a political office requires a "mature" occupant, the law stipulates a gross income of say "20,000 dollars" or that aspirants be at least "thirty-five years of age." Highway speed limits are meant to produce "safe" travel. The posted limit is a number of miles-per-hour, not the warning, "drive safely," and sometimes driving the limit is, in truth, dangerous. People who wish to marry must, as a matter of fact, be mature enough to understand what they are getting into and freely consent. But the law does not limit marriage to those, and only to those, who are "mature" and "free." The law says that one must be eighteen years old to marry.

Justice Scalia and the *Baker* judges suppose far greater coherence between a legal classification and its putative legislative purpose than they should. Then, and inexplicably, they make their inflated notion a litmus test of actual purpose: a purpose loosely wrapped around a legal class is not a purpose at all.

Goodridge made a related but distinguishable mistake about coherence in law. That court rebutted Massachusetts' claim that marriage is inherently procreative: "[T]he Commonwealth affirmatively facilitates bringing children into a family regardless of whether the intended parent is married or unmarried, whether the child is adopted or born into a family, whether assistive technology was used to conceive the child, and whether the parent or her partner is heterosexual, homosexual, or bisexual."[32]

The court observed that "[a]doption and certain insurance coverage for assisted reproductive technology are available to married couples, same-sex couples, and single individuals alike."[33] The *Goodridge* court concluded, "If procreation were a necessary component of civil marriage, our statutes would draw a tighter circle around the permissible bounds of non-marital child bearing and the creation of families by noncoital means."[34]

The court's mistake was to suppose that a commitment to marriage as procreative entails a much more extensive web of surrounding protective prohibitions than, in truth, it does. And this mistake was made possible—indeed, was sustained—by a variation of the Scalia/*Baker* error, which was an inexplicable failure to grasp the indeterminate relationship between ends and means in law. The error in *Goodridge* was, in other words, to suppose that the various liberalities it listed implied a propositional judgment by the lawmakers about marriage, which judgment, the *Goodridge* court further presumed, contradicted the judgment that marriage is procreative.[35]

But it is wrong to proceed so blithely from a legal norm to an underlying normative (moral) judgment. And it compounds this mistake to treat the asserted implicit bases of so many laws as propositions in one chain of reasoning, as if we are talking about one mind thinking through one problem.

Let me further explain this error.

The first step in the explanation is to cut the loose "circle" of permissive laws into two parts or groups of components: Group One is what the state does not prohibit (but which the *Goodridge* court says it should, and would, if it were genuinely interested in marriage as procreative).[36] Group Two is what the state more actively "facilitates"; that is, what the law specifically authorizes and promotes. Group One includes laws which regulate in-vitro fertilization ("IVF") as a laboratory procedure only or only under a description of it as a medical procedure, and not morally according to any overarching account of what is normative about human reproduction. This first group would also include the legal liberty of single women to have and to keep children without state interference and, we could add, without legally stamping these kids as "illegitimate."

Group Two includes a state agency's placement of foster children in a "gay" household and the eventual adoption of those children by the resident "gay" couple. This group could also include more active legal promotion of reproductive technologies, by government funding or other sorts of public endorsement.

As to the first group: in our legal order, liberty is the default position. In our constitutional system, what is not prohibited is permitted. People are at liberty to engage in all sorts of immoral and socially undesirable conduct. Their freedom reflects nothing more about the mind of the legislator than the default position. But this liberty is characteristically opaque: there need not be anything at all in the mind of the legislator who is responsible (in a very loose sense) for the liberty. All that is necessarily (always) true about liberty is that it is the residue of lawmaker inaction. Liberty as such implies nothing whatsoever about any lawmaker's opinion of the conduct at issue, much less about some other (assertedly intertwined) conduct, practice, or institution.

Sometimes the legislator is wholly unaware of the conduct which people are at liberty to perform. Sometimes the legislator is aware but has not had the time to seriously consider whether to legally prohibit the conduct at issue or not. At least in the early stages of development, even important novel undertakings, such as the internet, human growth hormones, and IVF, operate under the legal radar. They are initially unregulated because no lawmaking body has gotten around to crafting, proposing, debating and enacting regulations. Sometimes a particular act or practice or product is not obscure. But its potentially harmful consequences (or bad collateral effect upon something else which the law values) are unknown. Perhaps many legislators decided to leave assisted reproduction to medical ethics and to the market, believing that doing so had no effect on the meaning of marriage as procreative.

Sometimes liberty reflects a conscientious and studied judgment but not a judgment about the conduct at hand. The relevant judgment may be about the limits of the state's authority. These limits include norms arising from sound reasoning about the outer limits of the political common good or norms found in the fundamental law (such as the Constitution). Adults in the United States are at liberty to view pornography[37] and, according to the *Lawrence* decision, engage in consensual sex at home even if they are unmarried.[38] But these liberties are protected by the Constitution—the Court says—with no implied endorsement at all of pornography or of swinging.[39] Thus, it would be wrong to say about legislators who enacted a law to restrict supermarket displays of raunchy magazines that they could not have done so because they think the magazines corrupt people's character, because anyone who really thought so would prohibit all possession and sales of the saucy magazines.

Not so. Legislators possessed of a negative moral view of these magazines were likely blocked by other considerations from acting in the way demanded by our hypothetical liberationists. More generally, legitimate concerns about state intrusion into any adult's home and state supervision of sexual conduct limit good faith efforts to promote marriage as procreative.

We often label this complex of thoughts a doctrine about privacy. A close relative (but not twin) of privacy is tolerance. When public authority "tolerates" an act it means that, though the conduct is judged to be wrong or undesirable, people are at liberty to do as they please, even though (unlike with privacy) it would not be wrong in principle for the state to discourage, or even to prohibit, the act. Tolerance reflects the lawmaker's judgment that attempting to discourage or prohibit the act would, all things considered, do more harm than good. Various immoralities presenting little or no harm to non-consenting people—recreational use of marijuana, some sexual misbehavior, gambling, in some places prostitution—have gradually been decriminalized over the last several decades for this reason. At first they were merely legally tolerated; that is, lawful but still widely perceived to be immoral or at least unseemly. Over time, most tolerated behaviors came to be seen as morally indifferent, and if not, as morally valuable for those with certain appetites.

The decision to tolerate lamentable conduct is a judgment about the lesser of two evils. The decision is not dictated by logic. It is the product of experience, guided by prudent judgment. Making the right call depends upon local circumstances and carefully calibrated judgments about, among other matters, how widespread the demand is for the undesirable behavior at issue, and how bad the secondary effects of its tolerance would likely be. The costs of enforcing a legal prohibition must be considered too, as must the likely effects upon popular respect for the law as a whole. Sometimes the cultural sanctions against certain undesirable acts remain strong enough to contain the misconduct within acceptable bounds—as is probably the case early in an act's transition from prohibited to tolerated (to morally indifferent and, then maybe, to good).

Besides, many if not most laws are a combination of features attractive and unattractive to legislators, with the categories shuffled around according to the convictions of particular lawmakers. Legislators often vote for bills because they favor some parts of it, do not care about others, and positively oppose still more. The classic example may be an abortion restrictive law, one which prohibits, say, "all abortions performed in the third trimester," and which regulates in fine detail the remainder of permitted abortion procedures. A pro-life legislator could vote for it to prohibit as many abortions as he can, regretting the remainder. A pro-choice legislator might vote for it because it is the best compromise available with pro-life forces that would ban all abortions. This legislator might actually oppose the prohibition as a violation of women's privacy. A third legislator might be perplexed by abortion generally but prefer more rather than less regulation of any medical procedure. What does enactment of such a bill imply?

In the cases of artificial insemination and IVF, it could very well be that their legal availability reflects a judgment that they are to be legally tolerated notwithstanding their tendency to blur the law's message about marriage as procreative. Or, that their availability owes partly to a desire to extend the reproductive meaning of marriage to married couples unable to generate children from their own acts of intercourse. On this possible understanding, legislators could believe that, while it would not be unjust to limit these techniques to married couples—as some countries have done—it would do more harm than good to try. In the cases of placing kids in the foster care of a same-sex couple, it could be that the need for adults willing to take on the difficult task of sheltering troubled kids on a temporary basis is so great, and the institutional alternatives so grim, that placing kids notwithstanding the adults' sexual habits is the least unappealing available option.

The relevant flaw in the incoherence argument is by now bubbling to the surface. To conclude from any law in the first group (the group populated by liberties) that the lawmaker has gone back on his commitment to marriage as procreative, one would have to persuasively extract from the liberty—by implication or entailment or by strongly supported inference—some proposition about marriage (it takes two propositions on the same subject for there to be a contradiction). But no such extraction is possible. It could be the case that a particular lawmaker favors such liberties because he opposes traditional marriage. But this would be a matter of fact, awaiting proof in court. No such proof has been adduced in any case. All that we have in cases such as *Baker* and *Goodridge*, then, are free (and bold) assertions, which are no more intuitively plausible than the assertion that restrictions on smoking cannot and thus are not rooted in health concerns because, if they were, smoking would be banned altogether.

What about Group Two laws? Someone might say that the lawmaker can see and did see that licensing IVF clinics implies something contrary to the judgment that lies at the heart of the law's protection of opposite-sex marriage: that children ought to come to be through the marital acts of mother and father. Someone else might say that state agencies which place kids in "gay" households must be saying something—at least implicitly—at odds with restrictive marriage laws (Is the mother-father household morally normative for children, or not?). Let us grant this premise. Let us stipulate that at some time past, lawmakers established that marriage was limited to unions of a man and a woman because marriage is procreative. Let us further stipulate that lawmakers recently enacted a provision which inescapably implies an incompatible conviction about marriage—say, that it is in essence a purely adult relationship (in the sense earlier described here). This is essentially to grant the positions of the *Baker* and *Goodridge* courts, as well as that of Justice Scalia in *Lawrence v. Texas*.

What follows?

The position we are considering maintains that, from an incompatibility between two laws, it follows that the purpose of the prior law has changed, or at least that it has been abandoned. But what is revealed on the pages of the legislative record from the earlier time cannot now be erased or amended. The position therefore should be restated to be this: the older law cannot presently be maintained on its original basis because the original basis is irreconcilable with the grounds of a subsequent enactment.

Now, this could be the case where the subsequent legal act is by its nature superior to the prior act. For example: a blacks-only publicly supported college, founded in a southern state in 1910 for reasons which require no elaboration, cannot be maintained now against constitutional challenge on its founding basis (and could not, I should think, be sustained at all). But this is not at all like the same-sex marriage situation. For one thing, we are talking prototypically about two legislative acts—one way-back then and the other quite recent—possessed of equal authority within the system. For a second thing, we are not talking about incompatible operative legal norms. That is the case in our example. Now there is an operative norm which forbids racial segregation which clashes with, say, the by-laws of the college which forbid the attendance of any but "colored" students.

In the same-sex marriage cases, there is no such real-world operative impossibility of complying with both operative norms: a state can coherently limit marriage to men and women and place kids in the foster care of two unmarried men. The situation at hand involves an alleged incompatibility between an operative norm—no same-sex marriage—and the (alleged) implication or unstated basis of another law. But no one is aware of all that is implied or entailed by the positions he takes or the propositions he asserts. Insofar as one is unaware of these implications or entailments, one does not embrace them, for no one can adopt or endorse a proposition which he has never considered, especially one which was never brought to mind. It is true that the implications and entailments of any proposition are beyond the conscious control of anyone. Their existence is a matter of logic, not will, and people are in some sense committed to them. But the existence (which we are assuming) of a latent incompatibility does not mean that the implication later in time supplants what came earlier. The existence of a latent incompatibility does not establish a conclusion. It does, however, raise the question: would the lawmaker have acted as he did (later), if he were fully aware that a consequence of doing so was an effective repeal of the earlier act?

The relevant question would be, for example, whether the lawmaker who voted to license an IVF clinic or to approve foster care placements without concern for sexual orientation would have done so even if it meant legally recognizing same-sex relationships as marriages. The *Baker* and *Goodridge* courts never ask this question.

This argument from incoherence is therefore question-begging. From the observation that the law is of two minds about marriage, it does not follow that the law really is of one mind. It follows even less that the law is of this one mind rather than of that other mind. Careful analysis can expose incoherence, and logic calls for its removal. But there is no more reason to suppose that marriage law must be made coherent by recognizing same-sex relationships as marriages than there is to suppose that it must be made coherent by declaring same-sex couples ineligible to adopt. If one supposes that the legal regime of marriage must be coherent—and if one further supposes that courts are authorized to make it coherent—all that one has established is that a very important choice has to be made. But these courts have sought to escape the burdens and responsibilities of choosing precisely by exaggerating the role of coherence in law.

In what sense is an inflated understanding of coherence in law a characteristically liberal notion? I think that this inflation reflects and even proceeds from the distrust of ordinary politics characteristic of the liberal judicial activism of the last generation or so. By making a norm assertedly embedded somewhere within incoherent, muddled law a reform driver, courts acquire at once a breathtaking jurisdiction they would not otherwise possess, and a norm to guide its exercise which is intrinsically opposed to incrementalism, respect for precedent, and deference to legislation (warts and all).

II

The *Goodridge* majority found common ground with the dissenting justices when it said that "preferential treatment" of civil marriage owes to the legislature's judgment that marriage "is the foremost setting for the education and socialization of children" precisely because it "encourages parents to remain committed to each other and to their children as they grow."[40]

This optimal setting bears some resemblance to the "best interest" of the child standard which has long been the touchstone of custody battles and adoption proceedings.[41] But there is this huge difference: optimal setting is a statistical measure which does not purport to identify what is best for this child or whether those prospective parents will be a success. And another difference: statistics about what is optimal determine not who rears any child, but who may—as a rule—marry.

"Optimal setting" is an evaluative but non-moral yardstick. It is concerned with whether things such as kids' self-esteem, school performance, success in forming relationships, and various other psychological indicia are, generally speaking, higher in intact mother and father households than they are in same-sex households. There are by now many studies of this question.[42] The findings are mixed and the validity of some studies is hotly disputed. It is safe to say, however, that a legislator could reasonably conclude from these studies that "intact" households are generally better for kids such that they amount to the optimal setting for child development. Then limiting marriage to opposite-sex couples would be constitutional.

I said that optimal setting is evaluative but non-moral. I meant that "optimal setting" excludes consideration of parents' instruction and example on the morality of homosexual acts (and thus of sexual morality in larger part), and on the constitution (heterosexual or otherwise) of marriage. The reason for this exclusion is simple: optimal setting is intended to be an argument for conclusions about marriage and sexual morality. Uncontroversial indicators of emotional and psychological well-being are offered as debate-resolvers because they are traits which anyone would want for their kids no matter what they think of "gay" marriage. To include moral norms about marriage and sex would be to slip what needs to be established into the premises.

Sometimes optimal includes references to mothers and fathers as "role models" or as parental authorities. In the course of upholding that state's marriage law, the New York Court of Appeals noted the importance of "living models of what both a man and a woman are like."[43] But these references are underdeveloped and vague. They are meant to be; lest their non-controversial character be sacrificed by connection with more concrete gender roles and with moral claims about sexual acts and what marriage is. Perhaps it does not pay to press a point about so vague a claim. But one wonders what is left of these "living models" once they are stripped of disputed moral and cultural norms.

The *Goodridge* majority considered, but eventually rejected, the Commonwealth's argument that "confining marriage to opposite-sex couples ensures that children are raised in the 'optimal' setting."[44] The *Goodridge* dissenters stressed the state's legitimate interest in "promoting . . . the best possible social structure in which children should be born and raised";[45] "supporting an optimal social structure within which to bear and raise children";[46] and "ensuring . . . an optimal social structure for the bearing and raising of children."[47] The dissenters said that this aim was "normative," and at a couple points, they flirted with making a moral claim.[48] But they did not. Optimal was, for them, in the end reducible to social scientific indicia of well-being.[49]

Now, "optimal setting" does not purport to be the (or even, a) key to understanding what marriage really is. It is not an argument about moral truth. It is a claim rather about public authority's point of view, about the "state's interest" in marriage. It is an answer to the question: *why* does the government recognize and promote this relationship known as "marriage" at all? I have already (in Chapter Four) explained why separating the truth about marriage from the state's interest in it is a mistake. Here I should like to take up the "optimal setting" argument on its own terms, and ask: is it a sound way to explain and justify public authority's (perhaps) peculiar point of view about marriage?

It is not.

There is, first, a contingent problem of what could be called rhetorical *estoppel*. Massachusetts' position in *Goodridge* was undone partly by its concession that "same-sex couples may be 'excellent' parents," a concession magnified by state laws permitting same-sex couples to adopt children.[50] The *Goodridge* court further observed that "[n]o one disputes that the plaintiff couples are families, that many are parents, and that the children they are raising" need a secure and stable family environment.[51]

Wherever concessions of this sort are made—and they often are—it is untenable to assert that same-sex couples are so "sub-optimal" as to justify exclusion of them altogether from legal marriage. It is, moreover, practically impossible not to make these concessions where the organizing principle of legal marriage is "optimizing" child outcomes. So, the argument is self-defeating.

How so? Statistics tell one nothing about this or that same-sex couple as potential parents. Some such couples measure up just fine on the optimal dial, just as statistics do not guarantee that any particular opposite-sex couple will rate high. And many such couples are in fact abysmal parents. Foster care, child custody, and adoption proceedings are all couple-specific. Even assuming that optimum setting statistics justify excluding same-sex couples from marriage, that measure does not exclude them from adopting and, thus, from forming "families." As I said, there is nothing in statistical tendencies which suggests that same-sex couples invariably fall below some norm of child-care "success."

Besides, there is a grave danger of circularity in the optimal-setting argument. The argument is deployed (you will recall) to rebut claims that excluding same-sex couples from legal marriage is *arbitrary*. The *reason* on offer is that the state, relying upon statistical findings about parental cohorts, seeks to promote the most promising or best ("optimal") arrangement for certain child-rearing outcomes. The conclusion to be supported is, however, pretty blunt and not obviously "optimal" at all: any opposite-sex couple may marry; no same-sex couple may do so. Proponents of same-sex "marriage" might reasonably wonder why the state should be so lazy. These advocates could argue that, if the state were serious about "optim[izing]" child welfare, then public authority would consider further limitations upon marital couplings. Why not limit marriage to more educated couples, or to wealthier twosomes, or to some other combination of persons which predict for marital stability and childrearing success? No doubt competent social science could be mustered to support all sorts of refinements, so that at the end of the day children were raised by the best parents available. The looming circularity lies here. If the state relies upon "optimal setting" to bar same-sex couples' access to marriage but no one else's access, then is it not using that argument *arbitrarily*?

Excluding same-sex couples from marriage leads, in any event, to *de facto* families cut off from the law's protection of families. As the *Goodridge* court concluded, that makes "the task of child rearing . . . infinitely harder by their status as outliers to the marriage laws."[52] For good measure, Chief Justice Marshall wrote in *Goodridge* that, by focusing on the procreative potential of marriage, "the State's action confers an official stamp of approval on the destructive stereotype that same-sex relationships are inherently unstable and inferior to opposite-sex relationships and are not worthy of respect."[53]

Some other appellate courts have responded very strangely to this charge. I do not mean it strange that courts have responded. I mean that the response itself is very strange.

Take the high court of New York. In the course of upholding that state's marriage law, the New York Court of Appeals observed that "[h]eterosexual intercourse has a natural tendency to lead to the birth of children."[54] The legislature could find, however, that "such relationships are all too often casual or temporary."[55] There is, therefore, "greater danger that children will be born into or grow up in unstable homes than is the case with same-sex couples, and thus that promoting stability in opposite-sex relationships will help children more."[56]

One Indiana appellate court held that the state had a "legitimate interest" in what it called "responsible procreation."[57] The court described its distinguishing feature as "the ability to procreate 'naturally.'"[58] But the key predicate of this court's validation of Indiana's marriage law was an unflattering factual one: a man and woman may procreate irresponsibly; they have (in the court's word) "accidents."[59] Same-sex couples must "rely on adoption or assisted reproduction technology to have children."[60] They "are not at 'risk' of having random and unexpected children by virtue of their ordinary sexual activities"—as are opposite-sex couples.[61] Or, as the *Goodridge* dissenters—who would limit marriage to man and woman—phrased it, "[A]n orderly society requires some mechanism for coping with the fact that sexual intercourse commonly results in pregnancy and childbirth. The institution of marriage is that mechanism."[62]

These cases stand for the paradoxical conclusion that precisely because same-sex couples are by nature or necessity better parents—and as a cohort, optimal—they may be denied the status of marriage and its accompanying benefits. Neither the New York nor the Indiana courts considered that, while same-sex parents may not need marriage and its benefits, they might be better parents if they got them.

The optimal setting argument is not, moreover, an argument against same-sex *marriage* at all. It is an argument against same-sex couples raising children; that is, after all, entirely the "setting" which state promotion of marriage is claimed to "optima[ize]." But, because no two men or two women produce issue, recognizing them as married would not commit the law to placing children in their care. Unlike the situation with opposite-sex couples, in which legal recognition of them as married implies (or "licenses," if you will) their having and raising children, laws recognizing same-sex couples as married would not by themselves mean children. The law would have to take an additional, specifically child-focused, step before any children were placed in the care of a same-sex couples through agencies of foster care or adoption, or by a legally valid custody arrangement where one or both partners come to the marriage with children of his or her own by a previous relationship. Nothing in optimal-setting thinking would prevent such placements. Thus (again) the *Goodridge* court's point about the pointlessness of excluding *de facto* families from the world of de jure families. is left unrebutted[63]

None of the foregoing criticisms of "optimal setting" are meant to be an argument for same-sex marriage. Rejecting the whole "optimal setting" method implies no such favorable view. Indeed, the whole "optimal setting" mindset should be discarded. The reason for doing so is not that it succeeds—or not—as an argument for same-sex marriage. This reason is that "optimal setting" can only succeed in undermining the law's whole understanding of its obligations to marriage.

The "optimal setting" viewpoint starts in a state of nature: a hypothesized world innocent of sexual morality, where consenting adults engage in all sorts of mutually agreeable sexual acts. These acts (and resulting relationships) are all equally moral or amoral, or uninteresting to public authority; it is all private. And, so far considered, there is no such distinctive thing as marriage in the public legal realm.

The public realm and its law is engaged by virtue of the fact—and solely by virtue of the fact—that sometimes certain sex acts between certain couples have an intriguing result: a baby. Then questions leading to more questions about the baby's upbringing eventually trip a switch. The lights go on and illuminate something called "marriage." Then the whole legal marital regime—whatever exactly it is—is posited in the rawest sense. In the "optimal setting" world, the civil law does not supervene upon any pre-legal moral or cultural reality, which might be called by some the truth about marriage. This truth about marriage does not define the legal relation because there is no place for it in the "optimal setting" world. In that world, only a hazy and unstable notion of parents' rights over and against the state to rear and educate their children is possible.

Why? Because there is no moral truth about marriage, no natural right to marry and form a family, and no possibility of seeing that, though children are equal in dignity to their parents, they nonetheless are a perfection of their parents' marriage and thus part of it. Put differently, in the "optimal setting" world, kids' perceived non-moral (and statistically measured) needs determine what marriage—at least in law—is. In the real legal world a sound understanding of what marriage really is has long shaped the law of marriage.

How is the optimal setting argument characteristically liberal, even if conservatives have co-opted it to oppose same-sex "marriage"?

Up to a point, optimal setting is neither liberal nor conservative. Any sound guide to rhetoric counsels avoiding, wherever possible, reliance upon controversial premises. Basing decisions upon undisputed premises (including social science data) is often virtuous and productive of good results; at least, many decisions of public authorities are rightly made according to what will, in fact, work. There is nothing characteristically liberal or conservative so far.

Any sound decision about what the law should be, however, ultimately traces its justificatory way back to a moral premise which does not depend upon statistics for its validity. Many such decisions—such as those legally prohibiting torture, conviction of the innocent, capital punishment, and that marriage is a relationship of two persons (and no more)—are entirely (or almost entirely) matters of moral principle, decided against statistical evidence of unfortunate consequences. The strongest argument against legal recognition of polygamous unions as marriages is not that kids suffer in them. It is that such relationships are not really marriages. Monogamy has a legal monopoly because that is what marriage really is, it is the truth about marriage, notwithstanding statistics suggesting that children of polygamy do just fine. It is nonetheless characteristically liberal to be reticent about the role of controversial moral judgments when it comes to law. Liberal political morality famously seeks to be scrupulously "neutral" about moral judgments not embraced by virtually the entire populace. In this way, the optimal setting argument is liberal, even when made by conservatives.

III

At the root of many arguments for same-sex "marriage" is a very strong positive moral evaluation, not of marriage as such, but of the *persons* who wish to be "married" and for their *choice* to do so. These valuations are said to express "equal respect" for the "dignity" and "autonomy" of homosexuals and lesbians, for their "liberty" and, indeed, for *them* as persons and as citizens.

The most influential expression of this muscular respect for anyone's self-constituting choices is the breathtaking definition of liberty propounded by Justices Kennedy, Souter, and O'Connor, in the watershed 1992 abortion case of *Planned Parenthood of Southeastern Pennsylvania v. Casey*.[64] Its status as a lodestar of liberal constitutional law is obvious and undeniable.

"At the heart of liberty is the right to define one's own concept of existence, of meaning, of the universe, and of the mystery of human life. Beliefs about these matters could not define the attributes of personhood were they formed under compulsion of the State."[65]

This is the so-called "Mystery Passage" ("MP") upon which the *Lawrence v. Texas* majority explicitly relied to strike down Texas' antisodomy law and, some predict, prepare the way to gay marriage.[66] The most ambitious re-imagining of the law's interest in marriage is, indeed, that of *Lawrence*. There the majority said that "[p]ersons in a homosexual relationship may seek autonomy for the purpose" of marriage and family relationships, "just as heterosexual persons do"—and that homosexuals have the same constitutional liberty interest in this "autonomy" as do heterosexuals.[67]

Late-night comics might make sport of the proposal that people seek autonomy by getting married—the "ol' ball and chain" and that sort of thing. The more reflective among us might scratch our heads for a while, too, trying to grasp what it means to seek autonomy. Autonomy is about moral independence. Moral independence is partly about the absence of heteronomy, dependence, undue influence, about not being in thrall to another's desires or wishes for you, and about immunity from interference in making and carrying out one's choices. It is also about some degree of maturity and critical edge in one's own thinking and deliberations. Understood in this way, one does not so much seek autonomy in making choices, such as the choice to marry. It is more that autonomy is an existential condition of our choices. Yes, one could pursue a course of education to acquire some perspective and critical understanding of what is what. One might move to another town to be free of the hegemonic influences of family or close friends. But very few people enter a marriage for the purpose of exercising freedom or in order to seek and obtain autonomy.

Nonetheless, the strong notion of autonomy expressed in the MP, and the *Lawrence* Court's statement that it is (in some sense) what people seek in marriage,[68] call for a candid evaluation of this emerging complex thought. In my judgment, the MP undermines genuine liberty and the rule of law too.

I shall make three points in support of these two judgments. The first is that the MP is all sail and no anchor. It exalts—mistakenly, I shall argue—the freedom with which one comes to hold certain beliefs over the truth, validity, and soundness of those beliefs. The second is that the MP's account of what public authority should do to promote freedom—basically, leave people alone—is innocent of real-world requirements for enjoying effective freedom in political society. Third, the MP leads to a kind of Hobbesian impasse in which the liberty to create and inhabit one's own moral universe darkens the door to the public square, making it impossible to perceive and accept law as the structure of free cooperation among persons for the common good. In the MP's world, legal constraint can scarcely be more than brute restraint.

The MP holds that you would be inauthentic, not really what you—incipiently and at bottom really—are, if your beliefs were formed under compulsion. In respect to some matters, notably including religion, this is largely true. Religion involves free assent to truths about the nature of reality and human destiny (among other matters), and it involves (in some way, shape or form) voluntary participation in such religious acts as worship within a community of believers. Some other good things, such as friendship and marriage, are good for people, in part according to the freedom with which they enter and maintain the relationship. To a significant extent, the freedom with which people seek the truth about such matters and the freedom with which they embrace the truth they discover, do contribute greatly to their flourishing.

But the MP goes further than this, much further. Literally, the MP holds that the voluntariness with which we come to hold our convictions about an apparently boundless array of questions is not only the earmark of liberty—it defines us as "persons."[69] But this is mistaken. It is also potentially dangerous. The truth about the role of voluntariness in constituting each of us as the people we are is ordinarily denoted by terms such as "character" or "identity" or "personality." One's status as a person ordinarily means what one possesses or is by virtue of one's existence as a human being with a rational nature. The confusion between personality (to a significant extent self-shaped by choices) and personhood is linked to the confusion between making one's own judgments about how things really are (defining one's own concept of existence) and the way things really are. It is important that persons make their own judgments about many things, but it is also important that they not come to think that they possess a God-like dominion over reality.

The MP identifies the ability to choose one's world reality with being a person. But this proposition implies that where the imagination and the will have gone dark, the person loses human dignity and descends to some sub-personal status. This implication may not make the MP a foe of freedom. But by so exalting freedom—understood as voluntarily defining one's universe—the MP is surely no protector of persons without imagination or will.

In fact, we do not prize voluntariness over correctness, as the MP suggests we do, or at least should do. No one really holds that so long as one freely chooses to believe the earth is young and flat like an Olympic athlete or old and round like most Supreme Court Justices, it does not matter which it is. Our schools and laws surely do not treat those beliefs as equivalent, and they strain to inculcate the one over the other.

If one's decisions or judgments about certain aspects of reality are false because, for example, they deny that some class of human beings has dignity and rights (the dignity and rights they truly have), then these beliefs do not contribute to one's own dignity. These beliefs do not deserve to be accepted by others (society) as autonomous, that is, entitling the person holding them to act upon them. Though the person holding them must adhere to them—otherwise he loses his integrity—he should be restrained; for he may lose his moral liberty to act on them by reason of the belief's falsity, of which he is by hypothesis unaware.

Consider the case of racism. Racism—the belief, for example, that black persons are indelibly inferior to white persons—is false. Holding such a racist belief is certain to lead the one holding it to treat black persons unjustly. These unjust acts should, at least presumptively, be legally prohibited. But racism also mutilates and diminishes the racist. The racist is not capable of entering into genuine friendships, or into any other relationship grounded in equality, with a whole class of persons—all those thought to be part of the inferior race. No matter how freely one comes to credit a racist conviction—and bear in mind that such beliefs come in assorted packages, as founded in science, sociology, history, religion, and morality—holding a racist belief is a tragedy all around. A decent society does what it can (within limits) to extirpate racism, to help make it the case that no one is a racist.

The *Casey* joint-opinion writers offered the MP as the organizing principle—the theretofore unstated rationale or genius—of a generation's work. Here is what immediately preceded the MP in the *Casey* opinion:

> Our law affords constitutional protection to personal decisions relating to marriage, procreation, contraception, family relationships, child rearing, and education. . . . These matters, involving the most intimate and personal choices a person may make in a lifetime, choices central to personal dignity and autonomy, are central to the liberty protected by the Fourteenth Amendment. All one can say for sure about freedom in the absence of law, however, is that persons are thereby left in, well, a condition bereft of law. Whether persons are more or less free without law is another question-or a matter of many additional questions. I am not referring to the nasty and brutish life of people in the state of nature. I am rather referring to life in a hugely complex advanced society like our own. Individuals and groups in our society confront a huge framework of settled behavioral expectations and practices—

> a culture—which they are often powerless to resist, much less to commandeer and change. Persons and groups cannot call into existence all the opportunities, practices, and patterns which they wish to participate in and enjoy.[70]

This is certainly the case with marriage; it is an ineradicably socio-legal institution. The marriage available to persons as an option for choice is constituted, to a significant extent, by the law's important (though secondary) role in establishing and maintaining marriage. Indeed, that is the principal contention of the preceding chapter of this book. Now let us say that a particular society, which had always maintained a monogamous culture of marriage through its laws, changes. Now let us say polygamy is legally recognized as a legally cognizable form of marriage. Monogamy is no longer the exclusive, legally sanctioned marital relationship. After even a short time, one could reasonably expect a modest number of polygamous marriages to be solemnized. Or, let us say that a society, which long limited marriage to unions of a man and a woman because marriage is procreative, changes. Before long, there would be some same-sex marriages—but not too many because not many people experience same-sex attractions.

The relevant changes would go way beyond the modest numbers of novel marriages—polygamous or same-sex, as the case may be. The changes would be deeper and more pervasive. One recent experience seems to confirm this thesis: the no-fault divorce revolution a generation ago not only increased the number of divorces, it also dramatically affected everyone's tendency to define marriage as a relationship for better or for worse, until death do the spouses part.

In the first instance, the real change is that a much larger number of people would come to believe that no matter what their personal preferences or options might lead them to choose for themselves, marriage itself is not necessarily a bilateral relationship. After a generation or two, perhaps very few people would believe that the mutuality and equality of spouses, which an uncompromised monogamy implies, were necessary parts of marriage, even if the number of polygamists remained small.

In the second case, the real change is that over time, and regardless of the statistical frequency of same-sex marriage, nearly everyone's beliefs about the relationship of children to marriage, and thus the nature of marriage itself, would be affected by the legal redefinition. If so, then the marriage on offer in society would be different than the marriage on offer before the legal change. The older version would scarcely be available to persons for their choice, much as the older idea of marriage as permanent is, perhaps already, scarcely available.

Finally, the MP holds that everyone has a valid (at least from the constitutional point of view) liberty interest in doing whatever they desire to do. Of course, no organized society could afford persons the liberty to do as they wish. What is obviously missing is an illumination of responsibility and limits, some common and reasoned account of the point, justification, or value of limits.

Note well: I say *illumination* of limits, not the presence of them. For there is no question of there being limits or of persons being held responsible. The sheer volume of law and enforced restraint in modern societies is not especially low. In fact, there is a necessary relationship between the utter volume of legal regulation and restraint upon what persons wish to do—on the one hand—and the guiding principles of the regime managing the constraints. Put differently, it is not at all apparent that there would be less law in a society whose law was determined by the MP than there would be in a society whose law was determined by moral paternalism, by therapeutic criteria, or by the standard of forming good "citizens." And there might well be more.

Of course, the moral justification of legal constraint is, fundamentally, the common good. But what meaning can that term have in the MP's world of random morality and limitless mental horizons? The "common good" in the MP way of viewing things is just the liberty to inhabit a world of one's choosing. This leads, however, to a zero sum game, in which A's liberty to do X—say, to be free from being seduced—simply takes away from B's liberty to seduce. A has, or may well have, no reason to be chaste, or to respect the integrity of B's body, save fear of consequences.

This impasse is structurally similar to that engineered by Hobbes, who thought and taught that men had the most rights—and the largest liberty— in a state of nature, a hypothetical location bereft of legally enforced obligation.[71] "[I]n such a condition, every man has a [r]ight to everything; even to one anothers [sic] body."[72] But is this not also to say that no one has a duty to respect another's body? Is it not to say, then, that no one has a right to bodily integrity? Where law supervenes upon this understanding of rights and duties, legal constraints cannot be experienced as the recognition of pre-existing moral duties, such as the Golden Rule.[73]

That is, in the MP (Hobbesian) world, legal constraints cannot be experienced as the reasonable requirements of free and fair cooperation among persons for the common good. Or they are so experienced purely by accident, by random overlap between what the law stipulates and someone's moral universe. Legal constraint in the MP (Hobbesian) world has no internal guidance to avoid being understood, received, and experienced instead as brute restraint, shackles, fetters, and gross imposition, which by definition subtract one-for-one from genuine liberty.

CONCLUSION

The validity of a conclusion is logically independent of the arguments for its soundness. By exposing the flaws in three arguments for same-sex "marriage," this chapter has not, therefore, established whether same-sex relationships are, or should be treated by the law as if they are, "marriages." The answer to that question is "No." We saw the argument for that conclusion in Chapter Four.

CHAPTER 6

Are "Civil Unions" An Acceptable Compromise?[1]

On June 26, 2003 the United States Supreme Court overturned the convictions of two Texas men for "deviate sexual intercourse." Although the anti-sodomy law thrown out in *Lawrence v. Texas*[2] referred to a particular sexual act, the Court's reasoning focused on the rationale and far-reaching consequences of making homosexual sodomy a crime. The Court's stated reasons for striking down the law were broad. In a key passage, Justice Kennedy wrote (for the *Lawrence* majority) that "persons in a homosexual relationship" seek constitutionally protected "autonomy" for decisions "relating to marriage, procreation . . . [and] family relationships"—"just as heterosexual persons do."[3] This bold claim lay behind dissenting Justice Scalia's *caveat* that *Lawrence* "dismantle[d] the structure of constitutional law" which permitted states to limit marriage to opposite-sex couples.[4]

Within five months of the *Lawrence* decision the Massachusetts Supreme Judicial Court confirmed Scalia's prophecy. In *Goodridge v. Department of Public Health*[5] that court held that Massachusetts "failed to identify any constitutionally adequate reason for denying civil marriage to same-sex couples."[6] *Lawrence* figured prominently in the Massachusetts' court's reasoning in support of its conclusion that marriage henceforth was "the voluntary union of two persons as spouses, to the exclusion of all others."[7]

Legal recognition of same-sex "marriages" has since *Goodridge* spread to eight other states and to the District of Columbia. A large and growing number of municipalities and other political subdivisions have, moreover, extended marital benefits to same-sex couples who wish to marry—but who are not legally permitted to do so. These jurisdictions have done so by legislative enactment without judicial compulsion. Some courts which rejected same-sex couples' demands to marry required nonetheless that all marital benefits be extended to them. These quasi-marital legal arrangements are most often called "civil unions."

"Civil unions" possess the appeal of a reasonable compromise over a hot and seemingly insoluble social issue. Some courts and many legislators see it as the coveted middle-ground in a white-hot debate where law and morality intersect. The question in this chapter is this: *are* 'civil unions' really a viable *modus vivendi,* a stable compromise which reduces the temperature around marriage law from a boil to at least a simmer?

Many on both sides of the same-sex "marriage" issue reject 'civil unions' precisely because it is a compromise. One side opposes 'civil unions' for giving same-sex couples *all* that the law offers to marriage, except the name. The other side opposes them because they withhold the name "marriage." The first group focuses on the plenitude of benefits and privileges given; they would provide few or none to any unmarried couple. The second group focuses on formal recognition withheld. They say that, unless they "are allowed to call their committed relationships by the name of marriage . . . they are consigned to second-class citizenship."[8] These contending forces mean to carry on the fight, until the enabling laws are repealed (according to one side) or supplanted by full-fledged marriage (says the other).

Perhaps "civil unions" could serve as the basis of a fragile political armistice. But my interest in them is not political. It is, first, philosophical and, then, legal. My point in this chapter is that "civil unions" are wrong and that they should be abandoned as an option because they are incoherent. If there are good reasons why same-sex couples may not marry—and there are—those same reasons defeat altogether the case for 'civil unions' defined (as they are) to include a sexual relationship. In other words, for the law to *reasonably* deny same-sex couples access to lawful marriage is for the law to defeat the case for "civil unions." Conversely, to create 'civil unions' out of a sexual relationship is to evacuate any coherent ground for withholding the name "marriage" from them.

We saw in Chapter Five how so many courts applying the constitutional "rational basis" test are prone to overstate the role of coherence in sound constitutional reasoning. These courts are therefore very likely to recognize the instability of the "civil union" armistice, strike it down, and declare that same-sex "marriage" is the only rational alternative to rank discrimination against gays and lesbians. But even more careful judges will see easily enough that a legislature which establishes "civil unions" has abandoned the coherent bases for stopping short of same-sex "marriage." These courts may declare that legislators arbitrarily stopped short of where their own reasoning inevitably leads—straightaway to same-sex "marriage."

In the first part of this chapter I investigate whether 'civil union' laws really do predicate marital benefits upon the existence of a non-marital *sexual* relationship. After looking at many examples of such laws and opinions I conclude that, by plain implication, civil unions are defined (in part) by the presence or presumed presence of a sexual relationship between those "uni[ted]." Committed and caring *platonic* couples are at least implicitly excluded from these civil unions.

In Part II I look at United States constitutional law to see what the law's interest in marriage has been. I ask *why* the union of man and woman has been so generously protected and aided by the law. The constitutional tradition has been remarkably consistent (we shall see) in recognizing marriage of a man and a woman—and no other relationship—as the morally normative context for having sex and for having children.

Part III critically examines the reasoning of courts which have declined to recognize same-sex relationships as marriages. These courts often focus on marriage and "natural," "responsible" procreation. They often speak at length about the "welfare" of children in marital households. But they do not come close to identifying what the tradition has long regarded as the indispensable core of marriage.

I unpack (in moral-philosophical language) that core commitment in Part III, and defend its indispensable place in any coherent argument against legal recognition of same-sex "marriages." In my Conclusion I set out some important implications of this chapter's findings.

I

Many benefits long reserved to husbands and wives have recently been made available to unmarried couples in states and municipalities throughout the United States. These new laws describe the recipients' relationships in positive, normative terms. Los Angeles County's law describes an "intimate and committed relationship of mutual caring." Santa Monica's law is substantially the same. San Francisco's law states that the parties will have "chosen to share one another's lives in an intimate and committed relationship of mutual caring." Rochester (New York) specifies that partners be "committed to the physical, emotional and financial care and support of each other." Sometimes a similar evaluative intention is expressed by negative implication. Madison, Wisconsin describes the "relationship [as] of a permanent and distinct domestic character," and that individuals are "not in a relationship that is merely temporary, social, political, commercial or economic in nature."[9]

Other ordinances recognize new and different forms of "family," with additional normative modifiers thrown in. Ann Arbor's statement of purpose, for example, says: "Ann Arbor has an interest in strengthening and supporting "all caring, committed, and responsible family forms." Ithaca, New York's ordinance would strengthen and support "all caring, committed and responsible family forms." Santa Monica's law states that "domestic partners live in an intimate and committed family relationship."

Still other benefit-granting provisions are evaluative, in the peculiarly limited sense of endorsing what some persons wish themselves to be called. Cambridge, Massachusetts, for example, requires that the parties "consider themselves to be a family." Key West similarly requires that the partners "consider themselves to be members of each other's immediate family," and that they have "chosen to share one another's lives in a family relationship."

So far considered there is no obvious reason why these novel legal forms would be limited to same-sex couples, or to couples (same-sex or not) involved sexually with each other. Nothing in the evaluative descriptions would necessarily exclude qualitatively similar platonic relationships, such as elderly sisters[10] or bachelor brothers or best friends living together—Felix and Oscar ("The Odd Couple"), or even Will and Grace.

The statutory expressions viewed so far are a bit coy about sex. Use of the word 'intimate' suggests a sexual relationship. But that is just one possible meaning. Express references in statutory prefaces or findings to the plight of "gays and lesbians" more strongly suggest a sexual relationship. The San Francisco ordinance states, for instance, that its "purpose is to create a way to recognize intimate, committed relationships, including those of lesbians and gay men who otherwise are denied the right to identify the partners with whom they share their lives." Findings like these do not necessarily mean that a sexual relationship is required. It is a commonplace of statutory drafting and of legal interpretation that the occasion of a legislative enactment—here, the situations of "gay and lesbian" couples—does not settle the meaning or range of applications of a resulting law. What led to the law is one aid to its construction, in cases where the meaning of the enacted provision is doubtful.

Where verbal suggestions such as 'intimate,' 'gays and lesbians,' 'couples,' and 'families' surround delivery of all ('identical' or 'equal') marital rights and obligations, however, a sexual relationship is almost certainly intended. After all, if *marriage-in-all-but-name* is the objective, then a sexual relationship is meant. Any administrative or judicial application of these laws excluding platonic relationships would not only survive any "rational-basis" scrutiny. It would be correct. Statutory eligibility criteria make the case as well. California's domestic partnership law, for example, applies to "two adults who have chosen to share one another's lives in an intimate and committed relationship of mutual caring." These couples are granted almost every spousal right under state law, except for the ability to jointly file income taxes. So far, then, one may presume a sexual relationship. The eligibility requirements stipulate that partners not be related "by blood in a way that would prevent them from being married to each other" in California,[11] and that they be of the same-sex unless one of the partners is over the age of 62. These limitations confirm the presumption.

Let's look first at the consanguinity restriction. There is no possibility that a same-sex relationship could produce "issue"—children born of the genetic contribution of both partners. Thus there can be no fear of genetically-defective offspring behind this consanguinity limitation. Any consanguinity limitation upon civil unions would, therefore, be either a mindless imitation of marriage law, or wittingly grounded in the consanguinity rule's longstanding, basic justification. Either way a sexual relationship is implied.

Behind the consanguinity rules about marriage is not—at least not principally—fear of birth defects. Behind these rules lies the settled conviction that certain relationships important enough to be protected by law would be undone if romance and sex were introduced into them. Relationships among siblings are a prime example. To forestall ruinous romantic and sexual temptations between siblings (for example), marriage of siblings is prohibited. The consanguinity restriction reinforces, protects and extends the incest taboo.

Let's look now at the same-sex limitations in some civil-union laws. Plaintiffs in *Baker v. Vermont* were same-sex couples, each of whom had lived together for years. The court emphasized the State's interest in extending official recognition and legal protection to the professed commitment of "two individuals" in a "lasting relationship of mutual affection." "Identity" of legal benefits was mandated. Acting under *Baker* duress the legislature decided that parties to a Vermont 'civil union' must "not be a party to another civil union or marriage"; and must "be of the same-sex and therefore excluded from the marriage laws of this state."[12] Vermont also enacted a consanguinity limitation which, given "civil union's" limitation to persons of the same-sex, prohibited a man from entering a union with a host of strictly male relatives, and a woman from unions with corresponding female relations.[13]

The plain sense of excluding opposite-sex couples from these "unions" has two parts. The first: a man and woman interested sexually in each other do not need access to 'civil unions,' because they already have an equivalent option: they can marry. Same-sex couples with the same interest may enter 'civil unions.' There is therefore no unjust discrimination against the courting couple Bob and Phyllis.

Second: a man and a woman uninterested in each other sexually—an elderly brother and his sister, Will and Grace—will not want to marry (for marriage is a sexual relationship). The Vermont legislature evidently thought that they have no more business entering a civil union than they do a marriage: *each* is a sexual relationship. But excluding opposite-sex couples from civil unions is irrational unless civil unions are also off limits to platonic same-sex couples. So, I conclude that civil-union laws predicate benefits upon the presence (or presumed presence) of a sexual relationship.

II

Testimony in favor of marriage's exalted place in law and culture is strewn across the whole corpus of American law. Encomia to marriage can be found in constitutions, statutes, case reports, and legislative findings. One prominent example (from a late nineteenth-century Supreme Court decision) affirmed that marriage was "the most important relation in life," and that it had "more to do with the morals and civilization of a people than any other institution."[14] Similar encomia can be located in much more recent settings. The Supreme Court's 1965 *Griswold* opinions read at several points like odes to the wedded state: the "intimate relation of husband and wife"[15] is "a coming together for better or for worse, hopefully enduring, and intimate to the degree of being sacred."[16]

Parties to today's roiling debate recognize marriage's very high social and legal importance. That is one reason why, I suppose, they contend so fiercely over it. To be sure, some proponents of same-sex marriage make no claim of their own about the social value of marriage; theirs is a straightforward nondiscrimination argument which could be made against any alleged discrimination against homosexuals. Many other proponents sing high praises of marriage. Their lyrics usually stress, however, the subjective importance and meaning of the "marriage" bond to the couple, much more than the traditional emphasis upon the objective contours of marriage and its social worth. The disputants agree, however, that legal recognition of same-sex relationships as marriages implies social approval.

What explains the law's great and enduring interest in marriage? What, more exactly, is the indispensable core of our laws' interest in marriage? Fortunately, we have a compact but rich and sound explanation of the tradition's patronage of marriage in Justice John Harlan's 1961 *Poe v. Ullman*[17] dissent. *Poe* presented essentially the facts of *Griswold v. Connecticut,* four years before the Court in that case invalidated a state law restricting married couples' access to prescription contraceptives. Harlan would have decided the matter in 1961 as the Court later did in *Griswold*: he would have held that the Constitution denies states the power to so intrude upon the married couples' privacy. To that extent, at least, Harlan cannot be accused of being an old fogy.

In *Poe* Harlan stated that marriage was the distinguishing principle of sexual morality, and the morally-right context for children:

> The very inclusion of the category of morality among state concerns indicates that society is not limited in its objects only to the physical wellbeing of the community, but has traditionally concerned itself with the moral soundness of its people as well. . . . The laws regarding marriage which provide both when the sexual powers may be used and the legal and societal context in which children are born and brought up, as well as laws forbidding adultery, fornication and homosexual practices, which express the negative of the proposition, confining sexuality to lawful marriage, form a pattern so deeply pressed into the substance of our social life that any constitutional doctrine in this area must build on that basis.[18]

This is the indispensable core of our laws' solicitude for marriage, past and present: the "proposition" that marriage is the morally normative and uniquely appropriate legal context for sexual relations and for children to come to be.

Harlan's summation ties together the three non-marital sexual acts—"adultery, fornication, and homosexual practices"—and sharply contrasts them to the three intertwined aspects of the marital act—"sexual powers," children "born" and "brought up." Harlan rightly says that the law's hostile view of the former *owes* to the latter. The three linked acts are wrong *because* they are non-marital. Protecting marriage implies discouraging these acts. Protecting marriage *means* privileging it as the normative setting for sex and kids. Protecting marriage (so understood) also *means* discouraging non-marital sexual acts and relationships. These are two sides of the *same* "proposition."

Harlan's "proposition" means that legal discouragement of non-marital sex, up to and including criminal sanction, arises *not* from a paternalistic desire to correct and punish persons for their sexual misbehavior just for the sake of *their* moral improvement. Much less does it arise from idle or baseless opinion—sometimes called "majoritarian prejudice." The law's protection of marriage has nothing to do with dislike for persons who engage in the prohibited sex acts, even as the acts themselves are branded as socially harmful. Indeed, apart from these acts' adverse relation to marriage, it is hard to see what would be wrong with them. Harlan's "proposition" would also be absurd—inconceivable to implement, and perhaps unintelligible—if marriage and the family founded on it were in the eye of the beholder, if "moral soundness" was believed or deemed to be a matter of subjective opinion. The state's protection of marriage and discouragement of non-marital acts makes sense, in other words, only if there is an objective common good in marriage. The state seeks (among other objectives) to preserve a common cultural understanding of just what marriage is really about—so that people might flourish by participating in and supporting it.

Harlan describes the three particular acts as non-marital. There are two ways in which they are so. The first has to do with the status of parties to them; call this sense, "agent-centered." "Fornication" refers to sexual intercourse between two unmarried persons (think of college kids). "Adultery" refers to sexual intercourse between two persons, at least one of whom is married to someone else. "Homosexual practices" refers to sex between two men or two women, persons who by definition cannot be married to each other.

The second way is "act-centered." "Non-marital" here refers to *all* sexual acts other than the sexual intercourse of the spouses—the "sexual powers" which have to do with children coming to be. Fornication and adultery involve sexual intercourse outside this normative setting, even though kids may come. The reference to "homosexual practices" brings to mind, then, not persons who experience same-sex attractions, but the sexual acts ("practices") which they characteristically perform—anal and oral intercourse. These acts are of course not limited by nature or by emotional appeal to persons of the same-sex, or even to unmarried couples. These acts may be performed by married couples, too. Even their sodomitical acts are immoral, too.

The conviction that *all* non-marital acts are immoral lay at the heart of the tradition's profound solicitude for marriage. This conviction does not mean, of course, that all such acts must be treated the same way by the law. It does not imply that all of them—or any of them—should be crimes. But anyone taking Harlan's "proposition" seriously could not recognize any non-marital act as good, or predicate upon its performance favorable legal treatment or benefits. No one holding the tradition's view could coherently say that persons have a "right" to engage in non-marital acts, just as such. There can be no "right" to do a moral wrong. Saying that there is a "right" to fornicate, for example, implies that fornication possesses a value which in truth it does not possess. Saying that there is a "right" to engage in homosexual sexual acts is implicitly to deny what Harlan squarely asserted: such acts are morally wrong because they are non-marital, and as non-marital they are socially harmful.

That our constitutional and legal (and, for that matter, cultural) tradition held a decidedly negative moral evaluation of *all* sexual acts save the sexual intercourse of spouses is confirmed by *Lawrence v. Texas.*

The *Lawrence* Court supported its own very non-traditional holding by rehearsing the long-standing, specifically marital focus of the tradition the Court was there in process of abandoning. The *Lawrence* Court said: "At the outset it should be noted that there is no longstanding history in this country of laws directed at homosexual conduct as a distinct matter."[19] The Court said, more specifically, that "early American sodomy laws were not directed at homosexuals as such but instead sought to prohibit non-procreative activity more generally."[20] "Nineteenth-century commentators similarly read American sodomy, buggery, and crimes-against-nature statutes as criminalizing certain relations between men and women and between men and of men."[21] Not until the 1970s, according to the Court, did any state single out "same-sex relations for criminal prosecution."[22] The Court eschewed any Equal Protection basis for its holding, for that would leave open the question whether a prohibition which, unlike the challenged Texas law, reached "conduct both between same-sex and different-sex participants."[23]

Criminal "confin[ement] of sexuality to lawful marriage" ended in 2003, when *Lawrence* answered a question expressly left open in several

prior cases: do adults have a constitutional right to "engage in private con-
sensual sexual acts." The *Lawrence* Court said "yes." But the meaning of
the asserted "right"—and thus the scope of the "yes"—is uncertain.

We have already seen that the immorality of non-marital sex acts does
not imply or entail that they must be made crimes by the competent public
authority. Their immorality is a necessary but not sufficient condition for
affixing criminal penalties to their commission. Declaring these acts all to
be beyond the scope of criminal prosecution—as *Lawrence* declared neither implies nor entails nor presupposes a favorable moral judgment of
them (just as declaring that lying to one's spouse and treating your children
unfairly are beyond the criminal sanction implies that they are virtuous
acts). Insofar as the *Lawrence* opinion relies upon notions about the limits
of the criminal law and immunity from state interference in what consenting adults do within the home—call the confluence of these two streams of
thought a theory of *privacy*—*Lawrence* does *not* necessarily reject Harlan's
"proposition." The *Lawrence* Court said: "it suffices for us to acknowledge
that adults may choose to enter upon this relationship in the confines of
their homes and their own private lives and still retain their dignity as free
persons."

But the *Lawrence* majority ran in tandem with this tradition-compati-
ble chain of reasoning, a very different line of justification, one with
potentially very broad implications. *Lawrence* maintained that "persons in
a homosexual relationship may seek autonomy for the purposes" of "marriage" and "family relationships" "just as heterosexuals *do*," *and* that
"homosexuals" have the same constitutional-liberty interest in this "autonomy" as do heterosexuals. Apparently, the state may not "recognize" and
endorse marriage any more than it does same-sex relationships of (somehow) a roughly similar kind.

This extraordinary assertion is hard to fathom, or credit. Same-sex
couples cannot "seek autonomy" for marriage as do heterosexuals, for the
marital act is unavailable to them. Same-sex couples' relationships cannot
be recognized in law as marriages, unless the whole justification for recognizing anyone's marriage is overhauled. The *Lawrence* Court seemed
unwilling to go that far—or did not really understand what it was saying.

Neither the *Lawrence* majority, nor concurring Justice O'Connor,
denied the state's continuing authority to protect and promote marriage.
Both expressly reserved judgment on the question. The majority said that,
because the case was about privacy, "it does not involve whether the government must give formal recognition to any relationship that homosexual

persons seek to enter."[24] Justice O'Connor said: "Unlike the moral disapproval of same-sex relations—the asserted state interest in this case—other reasons exist to promote the institution of marriage beyond mere moral disapproval of an excluded group."[25]

But "promot[ing] the institution of marriage" is precisely *why* the state "moral[ly] disapprove[s]" of non-marital sexual acts and relationships, including those between persons of the same sex. If the state is constitutionally obliged to judge the morality of sodomy between two men just as it does the marital act, it is hard to see what "other reasons" are left to Justice O'Connor.

Justice Scalia said in his *Lawrence* dissent that the "people may feel that their disapprobation of homosexual conduct is strong enough to disallow homosexual marriage."[26] But "disapprobation of homosexual conduct" *follows* from an understanding of marriage which implies the impossibility of same-sex marriage. Scalia said too that apart from "moral disapprobation of homosexual conduct" there seems to be no possible justification "for denying the benefits of marriage to homosexual couples . . . ."[27] The moral impossibility of same-sex marriage, however, explains *both* the denial of marital benefits *and* popular "moral disapprobation."

III

There are three distinguishable elements or parts to Harlan's "proposition." They are not so many sub-propositions or implications. They are different but still inseparable aspects of the one reality—the marital act. Marriage is the uniquely normative moral context for when the "sexual powers" may be used, in which children are "born," and in which they are "brought up." Together they form what I call the "moral ecology" of the family. I discuss each property in turn.

A. The Marital Act and Sexual Morality

In and through their marital acts the couple actualize or express in a profound and special way their whole married life together. The genital intercourse of the spouses really unites them physically; in the reproductive act it is truly the mated-pair-which-acts-as-one. Marital intercourse thus truly unites the spouses biologically. But it also unites them emotionally (as feeling beings sharing this experience), intellectually (as thinking and choosing and acting beings), and morally (as two persons realizing the common good of their marriage by and through this act).

The marital act is a multi-layered, complex act, structured so that each spouse experiences it as a total gift of oneself and as receipt of the total gift of another. The moral justifying point of the marital act is, most important, *intrinsic*: it just *is* (to actualize, express, and experience) the spouses' marriage.

The moral value of the marital act is therefore non-instrumental. The spouses are two-in-one as no same-sex couple can be, as no couple engaged in any non-coital sexual act can be, and as no unmarried couple having intercourse is. The marital act is justified by the *marriage* which it actualizes; other sexual acts are wrong because they are non-marital.

The pleasure which usually accompanies the marital act becomes (in this understanding of the act's justifying point) a predictable and welcome effect, a sub-rational motive of the act—but *not* its object or intended end. The additional feelings of intimacy, connectedness, and openness which sexual acts, including the spouses' intercourse, often foster are not the object of the marital act either. As the "proposition" implies or at least suggests, neither pleasure nor these other feelings suffice to justify any sexual act.

The basic principle of sexual morality is not only pleasure. It is not merely consent. Nor is it a combination of the two: as if whatever two consenting adults find mutually pleasurable is, therefore, morally acceptable. Forcing sexual relations upon anyone is wrong for *that* reason. But all sexual relations save the marital act are wrong for another reason, even where no force or fraud is involved: all such acts damage personal and interpersonal integrity because they instrumentalize sex. Where sex is instrumentalized, the persons' bodies are reduced to the status of means to ends.

B. The Marital Act and the Moral Context in Which Children Come-to-Be

In and by one and the same act married couples express their two-in-one-flesh communion, *and* they do all that human persons can do to bring a child to be. When the spouses' marital acts bear the fruit of children, these children are perceptively called (in law) "issue of the marriage." Children can well be said to *be* their parents' marriage: just as the married couple is two-in-one-flesh, so too their child is the two-of-them-in-the one-flesh. The child *is* their union, extended into time and space, and thus into human history and the whole human community. Children conceived in marital intercourse participate in the good of their parents' marriage and are themselves non-instrumental aspects of its perfection; thus, spouses rightly hope for and welcome children, not as "products" they "make," but rather, as gifts, which, if all goes well, come to be through the same choice and act through which their parents expressed their marriage. Thus one may speak of children as "gifts" that "supervene" on marital acts.

Some understanding along these lines of the moral relationship of parents to the children they may conceive is essential to the rational affirmation of the dignity of children as *persons*: i.e., as *ends in themselves*, and not mere *means* of satisfying desires of their parents; as *subjects* of justice (including fundamental and inviolable human rights), rather than objects of will. Indeed, this view of the marital act and children permits us to see how the baby—weak, dependent, helpless—nonetheless enters into *this* family (*this* particular human community) as a real *partner,* equal to his mother and father in dignity.

This is not to suggest that there is anything wrong with spouses engaging in marital intercourse because they "want" a child. It is merely to indicate the description under which the "wanting" of the child is consistent with his or her dignity as a person, and to highlight the fact that the marital significance of properly motivated spousal intercourse obtains whether or not conception is hoped for, results, or is even possible. Children are to be desired under a description that does not reduce the child to the status of a product to be brought into existence at its parents' will, and for their ends. Children rather are to be treated as *persons*, possessing full human dignity, which the spouses are eager to welcome (and take responsibility for) as a perfective participant in the community established by their marriage (i.e., their family).

C. The Marital Act and the Moral Structure of the Family

Because all the married couple's children come to be in and through the *same* act—separated only by time—each child is equally and wholly the image of their parents' unique union. The siblings' family identity is just that: a matter of *identity*. All the children are, one compared to the others, equally and wholly the offspring of the same parents; mother and father are equally and wholly parents of each child, in whom they see (literally) so many unique, yet related and, in a sense, similar expressions of their own union. For each child is *their* flesh, their marriage.

This matrix of familial equality, mutuality and common identity is the wellspring and ground of love, duty, loyalty, care-giving—the whole moral culture of family life. The lifelong and unbreakable chords of fealty and relatedness which family members possess, one for the others, and which even distance and alienation never quite erase, depend upon it. No other "family" form can replace it.

These marital and familial relationships fuel the law's protection of marriage as the morally-appropriate context of parenting. This radical equality and mutuality is neither mysterious nor dreamily metaphysical. It is no more subtle or beyond the state's concern than is the correct judgment that the factor of *equality* of marital friendship lies at, or very near, the heart of the state's legitimate judgment that polygamy is not supportable, even to the point of making criminal a person's attempts (indeed, rendering their acts merely *attempts*) at plural marriage.

All the children who do come to be in and through the marital act come to be as gifts and on equal terms with siblings and parents. *All* the sexual intercourse of spouses—even those who cannot conceive by *this* or *that* marital act—retains the capacity to actualize their marriage as a two-in-one-flesh communion. For just as the marital act is structured (physically, morally) for couples who are fertile and who wish for children, so too it is structured for sterile couples: for *all* of them the marital act can indeed be *intrinsically* valuable. For *all* of them the marital act need not be instrumental to procreation or to pleasure or to any other ulterior end.

CONCLUSION

What's in the name 'marriage'? Is it a meaningless verbal preference— "six" says one; "half-dozen" insists another—for which no reasoned basis is *possible?* Are "civil unions" which presuppose sex really just marriage-by-another-name, a distinction without a difference? If so, then parallel strictures of this sort are necessarily irrational, and should be eliminated for that reason.

Or is there more to the name than that? One state supreme court said in a marriage case that it was "mindful that in the cultural clash over same-sex marriage, the word marriage itself—independent of the rights and benefits of marriage—has an "evocative and important meaning to both parties."[28] "Plaintiffs seek not just legal standing, but also social acceptance, which in their view is the last step toward true equality."[29] If this court is on the right track, parallel structures really do amount to "separate, but equal"—as if public facilities were in fact open to persons of both races, but signs indicating "coloreds only" were retained as a political concession to popular prejudice.

Obviously, this won't do.

The way out of this impasse is marked by the argument of this chapter. Any law which defines the union of man and woman—and no other relationship—as marriage does more than monopolize a name or brand. It excludes same-sex couples from the married state, and if that exclusion is defensible at all, it is because of Harlan's "proposition." And Harlan's "proposition" sets out what it is that law is doing when it recognizes and protects marriage: defining the morally normative context for having sex and having children.

A marriage-defining law *means,* therefore, that no *other* sexual relationship may be recognized and affirmed by the state. Such a law *means* that no benefits or privileges may be predicated upon the presence (even if presupposed or implied) of a non-marital sexual relationship. And where the legal definition of marriage (as the union of man and woman) is constitutionally specified, any statute or municipal ordinance or court decision purportedly creating sexualized "civil unions" (by any name) violates the fundamental law.

With the indispensable core of Harlan's "proposition" in view, it also becomes clear that norms against unjust discrimination and in favor of equality do not lead to same-sex "marriage." Traditional marriage laws do not imply inequality or "second class citizenship." At the same time, they do not preclude the prudent extension by competent authority of some benefits traditionally reserved to married couples, to unmarried couples, and even to groups living in household community.

III
RELIGIOUS LIBERTY

CHAPTER 7:

The Original Meaning of the
Establishment Clause[1]

"[M]any of the Framers understood the word 'religion' in the Establishment Clause to encompass only the various sects of Christianity."[2] So asserted Justice John Paul Stevens, the most ardent secularist to sit on the Supreme Court in the last half-century. Stevens presented what he considered to be evidence in support of his assertion in *Van Orden v. Perry*, a 2005 decision about the public display of a monument bearing the Ten Commandments. Cases about such public affirmations of religion are a staple of court dockets throughout the country. The factual variations include Yule-time nativity scenes, Christian crosses erected on public property, and prayers at public events like school graduations and at the opening of legislative sessions.

The results in lawsuits challenging these practices defy easy generalization. If I were to ask my law students on an exam whether student-led prayer during school hours is unconstitutional, the correct answer would be: sometimes it is, and sometimes it is not. That would be the correct answer too to similar questions about crèches at the courthouse and about posting the Decalogue in some public hallway.

In this chapter I am not concerned with judicial doctrines,[3] or with the right result (whatever it might be) in specific cases. I am interested rather in the fundamental challenge which Justice Stevens mounted in the *Van Orden* case against the whole possibility of interpreting the First Amendment according to the founders' original understanding of it. Stevens' basic argument is that if we take what the founders said seriously, we will saddle ourselves with an untenably intolerant reading of the Constitution, namely, that (in Stevens' view) Jews and Muslims were not protected by the First Amendment.

Let's call Stevens' assertion that the founders meant "Christianity" when they wrote "religion" in the Establishment Clause, Proposition A. Much of Stevens' evidence, however, supports a different proposition— call it Proposition B—which Stevens treated as indistinguishable from Proposition A. Proposition B is that the founders regarded America as a "Christian nation." Stevens concluded that his sources showed that the "original understanding of the type of religion that qualified for constitutional protection" "likely did not include" Judaism and Islam.[4] In light of this conclusion, Stevens asserted that the inclusion of Jews and Muslims within the First Amendment would be a "laudable act of religious tolerance." It was nonetheless, according to Stevens, an act "unmoored from the Constitution's history and text."[5]

I think that Proposition B is true: by and large the founders believed that America was a "Christian nation." But Proposition B does not mean nearly the same thing as Proposition A. As a matter of historical fact, A is false. Because Stevens' conclusion about Jews and Muslims depends upon the validity of A (and do not follow from B), it is false too. Jews and Muslims (and all other religions) are included within the First Amendment.

Let me explain by showing in Parts I and II why I think Proposition A—the one about "religion" meaning "the various sects of Christianity"— is false. In Part III of the chapter I show some important ways in which America was understood by the founders to be a "Christian nation." Doing that aids me in showing, also in Part III, how the founding generation understood the Establishment Clause. In Part IV I take up the question of giving coherent meaning today to what the Establishment Clause originally meant.

I

The founding fathers who wrote our Constitution in 1787 and who put it into practice shortly thereafter believed that Judaism and Islam were "religions." The founders invariably referred in speech and in writing to them *as* "religions," even though virtually none subscribed to either faith. The founders were, after all, Christians. Almost none of the founders thought that Judaism and Islam played, could play, or should play the same role in their republican experiment that Christianity played. Nonetheless, I have never encountered an original source from the founding era wherein the status of Judaism or Islam as a *religion* was denied. Justice Stevens cited none in *Van Orden.*

The founders' ecumenical usage of the word "religion" was not merely descriptive or demographic. The founders were not persons who would have predicated the word "religion" of whatever beliefs some sincere individual, or some serious group, happened to decide were "religious" to and for them. The founders were not shy about defining religion from a normative point of view. They did so repeatedly and with remarkable consistency in the constitutions and laws they enacted. The founders habitually conceptualized *religion* critically; that is, they used a normative definition of religion to develop a set of criteria or attributes which they thought truly distinguished *religion* from imposters, counterfeits, and knock-offs.

The most famous of these critical definitions is the one most prominent in the Supreme Court's modern church-state corpus. Madison took it verbatim from the 1776 *Virginia Declaration of Rights*, and inserted it into his celebrated "Memorial and Remonstrance." This document was a petition Madison circulated in 1785 against a proposed Virginia bill to publicly support teachers of Christianity. It has often been cited by the Supreme Court as somehow capturing the essence of what the founders thought about how church and state should be ordered. In the "M&R" Madison defined religion as "the duty which we owe to our Creator and the manner of discharging it."[6] Many other important legal sources at or near the founding said much the same about the nature or essence of religion. The New Hampshire Supreme Court in *Muzzy v. Wilkins*, an 1803 decision in favor of the public provision of "Protestant teachers of religion," defined religion as "that sense of Deity, that reverence for the Creator, which is implanted in the minds of rational beings."[7]

The term "sect" was often used by the founders. Almost always that word referred to the various divisions within *Protestantism*. "Sect" was synonymous with "denomination" and "persuasion."[8] "Sect" was never used to describe Judaism or Islam, and was rarely (but not never[9]) used to describe Catholicism. That huge subdivision of Christianity was instead described as the "Romish religion," "the Roman church," or, less respectfully, "Popery."[10]

During and after the American Revolution and therefore throughout the time when the Constitution came into being, many states "disestablished" religion. "Disestablishment" referred to removing any legal preference for one of the Protestant sects over the others. It was a matter of eliminating any preference for, say, Congregationalists or Anglicans over, say, Baptists. The language of disestablishment tracked this movement of thought. Disestablishment meant no *sect* preference, and that is what the earliest state constitutions said. The Delaware Constitution of 1776 (Art. 29) forbade the "establishment of any religious sect . . . in preference to another." The "no-preference" norm extended to "Denominations of Christians" in Connecticut; in North Carolina to "any religious church or denomination"; South Carolina eliminated all sect preferences in its Constitution of 1778, and explicitly declared the result to be the "estab-lish[ment]" of the "Christian Protestant *religion*" [my emphasis].

I think that the state disestablishment story undercuts Stevens' Proposition A. He reads the Establishment Clause—which uses the word "religion"—as if it meant to use the word "sect." Recall the very first sentence of this chapter, where Stevens asserts that the word "religion" was understood to encompass only "the various sects of Christianity." But the states' experiences strongly suggest that, if the First Amendment was sup-posed to mean "no-*sect* preference," then the founders would have put the word "sect" somewhere in it. They did not.

II

Justice Stevens nowhere considered what he could learn about the mean-ing of "religion" in the Establishment Clause by looking at the only other place in the Constitution where the word appears: the Article VI Test Clause. It says: "And no religious test shall ever be required as a qualifica-tion for office or public trust under the United States." Though the "no-test" clause was discussed nearly two years before the First Congress debated the Establishment Clause, and as long as three years before the states ratified the Bill of Rights, how the word "religion" was used in Article VI is still evidence of how it was used in the First Amendment. For when a term of common usage is put into a proposed constitution for pop-ular debate and, then, for ratification by representative assemblies, it is likely to be the case that its *meaning* in the constitution would be the com-mon meaning. In fact, many members of the First Congress which formu-lated the Establishment Clause in 1789 had debated the meaning of the Test Clause when they were members of the state conventions which considered ratifying the Constitution. Presumably, they retained a common under-standing of "religion" for the duration of these two constitutional moments (if you will).

What about the meaning of "religion" in Article VI? There was little discussion at Philadelphia about the no-test clause. The records from

Philadelphia confirm the observation of Luther Martin (a delegate from Maryland) that the Test Clause was "adopted by a great majority of the Convention, and without much debate."[11] Martin was scandalized. He left the Convention early (without voting on the finished draft), and attacked the proposed Constitution partly because he thought that "in a Christian country, it would be at least decent to hold out some distinction between the professors of Christianity and downright infidelity and paganism."[12] Benjamin Rush spoke truly (in a letter to John Adams) when he said that "[m]any pious people wish the name of the Supreme Being had been introduced somewhere in the Constitution." In other words, the Test Clause was a prime target for those who opposed the Constitution as, in one opponent's phrase, too "latitudinarian" in matters of faith.

This lament for a neglected God brought forth an ingenious defense of Article VI by Oliver Ellsworth, who later voted for the Establishment Clause in the First Senate and who after that served as Chief Justice of the United States. Ellsworth opined in his "Landholder" series of letters that the Article VI ban pertained to what he called a "particular" oath, one which discriminated among Christians. Ellsworth argued that a "general" oath—one which stated belief in a Supreme Being and a future state of rewards and punishments—was *not* constitutionally prohibited.[13] That is, Ellsworth proposed to understand "religion" as encompassing only the various sects within Christianity. Only a "sectarian" test was excluded.

Ellsworth's novel interpretation went against the popular understanding of what the Framers had wrought. That understanding was: federal offices and public trusts alike were open to *anyone* at all, due to Article VI. One New Hampshire anti-federalist objected precisely that that a "Turk, a Jew, a Roman Catholic, and what is worse than all, a Universalist, may be President of the United States." Similar arguments were made in the Virginia and North Carolina ratifying conventions, where "pagans," "deists," "heathens" and "Mahometans" were added to the watch list. In the Massachusetts Convention Baptist leader Isaac Backus addressed those "serious minds" (his words) concerned that, absent a test, "Congress would hereafter establish Popery or some other "tyrannical mode of worship." One serious mind present had already (before Backus spoke) "shuddered at the idea . . . that Popery and the Inquisition might be established in America" because of Article VI.

North Carolina's Convention bogged down in debate over a broadside which said that the Pope might one day become President of the United

States. The problem for federalists was that it was, indeed, literally possible due to Article VI. An anti-federalist name Lancaster elaborated:

> For my part, in reviewing the qualifications necessary for a President, I did not suppose that the pope could occupy the President's chair. But let us remember that we form a government for millions not yet in existence. I have not the art of divination. In the course of four or five hundred years, I do not know how it will work. This is most certain, that Papists may occupy that chair, and Mohametans may take it. I see nothing against it. There is a disqualification, I believe, in every state in the Union—it ought to be so in this system.[14]

Destined for a seat on the Supreme Court, but then the Constitution's leading proponent in the North Carolina Convention, James Iredell responded on behalf of the beleaguered test-ban:

> No man but a native, or who has resided fourteen years in America, can be chosen President. I know not all the qualifications for pope, but I believe he must be taken from the College of Cardinals; and probably there are many previous steps necessary before he arrives at this dignity. A native of America must have very singular good fortune, who, after residing fourteen years in his own country, should go to Europe, enter into Romish orders, obtain the promotion of cardinal, afterwards that of pope, and at length be so much in the confidence of his own country as to be elected President. It would be still more extraordinary if he should give up his popedom for our presidency.[15]

Records of the debate over the Establishment Clause in the First Congress suggest (but do not, in my judgment, compellingly show) that the debaters followed these conventions. The word "sect" referred to the divisions within Protestantism (Anglicans, Baptists, Methodists). The word "religion"—as in *"no religious test"*—referred expansively to Christianity, Judaism, Islam. The leading concern to which the Establishment Clause responded was surely Protestant *sect* hegemony. Madison said on the floor of the House that "the people feared" that "one sect might obtain a pre-eminence, or two combine together, and establish a religion to which they would compel others to conform." Madison clearly referred here to one (or two) of the divisions within Protestantism. One side-effect of language to forestall *that* evil (language like that of the Establishment Clause), however, was, according to New York's Peter Sylvester, a "tendency to abolish religion altogether." Benjamin Huntington of Connecticut wished not to deprive "religion" of that legal support which it customarily enjoyed in New England and which did not threaten private rights of conscience. In fact, only Protestant bodies were beneficiaries of that support.

Elbridge Gerry (of Massachusetts) tried to calm these fears by proposing in place of "religion" "no religious doctrine." Later in the Senate, on September 3, 1789, for example, a motion to strike the word "religion" and to replace it with "one religious sect or society in preference to others" carried. In light of these exchanges, I think that the eventual agreement to "religion" suggests a conscious choice of more expansive definition.[16]

The wider meaning of the word "religion" is confirmed when we bring into view the second First Amendment norm which pertains to the *same* "religion" that the Establishment Clause pertains to. After all, the word "religion" appears just once in the First Amendment, which says (in pertinent part), "Congress shall make no law respecting an establishment of religion, or prohibiting the free exercise *thereof*" [Emphasis added]. Unfortunately, Justice Stevens referred to "religion" throughout his *Van Orden* opinion as if there were no Free Exercise clause at all. Again, his claim is that the word "religion" in the Establishment Clause pertained only to the Protestant sects and had no extension to Jews and Muslims. Stevens never addressed this implication, of which he seems to have been wholly innocent: then non-Christians had no free exercise rights whatsoever. This implication leads to the following incongruity: though the Constitution protected the right of Jews and Muslims to become President, the Constitution gave them no protection whatsoever against persecution.

Stevens did refer to *state* constitutional protections for "free exercise." He asserted that "many of those [state constitutional] provisions restricted 'equal protection' and 'free exercise' to Christians."[17] But Stevens cited no such limited provision. He dropped instead a footnote to a scholarly article by Professor Lee Strange. But in those pages Professor Strange correctly reports that "free exercise" was, as a matter of fact, expanded after the Revolution precisely to include non-Christians, even though then and later (Strange also makes clear) the "religion" to which free exercise attached was defined critically, and limited to those who affirmed the existence of God. In fact, by the time the members of the First Congress proposed the Free Exercise Clause to the state legislatures for ratification, "free exercise of religion"—as a constitutional-legal term of art—unquestionably extended to *all* persons and to *all* faiths.[18]

Here is a brief sampling of the relevant evidence:

* The Georgia Constitution of 1777: "All persons whatever shall have the free exercise of their religion."[19]
* The Virginia Declaration of Rights (sec.16): "[A]ll men are equally entitled to the free exercise of religion, according to the dictates of conscience."[20]
* Madison in the M&R: "The religion of every man must be left to the conviction and conscience of every man; and it is the right of every man to exercise it as these may dictate."[21]

Judicial decisions shortly after the founding uniformly confirm this understanding, namely, that the "religion" protected by "free exercise" clauses extends as far as the reality of religion does and surely includes Judaism and Islam. In *Muzzy v. Wilkins* the New Hampshire Supreme Court wrote that "[e]very man may worship God according to the dictates of his own conscience and reason; and even those who deny their Maker this 'most reasonable service'. . . are referred for trial and punishment to him whose judgment cannot err." The Massachusetts high court wrote in *Barnes v. Falmouth* (1810) that "[h]aving secured liberty of conscience, on the subject of religious opinion and worship, for every man, whether Protestant, or Catholic, Jew, Mahometan or Pagan, the [Massachusetts] Constitution then provides for the public teaching of the precepts and maxims of the religion of Protestant Christians to all people."[22] Justice Stevens cited[23] *People v. Ruggles*,[24] a classic opinion by the redoubtable Chancellor Kent affirming a blasphemy conviction. Stevens omitted Kent's ringing affirmation of his state's constitutional protection of "the free, equal, and undisturbed enjoyment of religious opinion, whatever it might be, and free and decent discussion on any religious subject."[25]

Justice Stevens' evidence for Proposition A included this assertion: saying that Jews and Muslims were "inside the category of constitutionally protected religions would have shocked Chief Justice Marshall and Justice Story."[26] Then he turned to Justice Scalia, who in *Van Orden* held to the original meaning of the Establishment Clause, but who denied Stevens' challenge that "[g]iven [this] original understanding . . . one must ask whether Justice Scalia "has not had the courage (or the foolhardiness) to apply (his originalism) consistently."[27]

Stevens tried to support the Marshall claim, however, by evidence that Marshall adhered to Proposition B, the "Christian nation" view. But Stevens pointed to no evidence that Marshall dissented from the positions of, for example, the New Hampshire, Massachusetts, and New York courts (just noted here), which affirmed universal free exercise rights. In fact, Chief Justice Marshall consistently supported free exercise for everyone throughout his long public career.

Stevens relied upon this quotation from Joseph Story's *Commentaries on the Constitution of the United States* to make the other half of his case: "[A]t the time of the adoption of the constitution . . . the general if not the universal, sentiment in America was, that Christianity ought to receive encouragement from the state . . ."[28] Following Stevens' ellipsis, however, Story wrote: ". . . so far as it was not inconsistent with the private rights of conscience and the freedom of religious worship."[29] When Story wrote his *Commentaries,* the House of Representatives published a Committee Report rejecting petitions to suspend Sunday mail delivery. This 1830 document was authored by Kentucky's Richard Johnson. It stated that "The constitution regards the conscience of the Jew as sacred as that of the Christian."[30]

Justice Stevens asserted in *Van Orden* that the founders were "men who had no cause to view anti-Semitism or contempt for atheists as problems worthy of civic concern . . ."[31] This wooly but grave charge is obviously false in one sense: the founders had just as much "cause" to view such attitudes with "civic concern" as everyone else has—which is to say, a lot of cause. It is true that the founders had scarcely a positive word to say about atheism. They had little better to say about atheists, save that an unbeliever could (by dint of Article VI) become President. And no one at all, by force of free exercise guarantees, could be made to confess faith or attend worship which he or she did not conscientiously believe. So, *pace* Stevens, the founders viewed "contempt for atheists" with considerable though perhaps not enough "civic concern."

Stevens is even wider of the mark about anti-Semitism. He cites no evidence of anti-Semitism or of tolerance for it among the founders. Stevens seems, again, to read his charges off of Proposition B. He ignores considerable evidence of the founders' genuine respect, even affection, for Jews as their fathers in faith. We encountered Benjamin Rush earlier in this chapter, when he expressed some regret about Article VI. The same Rush was nonetheless quoted in a Philadelphia newspaper, speaking of "a most delightful sight" at the city's Independence Day parade in 1788. According to Rush, it was "The Rabbi of the Jews, locked in the arms of two ministers of the gospel." Rush further stated—this time with no regret—that the proposed ban on religious tests would open public office "not only to every sect of Christians but to worthy men of every religion."[32] While the First Amendment's fate was being decided by the state legislatures, President George Washington wrote to the Hebrew Congregation at Newport. Washington rejoiced that "toleration" is now "no more spoken of." Americans instead spoke of "inherent natural rights," which "gives to persecution no assistance," and in which "all possess alike liberty of conscience and immunities of citizenship."[33]

III

In *Van Orden v. Perry* Justice Stevens got the story about "religion" in the First Amendment very seriously wrong. But he got it right about "non-establishment." Stevens supposed that the basic norm about religion conveyed by the Establishment Clause is "non-preferentialism," or equality of treatment by the government of the various religions. This broad norm went beyond those of the state constitutions. But, then, so did the Article VI Test Clause.

We have seen that much of Stevens' historical evidence for Proposition A restated or tended to prove Proposition B—the "Christian nation" hypothesis.[34] Proposition B is true: Christianity was, in some important ways, pre-eminent—preferred, if you like—among religions at the founding. But, does not that fact imply that Stevens is correct about "religion"? After all, if non-establishment means no-preference and there is a preference for Christianity, then it must be true that the no-preference rule "encompass[es] only the various sects of Christianity."

No. Proposition A is false. Proposition B is true.

The way to unravel this apparent paradox is to carefully investigate the more precise meaning of Proposition B, that "America is a Christian nation." I propose to do so by letting the historical sources—some of the early state national constitutions, judicial decisions, and other authoritative public documents—speak for themselves. To that end I have collected some of those sources and arranged them (below) under three headings, where each heading expresses a constituent component of the "Christian nation" claim. I have added some commentary (noted as such) to be sure that the distinctions drawn by the founders are evident. My hope is that by unpacking the founders' complex understanding of what we call, in bulk, "public religion," we may discover the sort of government action which constituted a forbidden "preference."

The sources on offer below are meant to be illustrative. Though I firmly believe that each heading points to a component part of the common good of the polity as the founders understood such matters, I do not here try to demonstrate my belief by amassing a great quantity of supporting historical evidence.

A. *"The Religion of the People"*

"Blue laws"[35] mandating rest on Sunday were conspicuous pieces of civic furniture at the founding. These laws were often challenged by Saturday sabbatarians (typically Jews) who complained of an unconstitutional religious discrimination, because they would have to refrain from labor on both Saturday and Sunday, whereas Christians could work six days a week. Sunday laws were invariably sustained by the courts which heard challenges to them. These laws were almost never sustained by virtue of the truth of *any* religious doctrine or form of worship. The courts upholding blue laws ventured no answer to religious questions such as the right understanding of Scripture, the genuine requirements of the Third Commandment, when God really wanted people to take it easy, or the comparative validity of sectarian doctrines.

The major premise of these holdings in favor of Sabbatarian observance concerned public convenience. "All agree that to the well-being of society periods of rest are necessary," and at "stated intervals," one Pennsylvania court observed in an opinion characteristic of the genre.[36] The minor premise was the undeniable numerical preponderancy of Christians, almost all of whom were Sunday sabbatarians (a few Protestant sects maintained that Saturday was the biblical Sabbath). In response to Jewish plaintiffs' claim that Sunday laws exalted one religion's beliefs over another, the Pennsylvania court said: "In a Christian community, where a very large majority of the people celebrate the first day of the week as their chosen period of rest from labor, it is not surprising that that day should have received the legislative sanction." This coincidence "does not change the character of the enactment. It is still essentially a civil institution, made for the government of man, as a member of society." The obvious, and huge, incidental advantage to religion was not even a question.

Notwithstanding the presence of "blue laws" in every state, the national government moved and delivered mail on Sundays. This involved more than quiet backroom sorting; the mail stage (usually carrying passengers too) would often rumble into town during morning services, and unload at the store or inn doubling as the local post office. The resident menfolk would then excuse themselves to "check the mail"—and fall in for an afternoon of conversation and frivolity. The better class of folk (including wives who could relate to today's "football widows") complained bitterly to Congress over a period of many years.

The Congressional Committee to which the memorials were forwarded rejected all these prayers for relief. Sunday mail delivery was not ended until decades later. The Committee justified its denial by appeal to matters of public interest, convenience and necessity: the hinterlands would be cut off from news for an extra day; passengers would be delayed in their journey; news of commerce would be delayed reaching everyone. The Committee was especially keen to reject the petitioners' invitation to play minister or pious scold. "They [the petitioners] lay it down as an axiom, that the practice is a violation of the law of God." Because of the First Amendment, Congress could not take a position of what the law of God might require. "It is not the legitimate province of the legislature to determine what religion is true, or what is false."[37]

A different cascade of petitions engulfed Congress in the early 1850's. This time the complaint was too much religion, not too little. The gravamen was that Congressional chaplains violated the Establishment Clause. In an 1853 Report for the Senate Judiciary Committee, Wisconsin' Senator Badger wrote that, even though the chaplain selected were "in point of fact . . . always from some one of the denominations into which Christians are distributed," there was no Establishment Clause problem. Chaplains were as a matter of fact invariably always Protestants. But that fact did not owe, according to Badger for the Committee, to "any legal right or privilege," to the "voluntary choice of those who have the power of appointment." Instead it,

> . . . results from the fact that we are a Christian people—from the fact that almost our entire population belongs to or sympathizes with one of the Christian denominations which compose the Christian world. And Christians will of course select, for the performance of religious services, one who professes the faith of Christ. This, however, it should be carefully noted, is not by virtue of provision, but voluntary choice. We are Christians, not because the law demands it, not to gain exclusive benefits, or to avoid legal disabilities, but from choice and education; and in a land thus universally Christian, what is to be expected, what desired, but that we shall pay a due regard to Christianity, and have a reasonable respect for its ministers and religious solemnities?

Blasphemy prosecutions were sustained on the same demographic grounds combined with a different norm of public convenience. The norm this time was, in so many words: it won't do to permit some heckler to rile up a huge proportion of the populace by reviling or insulting their sacred religious figure—Jesus Christ. But blasphemy prosecutions did not presume, recognize, or enforce the truth of any religious proposition. To suggest otherwise would be to confuse blasphemy with heresy. All the antebellum appellate opinions upholding blasphemy convictions agreed that anyone might believe, profess, and argue for, orally or in writing, any religious position at all.

As the Delaware Supreme Court stated in *State v. Chandler*:

> [I]t is the open, public vilification of the religion of the country that is punished, not to force conscience by punishment, but to preserve the peace of the country, by an outward respect to the religion of the country, and not as a restraint upon the liberty of conscience; but licentiousness endangering the public peace . . .[38]

The *Chandler* court opined that "[i]n general, an offence which outrages the feelings of the community so far as to endanger the public peace, may be prohibited by the legislature. . . ." The court added that, because Christianity was presently the religion preferred by the vast bulk of the people, reviling it was subject to indictment. Reviling Mohammed would not be.

B. Public Morality

It is commonplace that the founders believed that a "virtuous" citizenry was a precondition for the success of republican government. Perhaps most famously, Madison wondered in Federalist 55 whether "nothing less than the chains of despotism" were needed "to restrain [men] from destroying and devouring one another." The founders believed that the answer was: no. They believed (gambled?) that sufficient virtue could be cultivated in the citizenry to keep liberty going. But, Madison cautioned readers of Federalist 55, "republican government presupposes the existence of [virtuous] qualities" in the citizens "in a higher degree than any other form of government."

"Religion and morality"—a complex unity more than a compound—was the key to liberty with safety. As Washington bade his countrymen Farewell: "of all the dispositions and habits which lead to political prosperity, religion and morality are indispensable supports." Not only Madison and Washington, but Adams and even Jefferson—among many others—concurred in the basic sentiment. One especially authoritative expression of this notion is the Northwest Ordinance of 1787, language which was incorporated by Congress in many subsequent acts organizing newly acquired territories: "Religion, morality and knowledge, being necessary to good government and the happiness of mankind, schools and the means of education shall forever be encouraged."

The *Falmouth v. Barnes* court made this argument quite elegantly. It wrote that "human laws cannot oblige to the performance of duties of imperfect obligation," such as the obligations of family members to each other; "duties of charity, benevolence and good neighborhood"; "and of real patriotism, by influencing every citizen to love his country and obey all its laws." For "[t]hese are moral duties flowing from the disposition of the heart, and not subject to the control of human legislation."[39]

The founders believed that inculcating sound morality included work for the state. Performing that job, the founders further believed, inescapably involved inculcating religion too. The founders recognized at least three knots in the cord binding together religion and morality. The first is evident from the blasphemy cases. Chancellor Kent wrote in *Ruggles* that "things which corrupt moral sentiment, as obscene actions, prints and writings, and even gross instances of seduction" tend to "corrupt the morals of the people, and to destroy good order."[40] Kent further observed "that we are a Christian people, and the morality of the country is deeply engrafted upon Christianity, and not the doctrines or worship of . . . imposters." As a matter of fact, Americans possessed "Christian" morals. Protecting Christianity promoted sound morals.

This is not to say that the founders viewed the relationship among law, religion, and morality from an ironic distance, as if these were integral parts of a posited system. It is not as if the founders were like modern political scientists, or anthropologists, perhaps. The founders surely *believed* in free government. And, while it would not be logically impossible, it would have been very odd if they did not believe in the morality which—they surely did believe—was essential to liberty. The morality which they affirmed and the religion which was its linchpin were, they thought, *true*. And so the Northwest Ordinance spoke of both "good government" *and* "the happiness of mankind."

The *Falmouth* court identified a second intimate tie between religion and morality. "Civil government therefore, availing itself only of its own powers, is extremely defective; and unless it can derive assistance from some superior power, whose laws extend to the temper and disposition of the human heart, and before whom no offense is secret, wretched indeed would be the state of man under a civil condition of any form."[41] The 1854 House Report on military chaplains echoed this intimate connection of religion as motive force and sanction for morality:

> Laws will not have permanence or power without the sanction of religious sentiment—without a firm belief that there is a Power above us that will reward our virtues and punish our vices. In this age there can be no substitute for Christianity; that, in its general principles, is the great conservative element on which we must rely for the purity and permanence of free institutions.

Falmouth concluded that the relevant "excellencies" of Christianity were "well known, and its divine authority admitted."[42] Even so, liberty of conscience in religion is secured to "every man, whether Protestant or Catholic, Jew, Mahometan, or Pagan."[43]

The "morality" upon which republican institutions depend required religion. It necessarily *included* religion. The third knot was a subset of natural moral norms about duties to God. Piety and a fear of God were moral virtues. That they could be and were known without adverting to revealed truths or to the authority of some religious figure or book. That these were within the law's portfolio is apparent from universal requirements to *respect* the Sabbath, incumbent even on those who did not believe in the Third Commandment.

These legal duties to religion extended to enforcing those which individuals had voluntarily undertaken. In an 1815 Supreme Court opinion, written by Story and construing Virginia's Constitution, the Court held that the legislature could not compel any belief or worship or create an establishment with "exclusive rights and prerogatives." "But the free exercise of religion cannot be justly deemed to be restrained by aiding with equal attention the votaries of every sect to perform their own religious duties, or by establishing funds for the support of ministers, for public charities, for the endowment of churches, or for the sepulture of the dead."[44]

C. Natural Religion

Confidence in human reason was a leading characteristic of the founding generation. To modern ears this might sound like saying that the founders were skeptical of religion, that they were *rationalists*. That is not what I mean. I mean that, at the founding, any reasonable person was expected to affirm the truths affirmed by the fifty-five who signed the Declaration of Independence: there is a divine Creator who providentially guides human affairs, chiefly by providing sufficient evidence of moral truths such as those concerning inalienable human rights. Most people affirmed these propositions, and they affirmed them as true—and not as (or not merely as) the presuppositions of our governmental system, "noble lies" to domesticate the rabble, or as conventional knowledge. Herein lies the "neutrality" of these propositions: being affirmable as true by virtue of proofs available to unaided human reason, they did not depend upon revelation or religious authority for their acceptance as sound. Call these propositions the elements of "natural religion," and contrast them with the tenets of positive theology or revealed truth.

These affirmations were—like Blue Laws—part of the founders' civic furniture. As the Supreme Court later said in the *Holy Trinity* case (in 1892): "Every constitution of every one of the 44 states contains language which, either directly or by clear implication, recognizes a profound reverence for religion, and an assumption that its influence in all human affairs is essential to the well-being of the community."[45] Many of these constitutions contained additional explicit acknowledgments of God and Providence and of specific blessings, such as free government, religious liberty, and civil rights.[46] Even so: *Donahue v. Richards*, an 1854 decision which affirmed the expulsion of a Catholic school girl for refusing to read from the Protestant Bible, turned upon the meaning of the 1820 Maine Constitution. Maine's highest court said that the constitution "recognizes the goodness of the Sovereign ruler of the Universe, it does not recognize the superiority of any form of religion or of any sect or denomination."[47]

It is not quite right to say that the religious truths affirmed were part of Christianity. After all, anyone with unclouded reason could see that they were objectively true. And did not Jews as well as Muslims believe in a Creator God and His provident governance of the universe? Because the political power to insert natural religion into the nation's law lay in Christian hands, however, there was no practical chance that anything so affirmed would be *contrary* to the beliefs held by Christ's followers. These truths naturally came to be embedded in the civil theologies of the day, too, thus making sure that they would acquire the color and flavor of the dominant brand of civil theology then on offer, the Christian "religion of the people."

These three components of public religion—the people's religion; religion as source, guarantor, and motive force of morality which made freedom possible; natural religion—all tilted discernibly towards Christianity. Call this a certain powerful "preference" for the "various sects of Christianity." Or call it, more simply, confirmation of Proposition B. Either way, the evidence is overwhelming that this religious "preference" raised no serious "establishment" issue for the founders. For the founders, an "establishment" transcended government acts which in effect advanced religion, even where Christianity was peculiarly promoted. A reasonable person's perception that government acts conveyed a message of "endorsement" for religion in general or, even, Christianity in particular, did not count for an "establishment" of religion, either.

What then did a prohibited "preference" consist of?

The prohibition that emerges from the foregoing material includes, I think, a norm of abstention concerning the lawmaker's *reasons* for action: the truth of *certain* religious propositions must never be part of a law's justification. This is what I call the "Incompetence Norm." It is that the Establishment Clause ordains that the *truth* of certain religious matters is outside the *competence* of the national government.

To which sorts of religious matters did the Incompetence Norm attach? Not to moral norms, even where those norms are related to religious belief in myriad ways (as described in heading B, above). The Incompetence Norm does not attach to what reason can affirm about divine things (see heading C, above). The Incompetence Norm (as perhaps best illustrated under heading A, above) attaches to theological beliefs and doctrines, modes of worship, and to wider matters of religious discipline and observance (again, consider the sweep of the lawmaker's abstention in regard to Sabbath observance). And so the original meaning of non-establishment emerges as this: the lawmaker must not make the truth of *any* religious doctrine, discipline, or worship a *reason* for his actions.

The *Muzzy* court went to the outer limit of this range when it justified (albeit in *dictum)* blasphemy laws. "Religious opinions form no ground of distinction. But we are not to infer from this that the civil magistrate may not lawfully punish certain offenses against *the unalterable and essential principles of natural and revealed religion*, for these principles are said to make a part of the common law." Of this description are the offenses of blasphemy, reviling religion, and "profanation of the Sabbath." The "principles of revealed religion" could be, but need not be, understood to include any matter of doctrine, discipline or proper form of worship.

The Incompetence Norm extended to every religion, even though Christians were the only religious group which possessed the political power at the founding to violate the Incompetence Norm. But everyone—especially including non-Christians—benefitted from the Norm's requirement that a law touching religion (Sabbatarian rest, a witness' oath, military or Congressional chaplains, and even public support for Protestant teachers of religion) had to be justified on grounds apart from the truth of some religious doctrine, form of worship, or matter of church discipline. So Justice Stevens' assertion that only Christians were "protected" by the Establishment Clause is not only off the mark. It is uncomprehending.

IV

How does the historical recovery project we have conducted in Parts I through III of this chapter fit into contemporary constitutional doctrine? Does the effort yield up an unusable past, an "original" understanding which is unsuited to today's pluralistic religious environment?

I think it does.

The Incompetence Norm is right in line with the minority position on the Supreme Court about what the Establishment Clause means. The dominant position is the requirement that government not "endorse" religion as such, not even all manner of religious belief over and against what the Court calls "irreligion" or "non-religion." The alternative is "non-preferentialism." "Non-preferentialism" holds that government is permitted under the Establishment Clause to encourage and promote and aid religion, so long as it does without discrimination among religions. The Incompetence Norm gives this statement muscle and specificity.[48]

The Incompetence Norm fits well with today's Free Exercise doctrine. In *Employment Division v. Smith*[49] the Court—largely based upon historical research—anchored Free Exercise in what looks like a mirror image of the Incompetence Norm. The *Smith* Court said:

> [A]ssembling with others for a worship service, participating in sacramental use of bread and wine, proselytizing, abstaining from certain foods or certain modes of transportation. . . [A] state would be "prohibiting the free exercise [of religion]" if it sought to ban such acts . . . *only* when they are engaged in for religious reasons, or only because of the religious belief that they display.[50]

The decisive feature here is the lawmaker's implicit *unfavorable* judgment (of falseness, invalidity, unsoundness) about someone's or some group's theological doctrine or belief or mode of worship. The Supreme Court subsequently recognized in *Church of Lukumi Babalyu v. Hialehah*,[51] a Free Exercise exemption to a municipal ordinance that forbade the ritual slaughter of animals, in a jurisdiction wherein animal slaughter for sport or food was permitted. The Court rightly inferred from this ensemble of laws that the local authorities banned the ritual sacrifice *because of*, or somehow *on account of*, the religious meaning the Santeria faithful ascribed to it. The selective prohibition implied that the religious beliefs in play were false, unsound, unworthy.

The Incompetence Norm may therefore be understood as the symmetrical counterpart to this Free Exercise doctrine. Both are Incompetence Norms. The one bans favoritism based upon certain reasons. The other bans hostility based upon certain reasons. In the one case the Incompetence Norm is violated by affirming the truth of a bracketed proposition (say, that Sunday is really the Lord's Day); in the other, by declaring a bracketed proposition (such as God's true pleasure at animal sacrifice) to be false.

Adoption of the "original" meaning would also make the jurisprudence(s) of the two "Religion Clauses" coherent with each other. The problem created by the Court's dominant position is obvious: how could government protect the free exercise of *religion* without thereby "endorsing" religion, just as such? In its most recent testimony that incoherence is afoot, the Court in *Cutter v. Wilkinson*[52] confessed that the two clauses are "frequently in tension."[53] "While the two Clauses express complementary values, they often exert conflicting pressures."[54] And: "The Court has struggled to find a neutral course between the Religion Clauses which, if expanded to a logical extreme, would tend to clash with each other."[55] Years ago Justice O'Connor put the point plainly, and correctly: the Court's interpretations of them put the two clauses on a "collision course" with each other.

CONCLUSION

Justice Stevens asserted in *Van Orden v. Perry* that requiring government to be "neutral between religion and irreligion would have seemed foreign to some of the Framers." Indeed it would have. Stevens further claimed that it would have seemed no more strange to the Framers than requiring "neutrality between Jews and Christians." This claim, we can now say with confidence, is spectacularly mistaken. Stevens then compounded his error by making the unpalatable (but erroneous) Proposition A an excuse for rejecting originalism altogether. Well, almost, according to Stevens. "Fortunately, we are not bound by the Framers' expectations—we are bound by the legal principles they enshrined in the Constitution."[56]

Leave aside that Stevens had seemed to propose Proposition A as, precisely, a "legal principle." It is more worth notice that Stevens' update did not stop—or, it seems, seriously consider stopping—at the more felicitous "legal principle" with which he clubbed Justice Scalia, namely, "neutrality" including Judaism, Islam and all other religions. The adventurous Stevens instead moved beyond "legal principles" having anything to do with religion. His improved touchstone was "belief systems," with surprisingly regressive modifiers (in italics): "government must remain neutral between *valid* systems of belief," and as "religious pluralism has expanded so has *our acceptance* of what constitutes belief systems."[57] Stevens thus ends up where his earlier church-state opinions show that he started, with a deep and abiding secularism—the complete *absence* of religion from the public square, as the only available "neutral" ground between religious and non-religious "valid belief systems."

CHAPTER 8:

"The Miracle":
Catholicism, Culture, and the Constitution[1]

In early November 1951 Supreme Court Justice Felix Frankfurter reached out to a former Harvard colleague, someone he addressed as his "unofficial theological advisor." George La Piana was an emeritus professor of church history, a man of prodigious learning and long association with the Catholic Church. Ordained a priest in his native Italy in 1900, La Piana earned a doctorate in 1912 and was on track for preferment in the Church. His path was blocked, however, by his adherence to "Modernism," a complex of views declared by Pope Pius X in 1907 to be incompatible with Catholic faith.[2] La Piana emigrated to the United States in 1913, drifted out of the priesthood, and eventually landed at Harvard. He is said to have been the first Catholic on the Divinity School faculty. In truth, his Catholicism was, at most, nominal.

Frankfurter expressed "gratitude" for his friend's "past intellectual beneficence." He specifically mentioned one such gift: a new monograph titled *A Totalitarian Church in a Democratic State: The American Experiment*. This compact book grew out of a series of lectures La Piana gave at Butler University in 1949.[3] In these talks he explored and defended the thesis that Roman Catholicism was incompatible with American democracy. Paul Blanchard acknowledged these lectures as the inspiration for his own popular and controversial indictment of the American Church, *American Freedom and Catholic Power.*[4] Frankfurter described *Totalitarian Church* (in his letter to La Piana) as "illuminati[ng]."[5]

The Justice made no apology for "turn[ing] once more" to La Piana for assistance. "Gratitude," wrote Frankfurter, "is the expectation of lively favors to come." He had a big favor to ask. The task at hand was reversing the New York Court of Appeals' decision in *Burstyn v. Wilson.*[6] The court had just upheld New York closure of Roberto Rosselini's film *Il*

Miracolo—The Miracle. At the time in New York, all movies (with minor and here irrelevant exceptions) had to be licensed by public authority before they could be publicly exhibited. The governing statute said that a license "shall" issue from the Board of Regents movie office, "unless the film or a part thereof is obscene, indecent, immoral, inhuman" or—as was found to be the case with *The Miracle*—"sacrilegious."

The central claim of *The Miracle's* exhibitor—Joseph Burstyn, the nation's leading importer of European films—was that "sacrilegious" was too vague a legal standard to pass constitutional muster. Burstyn maintained throughout his court challenge that any movie impresario (such as himself) would have to guess whether a film in which he had invested would ever reach the screen. And this, Burstyn held, was more than our constitutional safeguards of free speech permitted.

New York's highest court rejected Burstyn's claim, and upheld the state's action against *The Miracle* on October 18, 1951. Frankfurter took dead aim at that conclusion.

Frankfurter bluntly informed La Piana that "[t]his time I want from you a bibliography—authoritative of course but within the compass both of time and the understanding of a busy judge—on the concept of 'sacrilegious' as it has come down through the ages in the Church of Rome." This reference to the Catholic Church calls for some explanation. It was, after all, New York (through its Commissioner of Education Lewis Wilson) and not the Church which stood opposite Burstyn in court. The disputed term, "sacrilegious," was taken from a statute, not from a Catechism. The highest state court had, moreover, held specifically that the "dictionary . . . furnishes a clear definition" of it, namely, "the act of violating or profaning anything sacred."[7] The court said that there is "nothing mysterious" about the statutory provision: "It is simply this: that no religion, as that word is understood by the ordinary, reasonable person, shall be treated with contempt, mockery, scorn and ridicule. . . ." Burstyn's claim about vagueness was, the court concluded, "without substance."[8]

Why then did Frankfurter want a memorandum concerning the "Church of Rome"? It is tempting to consider the odd request as a reflection of La Piana's scholarly expertise. He was after all a scholar of church history and not of legal doctrines. But La Piana'a accomplishments were not the main reason for Frankfurter's specific reference. Francis Cardinal Spellman, Archbishop of New York, was. More exactly, an essential premise of the Supreme Court's holding in *Burstyn,* as well as the whole point of Frankfurter's essay concurring in the judgment, was the Catholic Church's considerable culture-forming political clout in New York and, as La Piana and Blanshard and Frankfurter surely believed, across America as well. Spellman was the mid-century avatar of this power. New York's political classes routinely referred to his Chancery offices as "The Powerhouse." For Frankfurter and to some extent for others on the court, the Regents' decision was transparent for Spellman's political muscle. Frankfurter was determined to use the *Burstyn* case to confirm Blanchard's (and La Piana's) theses about the Church's exaggerated cultural authority in America. The state courts may have lacked the nerve to unplug the Powerhouse. But the United States Supreme Court would harbor no such trepidation.

This chapter tells the story of the movie, and of the case.

I

The Miracle opened at Manhattan's leading "art house," The Paris Theater, on December 12, 1950. Almost immediately the Legion of Decency—the Church's office for the moral evaluations of movies—tapped into the city's Catholic power grid to shut it down. The Legion's charge was that *The Miracle* mocked the story of Jesus's miraculous birth, and that the film was (in the relevant legal terms) "blasphemous" or "sacrilegious," or both. At first the City's License Commissioner Edward McCaffrey unilaterally tried to close *The Miracle*. When the courts blocked that effort, the Legion's leaders asked Spellman for help.

The Cardinal responded with a message read at all Masses on Sunday, January 7, 1951. In this letter Spellman decried *The Miracle* as a "despicable affront to every Christian." He "censured" the Motion Picture Division for licensing such an "insult" to "millions of people. He lamented that "no means of appeal to the Board of Regents [was then presently] available to correct the mistake of the Motion Picture Division." Then the Cardinal supplied ample incentive to create those means. "[I]f the present law is so weak and inadequate to cope with this desperate situation, then all right-thinking citizens should unite to change and strengthen the Federal and state statutes" so as to make it "impossible" for anyone to profit by "blasphemy, immorality, and sacrilege."[9] Within days, *The Miracle*'s exhibition license was lifted.

"Perhaps I better tell you," Frankfurter wrote to La Piana, "the assumption on which I am turning to you for aid. . . . It is that the concept of sacrilegious is not fixed, final and definite, but has its own history of changes and chances, of diversities and distinctions, of conflicts and controversies." Frankfurter wanted to hear nothing in support of the Court of Appeals' conclusion. "If it" (meaning Frankfurter's "assumption") "is wrong," he told La Piana, then "throw this letter in the wastebasket."

On November 18, La Piana "apologize[d] for [his] delay in acknowl-edging" Frankfurter's appeal. "I was away for a few days. It gives me great pleasure to be of some use to my friends. . . . I have compiled a short sum-mary of the history and doctrine about Sacrilege and I hope it may be of some use to one like you who has no time to study such question in detail."[10] La Piana enclosed a ten-page essay on the concept of "sacrilege," chiefly as it developed under the aegis of the Catholic Church during the Middle Ages.

On November 26 Frankfurter asked for still more help. This time the former Harvard law professor asked: "could you refer me to the writings that establish" the proposition that "sacrilege had no fixed meaning." La Piana's lengthy response supplied that authority, though it too was delayed in coming. La Piana reported a bout with influenza, which he playfully speculated might be punishment for his own sins of sacrilege.[11]

The Supreme Court noted probable jurisdiction in *Burstyn v. Wilson* more than two months *after* the Frankfurter / La Piana correspondence ended.[12] On April 25, 1952—the day after oral argument—Frankfurter shared with the brethren what he described to them as the "product of our labors." "Our" referred, Frankfurter made clear, to the Justice and his clerks. He explained the existence of such a precocious product this way: "In anticipation of the case coming here, I got under way, with my law clerks, lines of inquiry without which, I was confident, the case could not reasonably be decided." The "laborious and time-consuming" studies could not wait upon argument, Frankfurter wrote, because the case would not be heard until the "home-stretch" of the term. He was loathe to have the case held over to the next term.[13]

On May 26 the Supreme Court unanimously reversed the New York court's ruling against Joseph Burstyn and *The Miracle*.[14] Writing for the Court, Justice Tom Clark said that "application of the 'sacrilege' test . . . might raise substantial questions" under what he described as the "First Amendment's guaranty of separate church and state with freedom of wor-ship for all."[15] These "questions" received no explicit answers, however; the Court decided *Burstyn v. Wilson* "from the standpoint of freedom of speech and the press."[16] From that position, *Burstyn* declared for the first time in the Court's jurisprudence that "expression by means of motion pictures is included within the free speech and free press guaranty of the First Amendment."[17] "Sacrilege" was, according to the Court, "far from the kind of narrow exception to freedom of expression which a state may carve out" to satisfy other societal interests.[18]

The Court made no acknowledged use of Frankfurter's (that is, La Piana's) exhaustive research in its opinion. But just as Frankfurter had recommended and as he wrote in his concurring essay, the Court held that "sacrilege" was so vague that it amounted to an open invitation for "the most vocal and powerful orthodoxies" to banish whatever they found offensive or displeasing. The implicit reference to "The Powerhouse" was sufficient to alert readers to the back-story especially in light of Frankfurter accompanying rendition of the whole *Miracle* saga.[19]

II

The majority opinion in *Burstyn v. Wilson* includes no description of the *The Miracle's* plot. There is scarcely a clue as to what the picture was about. Cardinal Spellman's turgid January 7 denunciation of the film described it only as "the seduction of an idiotic Italian woman." Frankfurter's *Burstyn* opinion (joined by Justices Burton and Jackson) began with a plot "summary" previously published by a "practiced hand," that of the *New York Times'* movie critic Bosley Crowther.[20] Frankfurter's Crowther is heard to recite, though, just the improbable facts of the matter. These were: a "simple-minded" goatherd named Nanni is "ravishe[d]" by a bearded stranger whom she believes to be Saint Joseph. The stranger plies her with enough wine to put her "in a state of tumult." Discovering herself in due course to be with child, Nanni is mocked and rejected by villagers upon whom she presses her story of impregnation by "the grace of God!" "Even abused by the beggars, the poor girl gathers her pitiful rags and sadly departs from the village to live alone in a cave." When the period of her confinement ends she retreats to an empty church on a hill. "A goat is her sole companion." Labor pains are etched on her face just before an unseen baby cries. The movie ends with mother suckling her infant boy.[21]

I have shown *The Miracle* to my Civil Liberties class, comprised of second- and third-year law students. My students saw what Crowther (and Frankfurter) described. They saw the "idiot" Nanni, the bearded stranger, the wine, the mocking villagers, and the goat. They heard the baby cry. Still, the students had no idea what the movie was about. The reason is, what is *depicted* in *The Miracle* reveals almost nothing about the movie. *The Miracle* is no more really about a ravished idiot than *Animal Farm* is about the life of pigs.

No one could reasonably deny Anna Magnani's bravura performance as "Nanni."[22] But there is otherwise very little acting in *The Miracle*.[23] The "bearded stranger" never speaks. He conveys little by his looks, save bemusement. The photography is competent, but scarcely more than that. The story was cooked up on the eve of shooting by Frederico Fellini, who was already a regular script doctor on Rossellini's projects, and who also played the role of taciturn stranger.[24]

What *The Miracle* is really about is, in other words, a matter of interpretation. As Frankfurter's "practiced hand" wrote immediately after it opened: Nanni "may be interpreted two ways. She may be logically accepted as a symbol of deep and simple faith, horribly abused and tormented by a cold and insensitive world; or she may be entirely regarded as an open mockery of faith and religious fervor—depending upon your point of view."[25] A few days later, Crowther wrote in the *Times* that "[o]bviously, this story with its symbolic parallels, might by some be considered a blasphemy of the doctrine of the Virgin Birth. And with its poor crazy woman crying desperately to God while goats bleat at her, it might also be considered a mockery of religious faith. But because of the humble framing that Rossellini has given this simple tale and because of Magnani's great performance, it seems to this reviewer to be just a vastly compassionate comprehension of the suffering and the triumph of birth."[26]

On one reasonable interpretation of *The Miracle*, the viewer is given to understand that belief in the "miracle" of virginal conception is fit only for the delusional, that it is a fable fit for children and child-like adults. On another reasonable interpretation of the film, it is a testimony to the power (and even the appeal) of a simple but profound faith, and to the callousness of the world to this precious gift (given, as it were, to the child-like). *The Miracle* is, in other words, ambiguous.

Ambiguity is part of the film's appeal precisely as art. Justice Frankfurther (among others) attempted to resolve this ambiguity by appeal to the artist's (Rossellini's) intentions.[27] Others sought the interpretive key in the principals' alleged Catholicism.[28] Both these appeals miss the mark. The artist's work is the product of his or her intentions, and those intentions shape the work so as to limit the range of plausible interpretations. But the artist possesses no authority to settle what the work *means*. An artist of Rossellini's   sophistication,   moreover,   could   not   have inadvertently produced so indeterminate a film as *The Miracle*. He surely knew that it operated on two levels of understanding.

Indeed, most (but not all)[29] of those engaged in *The Miracle* dispute treated the film as univocal; it was *either* a mockery of Christian faith *or* a sublime testimony to its power and appeal. One or the other. But not both. These disputants tried to settle the question about the law ("sacrilege") by settling the question about what the movie means. *The Miracle* is, however, deliberately ambiguous.

The Supreme Court followed the well-trod path. The Justices asked: Is *The Miracle* "sacrilegious"? The Court misunderstood even this question. One of these misunderstandings confused "sacrilege" with disagreement, as if *The Miracle*'s "sacrilege" lay strictly in its implication that the Catholic doctrine of Mary's virginal conception is untrue. No one involved in *The Miracle* controversy—not Cardinal Spellman and certainly not the New York courts—defined "sacrilege" as a departure from doctrine, as heterodoxy. They never suggested that *The Miracle*'s offense was (even in so many words) heresy.

The other misinterpretation zeroed in on the emotional reaction of a doctrine's adherents, as if *The Miracle* was "sacrilegious" because Catholics found it disgusting or offensive. But this confuses one contingent effect of "sacrilege" with its meaning. No party to *The Miracle* controversy—not Cardinal Spellman and certainly not New York's courts—made this mistake, either.

Frankfurter nonetheless compounded these two errors by running them together.[30] He suggested that a movie which treated the Catholic doctrine of Transubstantiation favorably, or even "neutrally," would be "offensive" to a "great many Protestants," evidently because Protestants do not believe in Transubstantiation. Such a movie would be "therefore for them sacrilegious"[31] Frankfurter thus implicitly committed himself to the absurd view that *Going My Way*—that endearing depiction of the Catholic priesthood—might be a "sacrilege" to Protestants who rejected the Catholic sacrament of Holy Orders. But no one in *The Miracle* controversy—not Cardinal Spellman and certainly not the New York courts—made this mistake, either. None asserted that a mere deviation from doctrine—even one which "offended" its adherents—was perforce "sacrilegious."

"Is *The Miracle* 'sacrilegious'?" is not (again, *pace* Frankfurter and LaPiana) a question about ecclesiastical usage of the term. It is not about medieval legal history or even about how the English or American common law of yore apprehended the term. The relevant usage is in a New York licensing statute. The aim and desired effect of the New York motion picture law were not penal. The license law's purpose was not to identify persons who intended to cause some specific harm, then to deny them some valuable opportunity (such as exhibiting a film) as a just punishment for their bad choice and action. The licensing law's aim was instead to forestall certain cultural injuries, namely, bringing religion and the religious into disrepute by treating religious belief as unworthy of the intelligent and discriminating mind, by portraying religion as credible only to the deluded and idiotic, by "mocking" or "ridiculing" religious belief.

One reason why such a law might make sense is that in a country populated by three hundred different religious sects (as Frankfurter alleged about the American demographic), a culture of respectful and serious dialogue among those holding incompatible religious positions would be a welcome amenity. Such a culture of civilized disputation could promote mutual understanding, interfaith cooperation, and even civic peace. Such a culture would also promote religious liberty. For the freedom to believe (or not) is potentially diminished wherever those who are seriously searching for the truth receive the signal from their cultural betters that religion is for the stupid or the demented. Religiously-convinced "idiots" in such a cultural milieu would likely feel disrespected, inferior, and maybe like they were second-class citizens.

A government minded to protect public morality and to promote religious liberty and cognizant of the fact that we are, as the Supreme Court affirmed in *Zorach v. Clausen* just three days after the *Burstyn* oral argument, "a religious people whose institutions presuppose a Supreme Being,"[32] could reasonably conclude that it bears *some* responsibility for maintaining the cultural conditions just described. But even if not, or even if that responsibility does not extend so far (or, perhaps, nearly so far) as prohibiting public exhibition of a "sacrilegious" film, it should be apparent that the relevant meaning of "sacrilege" has to do with reasonable receptions of a work, with what an average person might plausibly understand the work to communicate, with the *effects* of such a film. The intermediate New York appellate court captured all of these considerations pretty well. That lower court said that the question was whether a movie "may fairly be deemed" by the competent public authority "sacrilegious to the adherents of any religious group."[33]

III

The Miracle lacked sex appeal. It was not an action flick. It conveyed no political message. Not surprisingly, the movie flopped in Italy. Box-office receipts there amounted to about half its modest cost of 60,000 dollars.

Rosselini entered *The Miracle* in the 1948 Venice Film Festival. It won no prize. It won the attention, however, of two unquiet Americans.

Mrs. Mary Looram was a seasoned Legion of Decency film reviewer, and she was in Venice.[34] She saw *The Miracle.* Then she saw Joseph Burstyn speaking with Rossellini[35] or (according to another account) Rossellini's lawyer.[36] Either way, Mrs. Looram figured that Burstyn was inquiring about rights to the film. She walked up to Burstyn and said, "You aren't going to buy *that* film, are you?" Burstyn laughed and told her that "Lots of things are all right for the Legion after cuts, aren't they? You approved *Forever Amber*[37] and we'll see what can be done with *The Miracle.*" Mrs. Looram expressed doubt that any set of "cuts" would save *The Miracle.*[38]

Burstyn did not obtain the rights to *The Miracle* while he was in Venice. Film importer Ilya Lopert did. Later Lopert sold them to Burstyn. Without a fuss the state's Motion Picture Division, headed by Hugh M. Flick, licensed *The Miracle* as part of a trilogy of foreign films called *Ways of Love*[39] on November 30, 1950.[40] Meanwhile, Mrs. Looram reported back on the sacrilegious character of *The Miracle*, and the Legion of Decency promptly condemned it. The Italian equivalent of the Legion had done likewise in 1948, branding the movie an "abominable profanation."[41]

The Ways of Love opened at The Paris Theater, on 58th street just off Fifth Avenue, on December 12, 1950, with Burstyn and the theater splitting any profits from the exhibition. At first their financial prospects looked grim. Reviews of *The Miracle* were mixed, as were those of the entire triptych. Attendance the first week was disappointing, and the trilogy seemed destined for a short run notwithstanding Bosley Crowther's over-the-top review. Crowther liked all three pictures. In his December 13 *Times'* review, however, he hailed *The Miracle* as "by far the most overpowering and provocative of the lot," "probably the most intense dramatic piece that we have had from the sensational" Rossellini.[42] Crowther added, presciently, that *The Miracle* "will certainly cause a lot of stir."

Rev. Patrick Masterson, head of the American Legion of Decency, was at the Paris Theater on opening day. Established in 1933, the Legion was part of the Catholic Church. It was from the beginning (in Crowther's words) "the most forceful and consistent arbitrator of the 'morals' of films in this land." Historian Frank Walsh maintains that in 1950 "the Legion seemed as powerful as ever."[43] Many in elite cultural circles and, perhaps, on the political left generally, would have agreed with Arthur Schlesinger, Jr.'s complaint that (in Walsh's words) "the movies were being filmed according to the ground rules set by a minority religious faith."[44] One such observer asserted that "the Legion holds the whip hand over Hollywood and nothing can be done about it."[45] Many others credited the Legion with preserving American cinema from a race to a tawdry, suggestive, and just plain filthy bottom. There was nonetheless festering resentment about Catholic power over the American cinema. Frankfurter, for example, repeatedly appealed to this resentment in his concurring essay, at one point succinctly asserting: "The effect of such [sectarian demands] upon art and upon those whose function is to enhance the culture of a society need not be labored."[46]

Legion leadership worked closely with the movie industry's own Production Code Administration, by which Code the Hollywood studios hewed to standards of decency very much in line with those used by the Legion of Decency. Hollywood would never have considered producing such a religion-ambivalent film as *The Miracle*.[47] Foreign film directors had a different set of cultural constraints in mind, partly because their films were not subject to the rigors of the American industry's code. One telling measure of the different sensibilities and constraints is the Legion's list of "condemned" films for 1952: only one of the fourteen was produced in America.[48]

"As the lights went up following *The Miracle*'s initial showing, Father Masterson told the management to cease showing the film. It refused."[49] Within days Masterson (or someone at his direction) contacted Edward McCaffrey,[50] the City official responsible for licensing all sorts of business venues, including motion picture theaters.[51] McCaffrey did not consider his portfolio to be merely ministerial, and he often used his authority to act in favor of public morality as he understood it to be.[52]

McCaffrey subsequently asked Hugh Flick (whose office had already licensed the film) to join him and Fr. Masterson at The Paris for the December 21 afternoon show. This was very likely the first time Flick saw *The Miracle*; as Movie Office Director he personally viewed only problem films and, prior to December 1950, *The Miracle* had not been one.[53] After the curtain came down on the December 21 screening, Flick told his two companions that he had decided to "abide by the majority decision of his board."[54] Flick said that he saw "no blasphemy or sacrilege; he saw a film that was 'a good illustration of man's inhumanity to man,' a film that deserved a license."[55]

The surviving evidence does not reveal whether McCaffrey or Masterson had a plan of action beyond persuading Flick to withdraw *The Miracle*'s license. When that failed, however, McCaffrey forged ahead upon the strength of his own judgment that *The Miracle* was "personally and officially" "offensive and blasphemous."[56] On December 22 his office called The Paris to say that its license would be suspended if *The Miracle* were shown as scheduled at 1 pm. McCaffrey's message was confirmed by letter delivered later that day. Unable to reach the Commissioner to try to work things out, Lillian Gerard, the theater's artistic director,[57] cancelled the afternoon showings, only to resume them that evening after Burstyn told her that he considered the cancellation a breach of contract.

By a second letter delivered on Saturday, the 23rd, McCaffrey told the theater management that its license was indeed suspended, a suspension to take effect "upon any further showing of *The Miracle*."[58] Burstyn and Gerard agreed that they would try to keep the ban out of the news, pending negotiations with McCaffrey. But a *New York Times* editor attending the cancelled December 23 show "became curious about the substitution and broke the news in his paper."[59] After unsuccessfully trying again to reach McCaffrey, Gerard and Burstyn decided to substitute *Riders to the Sea,* an Irish film on his shelf, for *The Miracle.* "As a precaution Joe phoned Albany and spoke to Hugh Flick," Gerard later recalled. Flick "said he would personally see the ... film and grant it a seal."[60]

During Christmas week New York Mayor Vincent R. Impellitteri tried to broker an agreement between his own License Commissioner and the Burstyn/Paris Theater partners. One might reasonably presume that Masterson hovered somewhere in the background, and that he might have been in touch with "The Powerhouse." But there is no direct evidence to confirm the presumption. A native Sicilian, Impellitteri was sworn in as Mayor in August 1950 when William O'Dwyer resigned in order to become Ambassador to Mexico. "Impy" won the November special election as an Independent, one especially fluent in populist rhetoric. He had some initial success in untangling *The Miracle* imbroglio: the *Times* reported on December 27 that a "satisfactory solution" was imminent. By that time the ACLU had entered the fray in support of *The Miracle.* The American film industry was rattling its sabers, too.[61] The Catholic War Veterans of New York had endorsed McCaffrey. But within two days and without a published explanation, the Mayor backed off. He declared that the matter "was to be litigated."[62]

From our vantage point we can see that compromise was impossible. Joseph Burstyn was not in the mood; he reckoned that the Legion of Decency was trying to establish itself as the *de facto* arbiter of his livelihood—the imported film—and he could not afford to operate under that constraint. Burstyn opined in a published interview that Cardinal Spellman was assisting the Legion in its "harsh" and "quite tough" approach to foreign films. "It is my impression that the Legion is trying to establish itself as the official censor of the City of New York."[63] For Burstyn, the fight over *The Miracle* became a "bet the company" case.

One reason for Burstyn's boldness was the obvious weakness of McCaffrey's (and thus the Legion's) legal position. The state Supreme Court in Rochester just a few years before (in the *Forever Amber* case) had ruled that the Regents' authority over licensing pre-empted local laws which purported to vest coordinate licensing authority in city officials. McCaffrey could not claim even so much discredited authority. Nothing in his job description expressly authorized him to second-guess Hugh Flick.

McCaffrey and the Legion of Decency, on the other hand, could have accepted less than a whole loaf. Imported films were growing slowly in popularity. None was likely to break out of the "art film" circuit. None realistically could do so without obtaining a Production Code seal. Thus, while Burstyn's back was up against the wall, his adversaries had room to negotiate. They could not, and evidently did not, accept Burstyn's terms, which must have conceded too little or nothing to them.

To the chagrin of many but to the surprise of few, McCaffrey dropped his ban on December 29, minutes after a Manhattan state judge told him that a temporary injunction was imminent.[64] Burstyn secured an injunction anyway on January 6, 1951. That court, citing the Rochester precedent, ruled that "the right to determine whether a motion picture is . . . sacrilegious is vested solely and exclusively" in the state Education Department. Should that body err, "any individual can seek," according to the court, "to have the Board of Regents revoke its permit."[65]

On January 7, Francis Cardinal Spellman seized that opportunity.[66] The Archdiocese of New York had not previously spoken publicly about *The Miracle* fracas, save for Monsignor Walter Kellenberg's December 30 published remarks, in which he called the exhibition "an open insult to the faith of millions of people in this city and hundreds of millions throughout the world."[67]

Spellman did not view *The Miracle* before January 7, or (as far as we know) ever afterwards. He was likely convinced of its defects as early as December 30, for it is likely that Kellenberg's caustic remarks were vetted with the Cardinal. Justice Steur's decision was reported in the newspapers on January 6, and Masterson went immediately to Spellman for help. Masterson probably asked specifically for the type of condemnation which the Cardinal had earlier directed at *Forever Amber.* That is, in any event, what he got.

Denouncing *The Miracle* in almost hysterical terms ("only Satan" could have made such a film) Spellman challenged public authorities above McCaffrey's pay-grade to make things right.[68] He lamented the apparent fecklessness of the Regents, thus pointing at one solution satisfactory to him: revocation of *The Miracle*'s license by action of Hugh Flick's bosses. But in a surprising relaxation of traditional Catholic opposition to state censorship, and in a startling repudiation of an unbroken line of hostility to federal censorship, Spellman raised the possibility of supporting both.[69]

The Regents got the message. In short order they established a three-man subcommittee—yes, comprised of a Protestant, a Catholic, and a Jew—to view the film and to review the decision to grant it a license. The subcommittee viewed the film on January 15. On January 19 the subcommittee reported that there was a basis for deeming *The Miracle* to be "sacrilegious,"[70] and ordered its exhibitor to show cause on January 30 why its license should not be revoked. After viewing the movie *en banc*, the Regents on February 16 ordered Commissioner of Education Lewis Wilson to rescind the movie's licenses—both that granted on Nov. 30, 1950 for *Ways of Love,* and the earlier (March 1, 1949) license to Lopert Films to show *The Miracle* alone.[71] It was the first time the Regents had reviewed a decision of the motion picture division to *grant* a license and, therefore the first time a license had been revoked. That same night New York judge Kenneth McAffee denied Burstyn's application for a stay of the Regents order pending judicial review of precisely this question: did the Regents have the power to revoke an exhibition license? Both the Appellate Division of the Supreme Court[72] and the New York Court of Appeals[73] held that the Regents possessed that power, and that *The Miracle* could reasonably be judged by that body to be "sacrilegious."

In light of the United States' Supreme Court's unanimous ruling against his position, and especially given that he never saw *The Miracle,* one might reasonably ask: why did Cardinal Spellman go so far in his opposition to the film?

Spellman understood enough about the movie to share the worries of Mrs. Looram, Father Masterson, and Commissioner McCaffrey. He understood, too (as did they) that the domestic sentinels against such impiety—the Production Code Administration and the threat of a Catholic consumer boycott—promised no relief. The Code was irrelevant to imports, and "art houses" were not sensitive to the blue-collar trade which a Catholic boy-cott would deny them. The Legion of Decency stood alone against the growing (but still small) array of European imports. Spellman could not have expected the Legion to acquire such clout over imports as it enjoyed with Hollywood productions. He could have reasonably aspired, though, to a practical veto over hostile depictions of the Church or its doctrines in any movie exhibited publicly, no matter where it was made. His political mus-cle was substantial enough for the task. When Masterson asked the Cardinal to fortify the Legion, then, Spellman understandably consented.[74]

One might still reasonably ask about the provenance of the Cardinal's hyperbolic and even bitter rhetoric. One part of this explanation is pique. Monsignor Edwin Broderick, who worked for Spellman from 1947 to 1964 and was for a decade his secretary, wrote that Spellman's "most glaring fault was his temper. He could fly off the handle easily when confronted with something he found offensive, such as movies like *The Miracle*, *The Moon is Blue*, and *Baby Doll*."[75] Broderick added that on these occasions the "staff would have to calm him down and urge him to act with more deliberation. And often he would."[76]

Spellman revealed another factor contributing to his vehemence when he said on January 7 that the "picture should very properly be entitled 'Woman Further Defamed' by Roberto Rossellini." This is an unmistak-able reference to the director's affair with Ingrid Bergman, who had become—by dint of her fresh beauty, her apparently happy marriage to Dr. Peter Lindstrom, and her winning roles such as that Ilsa Lund in *Casablanca* and especially that of Sister Benedict in *Bells of St. Mary's*—American Catholics' favorite actress. Even though Bergman's *Joan of Arc* was a financial disappointment, it earned her further praise for doing a "spiritual picture" and best actress awards by 1949 in Belgium and France. Shortly after Anna Magnani broke off her own affair with Rossellini in 1949, he got together with Bergman. Before long, they were expecting. Although there is plenty of evidence that Bergman pursued him as much as he did her, disappointed fans of Sister Benedict preferred to censor Rossellini for seducing and "despoiling" Bergman. Spellman was evident-ly such a fan.

Joseph Burstyn seems to have pushed the Cardinal too, so far so that Spellman took steps he might otherwise have resisted as imprudent. The impresario's stubborn refusal to negotiate peace raised the ante and denied the initiative to Spellman (and to the Legion). Bosley Crowther wrote in his *Atlantic* essay: "the Catholic artillery was assembled in mounting arrays as it was seen that the distributor and the theater were far from minded to heed the special objections of the Church."[77]

Once engaged, Spellman took no prisoners. Two Catholic columnists who criticized Spellman's response to *The Miracle*—William Clancy in *The Commonweal* and Frank Geitling in the Davenport Iowa *Messenger*— lost their positions on the faculties of The University of Notre Dame and Fairfield University, respectively. Spellman was behind their firings.[78] Thomas Pryor was one of Crowther's team of *Times'* movie critics. He told one scholarly investigator of *The Miracle* fracas that he went to the Archdiocese to reason with "church authority." "He was told [by whom is not said] that if he saw merit in the film, he should be promptly excommunicated."[79] Early in 1950 Fr. Masterson learned that a Dominican priest who was close to Bergman and Rossellini praised Bergman for having the courage to accept her responsibilities as a mother. Fr. Felix Morlion said that parenthood would bring the couple closer to God. "When Masterson learned that Morlion was planning a trip to New York, he contacted Cardinal Spellman, who was able to keep him out of the country."[80]

IV

Justice Tom Clark's opinion for the *Burstyn* Court is exceptionally lazy. Frankfurter's concurrence is more ambitious (with a considerable assist from La Piana). But Frankfurter's reasoning is no more cogent than is Clark's. Neither is convincing.

The primary burden of Clark's opinion is to shore up the major new doctrine of the Court's ruling, that movies are protected First Amendment "speech" or "press." The primary obstacle to doing so in *Burstyn* was the Court's 1915 decision in the *Mutual Film* case.[81] But not quite; that case arose before the First Amendment was "incorporated," and so *Mutual Film* could not have held that movies were *not* protected First Amendment "speech" or "press." *Mutual Film* held instead that movies were not covered by the *Ohio* constitutional guarantees of free speech and press.[82] Clark said that *Burstyn* was the first case to "squarely" present the federal constitutional question.[83] The Court held that movies are indeed protected First Amendment expression, an idea whose time evidently had come. But Clark did nothing to justify that conclusion.

Clark gave every appearance of taking over Ephraim London's (Burstyn's attorney) view of the problem. At oral argument London said that "the basic reasoning of [*Mutual Film*] is directly opposed to our

position here. There is no question about it. . . . The two fundamental principles of the *Mutual Film* case are . . . that motion pictures are merely a
form of entertainment and not a form of communication. And second is
that motion pictures is a business and therefore not a means of communication."[84]

Clark went right to work. He asserted that it "cannot be doubted that
motion pictures are a significant medium for the communication of ideas,"
even if they are produced and distributed "for profit," like "books, newspapers, and magazines."[85] But no one possessed of sanity ever asserted
otherwise—not the *Mutual Film* Court,[86] not the attorneys for New York in
Burstyn,[87] not even Cardinal Spellman.

Clark noted in passing the true obstacle in his path: the "hypothesis"
(Clark's term) that "motion pictures possess a greater capacity for evil, particularly among the youth. . ."[88] Clark conditionally "accept[ed] this
hypothesis," then declared that "it does not follow that motion pictures
should be disqualified from First Amendment protection."[89] Indeed, it does
not follow; the alleged "capacity for evil"—which the state's attorney
vividly described at Oral Argument[90] and which the *Mutual Film* Court
detailed[91]—is an argument for a conclusion which is *not* compelled by
logic. Movies' "capacity for evil" was offered (by New York Solicitor
General Wendell Brown, for example) as a crucial premise in a chain of
reasoning in support of the Regents' authority. Clark may have been right
to reach a contrary conclusion. But the only reason he offered for doing so
was the opinion's *minor* premise: the "substantially unbridled censorship
such as we have here" was simply incompatible with the First
Amendment.[92] That is to say: the "sacrilege" standard is an empty vessel,
helpless to resist content foisted on it by (in Clark's words) "the most vocal
and powerful orthodoxies."[93]

What did Clark do to shore up this minor premise (upon which the
major seems to depend)? Unfortunately, nothing. Clark recited the two mistaken interpretations of "sacrilege" explored earlier in this paper: departure
from doctrine[94] and felt offense.[95] Clark burnished these confusions by
appealing to the Court's opinion in *Winters v. New York*,[96] specifically refer-
ring to the allegedly evanescent lines between "informing" and "entertain-
ing" and between "one man's amusement" and "another's doctrine."[97]

The *Burstyn* Court surely believed that New York's "sacrilege" standard did not comport with the First Amendment. The question remains:
what evidence or argument did the Court muster to vindicate that belief?

Clark wrote that in "seeking to apply the broad and all-inclusive definition of 'sacrilegious' given by the New York courts, the censor is set adrift upon a boundless sea amid a myriad of conflicting currents of religious views, . . . New York cannot vest such unlimited power over motion pictures in a censor."[98] But the Justice cited no other case where New York banned (or tried to ban) a "sacrilegious" film. In fact, he cited no other instance of New York film censorship of any type. The burden of proving the minor premise true is to be carried, therefore, by *this* instance—*The Miracle* fracas. Clark does not describe the controversy, however, and he mounts no explicit argument about what *The Miracle* episode is supposed to mean. Evidently, the reader is supposed to have *already* concluded that any legal standard which censors that film "is far from the kind of narrow exception to freedom of expression which a state may carve out to satisfy the adverse demands of other interests of society."[99]

Felix Frankfurter's concurrence is an epic account of the winter war over *The Miracle*. Frankfurter named names, and the reader can easily identify Spellman and the Legion of Decency as the villains of the piece, and as philistines. Frankfurter's concurrence also includes substantial portions of La Piana's (mostly) medieval history, the source of which is acknowledged nowhere in Frankfurter's opinion. There is much additional legal research, too, supplied by Frankfurter's clerks. The result is a vast display of learning. But it is all analytically inert. Frankfurter (La Piana) labors mightily, for example, to establish the fluidity of the concept of "sacrilege" throughout Christendom. Frankfurter suggests that this historical "indefiniteness" belies that dictionary clarity for "sacrilege" claimed by the New York high court.[100] Not so. The Court of Appeals was neither distilling nor summarizing the wealth of human experience. It was instead authoritatively defining a statutory term.

Frankfurter repeatedly snarls himself in the twin confusions about "sacrilege" which we have already identified. He asserts, for example, that "[c]onduct and belief dear to one may seem the rankest 'sacrilege' to another."[101] Maybe so. But Frankfurter's "few examples"[102] instead indicate only that people adhere to different and sometimes incompatible religious positions. His point is nonetheless clear enough: at least when Cardinal Spellman screams "sacrilege" in a crowded metropolis, the politicians will throw any other man's "dear belief and conduct" under a bus. The trouble with Frankfurter's effort is the same as it is with the Court's: if one is not *already* persuaded that New York's law is a perfect open channel for Catholic suppression of films which annoy Cardinal Spellman nothing in *Burstyn v. Wilson* would change one's mind.

CONCLUSION

Burstyn v. Wilson did not pull the plug on prior restraint on movies.[103] The Court did not reach that conclusion until 1965, in *Freedman v. Maryland*.[104] In the meantime and starting just a week after *Burstyn* was decided, the Court issued a series of five one-sentence *per curiam* reversals of state censorship actions, citing *Burstyn v. Wilson*.[105] Together with the more substantial *Kingsley v. Regents of New York*,[106] invalidating "immoral[ity]" as a grounds for prior restraint and thus saving *Lady Chatterley's Lover* for the viewing public, the practical effect was to isolate "obscenity" as the sole ground consistent with the First Amendment for prohibiting the exhibition of a movie. That hardy survivor's experience is an engrossing story, too, one which must be left to another day to tell.

CHAPTER 9

Emerging Century Challenges
to Religious Liberty[1]

INTRODUCTION

The gravest challenges to religious freedom in most parts of the world bear little resemblance to those in the United States. The most dramatic threat elsewhere is the unwillingness of governments in Nigeria, Sudan, India, and Pakistan (among other countries) to curtail private violence against religious minorities. This impunity is often aggravated by the government's unwillingness to bring offenders before the bar of justice.

American public authorities face no such challenges. Only rarely in the United States is violent crime directed specifically at a religious group or activity. Where it occurs, public authorities have proved themselves willing and quite able to enforce the law. They do sometimes have to contend with religious communities that use pressure tactics when trying to recruit or retain members and, occasionally, to retaliate against those who have left the fold. These practices calls for a creative and supple but (as need be) decisive response by the state. Any suitable response to intimidation by religious groups must be animated by the demands of justice and of genuine religious freedom, just as it must be shaped by a realistic appreciation of the limited good that legal intervention into a religious community can do.[2]

Anti-proselytizing laws are an emerging challenge to religious freedom in many countries. But they are not in America. Laws against blasphemy, apostasy, or the vilification of others' religious beliefs are not issues in the United States, either. From the American founding up to the Civil War, there were occasional prosecutions of a blasphemer or contemnor of religion. In the most famous of these cases, one Ruggles opined loudly that

"Jesus Christ was a bastard, and his mother must have been a whore."[3] The purpose of these infrequent prosecutions was not the spiritual reform of the speaker. Nor was it to buttress the people's belief in the Christian religion as true. The point of these proceedings was well-expressed by the Delaware Supreme Court, when it upheld a conviction for utterances by one Chandler which were indistinguishable from those of Mr. Ruggles. The court in *State v. Chandler* said that "it is the open, public vilification of the religion of the country that is punished . . . to preserve the peace [by enforcing] outward respect" for the socially prevalent religion.[4]

By around 1950 the last traces of this older American tradition, which was somewhat hospitable to the conceptualizations of religious freedom and social harmony upon which restrictive laws abroad today depend, were finally eliminated by constitutional decision.[5] Since then and notwithstanding the recently growing view that religious belief is a sub-rational source of identity, and notwithstanding substantial gains made by an "identity politics" in which disagreement with another's defining beliefs is considered tantamount to denying him or her equal respect, and notwithstanding considerable confusion in law and culture about the foundations of religious liberty, there is nonetheless no appreciable support in America for anti-proselytizing or religious libel laws.

For anti-proselytizing laws are a corollary of anti-conversion strictures. Together they form a coherent matrix, even where they are supplemented by laws against blasphemy and apostasy. This matrix is often justified elsewhere as protecting "religious liberty," in the special sense of vindicating a "community's right to be left alone to its traditions,"[6] where a "stance on non-interference is central to those traditions."[7]

This sort of claim has never had much traction upon American thought or practice. The early blasphemy prosecutions were meant to vindicate public order and public morality; they were not justified as protections of religious liberty (except in a very attenuated sense). These sorts of claims have zero traction now. The reasons are many, and they are related to each other in complex ways. Americans have always understood their religious commitments to be more tentative and subject to revision than those tempted to support anti-proselytizing laws believe theirs to be. America's comparatively deeper commitment to *individual* freedom of religion further explains Americans' disinterest in restrictive laws, which presuppose that group identity and harmony is rather more important. In addition, America's overarching constitutional commitments to freedom of expression—including religious expression—have contributed to a culture of robust religious disputation, a milieu incompatible with such restrictions. This critical theological culture owes most, however, to the traditions of inquiry, argument, and evidence internal to the Christianity which has been paramount in the American religious experience. Transcending all these contributory factors is an important and unbreakable connection between the nature of religious freedom and the pursuit of religious truth. This pursuit of truth tames any temptation to leave believers in the undisturbed possession of whatever their "traditions" happen to be.

French *laicite* and Turkish *laiklik* are forms of secularism which are readily distinguishable from American separation of church and state. The former emerged historically from the *ancien* regime. Its propellants included anticlericalism (specifically, hostility to the Catholic Church's authorities). The latter was the work of Ataturk in the 1920s, and was a conscious response to what we would today call the possibility of Islamism. But America's original constitutional settlement had nothing to do with either Catholicism or Islam. It was (as we saw in Chapter Seven) mainly about eliminating government favoritism towards one or another Protestant denomination. We saw in Chapter Eight, though, that widespread fear of Catholic cultural and political influence shaped judicial doctrines about church and state around the middle of the last century. In fact, that worry has greatly influenced Establishment Clause doctrine since, especially because so many important cases concerned public aid to Catholic schools. Finally, anyone can see that today concern about Islamic militancy is shaping American security policies, both at home and abroad. Whether, and if so *how*, these worries might impact our law of religious liberty remains to be seen.

Today there is a lively jurisprudence in America about religious expression by the government and about its display of religious symbols. Constitutional litigation over Ten Commandments plaques and "under God" in the Pledge of Allegiance are illustrative of the genre. The case results are mixed. These debates reveal a minority opinion in America—call it, "strict separationism"—which favors a secularism scarcely distinguishable from, for example, *laicite*. By and large, however, Americans support such non-coercive government affirmations as those recently litigated. Public officials routinely speak in religious tones and terms which are unimaginable in, say, France. President Obama is more secular-minded than any of his predecessors save, perhaps, for Thomas Jefferson. Obama is still no exception to the prevailing norms of rhetorical indulgence. The whole political culture of the United States is much more religious, in content and in language, than is the politics in laicized countries.

The burka and the veil are not significant issues in America. Although the day might come to America when security and identity concerns clash with the niqab, for example, there is no chance that an assimilationist impulse just as such would produce any such conflict. Uniform dress policies abound today, not just for military and police personnel but for many other classes of government employees. A growing number of public elementary and secondary schools are turning to student uniforms. Often enough, religious liberty claimants petition public authorities for exemption from these policies, and they do so with occasional success. The policies themselves originate, though, not in any aversion to public display of religion-distinctive clothing or symbols. The policies are rooted in nonreligious considerations about grooming and uniformity of appearance. In the case of student uniforms, school authorities are moved by considerations of modesty, expense to parents, and about ghoulish or outlandish—and thus distracting—dress. And any state-sponsored uniform dress policy which originated in distaste for a specific religion or which targeted religious dress in particular would be patently unconstitutional.[8]

Little in the American tradition resonates with the overseas secularism which is intolerant of religious dress. In the late-nineteenth and early-twentieth centuries, some American states enacted laws restricting what public school teachers could wear to work. The meaning and transparent aim of these laws were to prevent Catholic nuns from taking such jobs. The deeper objective of these laws was to stymie maneuvers whereby municipalities with heavily Catholic populations blurred the line between public and parochial schools altogether, through various shared cost and facility plans (today's charter schools bear some resemblance to these experiments). If the nuns could not teach in them, there was little incentive—given the circumstances of the time—for Catholic authorities to seek control of "public" schools. In any event, the teacher garb laws have fallen into desuetude.

The most urgent challenges to religious freedom in the United States today involve conscience protection. There are two contexts in which the challenge is especially grave. One is healthcare. In years past, protecting conscience in this realm was mainly about a religiously scrupulous patient or parent of a patient—a Christian Scientist or a Jehovah's Witness, perhaps—who sought legal immunity from the administration of unremarkable and all but universally accepted medical procedures. Rarely was the issue about health care providers and their scruples about particular services. In years past there was a flourishing legal culture of granting generous relief to persons and institutions which, because of religious or moral convictions, could not conscientiously undertake certain duties or undergo certain procedures.

The 2010 enactment of the Patient Protection and Affordable Healthcare Act [PPACA] changed this picture or, more exactly, brought together and further aggravated a situation which had already begun to be perilous for conscience protection. Now the conscientious objectors include large institutional providers sponsored by mainstream religions. The largest of these is the Catholic network of some seven hundred facilities. Objectors today are predominantly providers—doctors, nurses, pharmacists, institutions—who seek to avoid complicity in morally controversial medical treatments, such as abortion. In August 2011, for example, the Obama Administration published proposed federal regulations which would require practically all health insurance plans to cover (without co-payments) all FDA approved "contraceptives," including some (*ella*, for instance) which act as abortifacients. In Part II of this chapter I critically examine this set of challenges to religious freedom.

The second conscience-protection context pivots upon the remarkable, and remarkably swift, turnaround in legal attitudes towards homosexual and lesbian behavior. Not just in America but in other English-speaking jurisdictions such as Canada, Australia, and the United Kingdom, legal norms mandating non-discrimination in employment and social services have been applied to religious schools, universities, and charities, notwithstanding their claims that religious freedom principles (properly understood) require their exemption from these laws.

This challenge is heightened where same-sex couples can legally marry. Otherwise, at least some religious institutions might not violate the non-discrimination stricture by dint of their treating *all* unmarried persons (gay or straight) the same. The recent abandonment of charitable ministries by Catholic authorities in two American jurisdictions—Boston and Washington, D.C.—indicate the high stakes involved and, probably, the pattern of the future. In Part III of this chapter I look at how public authorities—judicial and legislative—in overseas English-speaking jurisdictions as well as at the United States have navigated the issue. In Part III I also unpack the values which are at stake, lest the serious misunderstandings of them—more or less common to all the jurisdictions considered—lead one astray.

In Part I of this chapter I consider what some other writers might propose as the leading emerging challenge to Americans' religious freedom, namely, the Supreme Court's interpretation of the First Amendment's Free

Exercise Clause in the case of *Employment Division v. Smith*. In this Part I explain why I think their proposal is misguided.

In a brief Conclusion, I trace the possible, and perhaps probable, future trajectory of the twin main challenges herein examined.

I

More than a few informed writers would place a very different emerging challenge to religious freedom at, or near, the top of their lists. They would not replace abortion or sexual orientation equality with a different issue cluster. These writers would not give pride of place to any particular propositional statement about the content of religious freedom (like those found in leading international documents declaring in favor of, for example, "belief, worship and expression, in public or private"). These other writers would feature the following more formal statement: "the state must not burden anyone's conduct which is motivated by a sincere religious belief, unless the burden is the least restrictive means by which the government is able to achieve a compelling interest." But these writers would not make this test—just as such—their prime concern. They would instead claim that the Supreme Court's *abandonment* of it, in 1990, as the meaning of the First Amendment's Free Exercise Clause is the leading threat to religious freedom in America today.

I think that this view is mistaken.

The test spelled out above was established in 1963 by the Supreme Court as Free Exercise doctrine in *Sherbert v. Verner*.[9] The test's establishment put courts under an obligation, not to finally rule in favor of any religious freedom claimant, but to subject such claims to an ostensibly religion-friendly test which would (again, ostensibly) place governments under a stringent duty to give as wide a berth to religion as possible. In the event, courts from 1963 until 1990 (when the Supreme Court abandoned the "compelling interest" test) very rarely ruled in favor of claimants.[10] That is one reason for my judgment that the writers of whom I speak are mistaken: they exaggerate the importance of the *Sherbert* doctrine to the overall protection of religious freedom in the United States.

The case which abandoned the *Sherbert* test is called *Employment Division v. Smith*.[11] Decided in 1990, *Smith* held by a 5-4 vote of the Justices that the Free Exercise Clause did *not* authorize the judiciary to craft conduct exemptions for religious believers. *Smith* said that "the right of free exercise does not relieve an individual of the obligation to comply with a valid and neutral law of general applicability on the ground that the law proscribes (or prescribes) conduct that his religion prescribes (or proscribes)."

Smith limited the judicially enforceable scope of the Free Exercise clause to laws which "target" religion for adverse treatment. "[A]ssembling with others for a worship service, participating in sacramental use of bread and wine, proselytizing, abstaining from certain foods or modes of transportation, a state would be prohibiting the free exercise [of religion] if it sought to ban such acts only when they are engaged in for religious reasons, or only because of the religious belief that they display." After *Smith* the Free Exercise Clause would invalidate a law which, for instance, barred the use of single-family homes for religious meetings but not for pool parties or other large non-religious gatherings. The Free Exercise Clause would after *Smith* invalidate a law which prohibited ritual slaughter of animals, where slaughter for sport of for food was not similarly banned.[12] Perhaps the simplest way to express the norm of Free Exercise after *Smith* is to say that public authority may never make its disapproval—including its belief in the falsity—of a theological doctrine the basis for regulatory action. One might call this a deep *neutrality* about religious truth, so long as one understands the term "religious truth" to encompass, not every claim about God or the transcendent, but instead finer points of doctrine, modes of worship, and felt obligations about how a church's governance and internal communal life should be ordered. This "neutrality" does not extend, in other words, to natural religion (as we saw in Chapter Seven).

The *Smith* majority (in an opinion by Justice Scalia) rested its case upon an historical analysis of the original understanding of the Free Exercise Clause. I have argued at considerable length elsewhere that this analysis was basically sound, and that the Court's conclusion was correct.[13] The correctness of *Smith* as history and even as constitutional law does not by itself mean that it is good for religious freedom. After all, the founders could have been less solicitous of religion than they should have been. But the correctness of *Smith* suggests that fears of it for religious freedom's sake are exaggerated. For there is ample evidence that the founders who enacted the Free Exercise Clause were quite keen to protect religious freedom.[14]

It is important to note that *Smith* had solely to do with the courts' power under one clause of one document, the federal Constitution. Nothing in *Smith* or in any other Free Exercise case decided since 1990 casts doubt upon courts' authority to enforce exemptions from general laws, such as the exemption put into our military conscription laws in favor of conscientious objectors to killing, when legislators put such exemptions in them. Much less has any Free Exercise case since *Smith* cast doubt upon legislators' authority to craft exemptions. In other words, the *Smith* court did not say or imply that Congress or the state legislatures should treat religion or any particular religion badly, or even indifferently.

As a matter of fact, the "compelling interest" test remains the law across a vast swath of American jurisprudence. Congress partially reinstated it by a statute enacted in 1993, called the "Religious Freedom Restoration Act." The practical effect of this law is that every national government action which "burdens" religion must meet the "compelling interest" test. A separate Congressional enactment imposes the same justificatory requirement upon states and localities for laws involving land use and institutionalized persons. A multitude of state laws—constitutions, statutes, administrative rules, court decisions—contain "compelling interest" tests. This is another reason why *Smith* is not the threat to religious freedom that many say that it is: the "compelling interest" test is alive and quite well, reports of its demise notwithstanding.

Much of the widespread lament about *Smith* owes to the perceived truth in the following concession in the majority opinion: "It may finally be said that leaving accommodation [of religious freedom claims] to the political process will place at a relative disadvantage those religious practices not widely engaged in; but that unavoidable consequence of democratic government must be preferred to a system in which each conscience is a law unto itself or in which judges weigh the social importance of all laws against the centrality of all religious beliefs."[15] Incautious critics said that *Smith* declared "open season" on minority faiths.

Not so. Criticisms of this sort depend upon interlocking assumptions about comparative legislative and judicial behavior when it comes to smaller religious groups. They also depend upon a prediction which is laden with normative judgment, one to this effect: putatively less popular groups deserve a better deal than they are going to get at legislators' hands; minority faiths fare much better when judges are free to help them according to the *Sherbert* terms.

But the evidence that American judges are, as a whole, more religion-friendly than are American legislators is scanty. The courts' comparatively tepid attitude towards religious freedom is unlikely to improve as emerging challenges come to maturity. In years past what might have accurately been called outsider religious groups filed complaints against, chiefly, administrative burdens or routine procedures to which an exception could be made without implicating the rights of anyone else in particular. No one said, for example, that a doctor is somehow deprived of her rights in not transfusing a Jehovah's Witness or that excusing a child from, say, a flag salute violated the rights of children without such scruples.

In years past, religious freedom claimants were usually seen to be acting either immorally (guilty of child neglect or polygamy, for instance), or abnormally, statistically speaking (as with Amish buggy drivers or those conscientiously opposed to having their photos taken). The template then was that of marginal and even unpopular religious groups seeking relief from the broader common morality or majoritarian practices. It might have been the case that legislators dependent upon popular electoral approval for their offices were unsympathetic to some of these smaller groups.

The situation today is different. Legislators are probably no more morally conscientious than they used to be (probably, no less so). It is the rest of the equation which has changed. As the common morality which used to sustain American society continues to evaporate (and even boil off), the great religious traditions which were in harmony with the moral underpinnings of society's law have found themselves marginalized in a growing number of situations, including healthcare and family services. Some of the conduct for which conscience protection is now sought was not long ago considered to involve injustice. Claimants for conscience protection today are as likely as not to constitute (in one term for it) a "moral majority."

The key moving part in the emerging situation is really the upside-down moral valuation of the actions from which conscience protection is sought. Abortion is the chief example; same-sex sexual relationships, contraception, sterilization, and euthanasia are others. There is no reason to suppose that courts would, if given the opportunity to do so by legal doctrine, side with conscientious objectors on these issues with a frequency greater than would the first hundred persons listed in the South Bend, Indiana phonebook. On the contrary, courts in America have been the vanguard of legal protection for abortion rights and sexual orientation equality. The underlying assumption about latent institutional affinities—chiefly, that courts side with "minorities" whose moral conviction or family practices are deemed unorthodox by electoral majorities—would (if valid) lead courts to oppose conscience protection.

II

Conscience protection in American law is as old as the American republic. The Constitution itself protects those scrupulous of swearing an oath, providing (in Article VI, cl. 3) that government officers "shall be bound by oath *or affirmation*, to support the Constitution" [my emphasis]. Relief for those conscientiously opposed to bearing arms was commonplace at the founding, at least for adherents of "peace churches" like the Quakers. Exemption for Saturday Sabbatarians from conflicting civic obligations (such as giving court testimony) was more patchy. But the question was surely a legitimate one: almost everyone agreed that, if conditions permitted, Jews and Saturday-observant Christians ought not to be disturbed in their Sabbath observance.

Conscience protections of various sorts are strewn about the federal legal corpus, so many bits of evidence of this long-standing tradition of respect for religious freedom. The most famous of the exemptions may be those not enumerated in but nonetheless required by the Constitution, according to the Supreme Court. These include rulings in favor of Jehovah's Witnesses (in 1943, against compelled participation in flag salute ceremonies),[16] and the Old Order Amish (in 1972, releasing secondary school-age children from compulsory education requirements).[17]

Statutory conscience protections are plentiful, both at the state and at the national level. Included among these is a federal law which provides an exemption regarding capital punishment. No employee of any governmental unit (national, state, or local) may be required to "attend" or "participate in . . . any prosecution or execution" if doing so "is contrary to the moral or religious convictions of the employee." The protective shield around the objecting employee is large. "Participation in executions" includes personal preparation of the condemned individual and the apparatus used for execution and supervision of the activities of other personnel in carrying out such activities."[18]

Federal law for a long time exempted religious health plans from certain contraceptive coverage mandates; that is, from laws which require any health insurance plan which covers prescription drugs to include prescription contraceptives. Federal law has also protected individuals who refuse to prescribe or provide contraceptives due to "religious beliefs or moral convictions."[19] Congress has approved every year since 2000, for example, a resolution expressing its "intent" that District of Columbia officials include a "conscience clause" in any law that they should enact mandating that health insurance plans cover the cost of prescription contraceptives.[20] But the new federal regulations styling contraceptive drugs (including some which induce early abortions) as "preventive services" cuts very deeply into these protections.

The 1973 "Church Amendment" (named for its sponsor, Idaho Senator Frank Church, and not for its contemplated beneficiaries) stipulated that hospitals or individuals who receive federal funds may not be required to participate in abortion and sterilization procedures, so long as their objection to doing so are based on moral or religious convictions. It is still operative law, and it also forbids hospitals receiving federal funds from making anyone's willingness or unwillingness to perform these procedures a condition of employment. Another provision prohibits entities that receive public health service funds from discriminating against applicants who decline to participate in abortions or sterilizations on account of religious beliefs or moral convictions.

The 2004 "Hyde/Weldon Conscience Protection Amendment" protects physicians and nurses, hospitals, health insurance companies, and other health care entities from being forced by state or federal governments to perform, pay for, provide coverage of, or refer for abortions. Congress has approved it every year since 2004.

This tradition of solicitude for religious freedom in the healthcare field is the framework within which to evaluate the conscience protections contained in PPACA, the Obama Administration's comprehensive reform of America's leading industry. This law contains some important positive developments on the matter of conscience protection. Section 1553 of the Act says that governments at all levels (federal, state, local) are forbidden to discriminate against conscientious objectors with respect to assisted suicide, mercy killing, and euthanasia. So far so good, one might observe. The great worry about PPACA, however, is that it generates new threats to religious freedom, especially by creating distinctive funding streams and new categories of services to which existing protections do not apply, without including any protection comparable to, for example, "Church" or "Hyde/Weldon."

This deficiency cannot be attributed to oversight. Many affected healthcare providers, including most notably the leaders of the Catholic Church in America, and many members of Congress, including most notably Representative Bart Stupak and Senator Tom Coburn, issued repeated, urgent calls to bring PPACA into line with the existing framework of conscience protection. Some early versions of the Obama Administration healthcare overhaul did as much; their deletion from the enacted version was certainly not inadvertent. This is especially certain given that President Obama implicitly recognized the problem when he promised to issue an Executive Order which would supply "adequate conscience protection," a phrase which the President had elsewhere used to describe his own determination to align healthcare reform with religious freedom.[21]

The Executive Order unfortunately delivered far less than promised. The President declared that the "Church" and "Hyde/Weldon" amendments "remain intact." Indeed they do. But neither provides any relief from the new conscience challenges engendered by PPACA. That Act does contain some valuable but limited conscience protections, and the Executive Order highlighted them. It also contains some gaping holes in its conscience protection, and nowhere did the President supplement them (even where he possessed discretion to do so), in his Executive Order.

The text of the PPACA focuses upon conscience protection for healthcare providers, both individuals and institutions. Patients are, however, put in an unprecedented predicament by PPACA. This new burden arises, ironically, from the law's attempt to avoid using federal funds to finance abortion, in keeping with the longstanding tradition of sparing taxpayers who oppose abortion from paying for other people's abortions. The PPACA segregates abortion funding, so that anyone who enrolls in an abortion-covering health insurance plan must make two premium payments, one of which goes exclusively for abortion coverage. Because some people conscientiously opposed to abortion may have very strong reasons for choosing such a plan (the only non-abortion covering plan available may be vastly inferior in some other respects), they are faced now with the prospect of paying into a fund which does nothing but pay for abortions.[22]

Even in advance of full implementation of the PPACA we can identify five areas of urgent importance for conscience protection.

First. The reform is on balance a sharp departure downward from the established level of conscience protection. Second. This downward departure was taken in the face of assertions by spokesmen for some large providers (including the huge Catholic hospital network) that the PPACA might cause them to withdraw from some fields of treatment—and possibly even to close—in order not to compromise their integrity. Third. The downward departure reflects a conscious value judgment on the part of those who favored it. The American Civil Liberties Union said that those seeking conscience protection would "take patients out of the equation" (the ACLU sided with patients, as they saw the situation). The National

Women's Law Center said that it opposed conscience protection even for pharmacists, regardless of whether a particular service (such as chemical abortion) could be readily obtained elsewhere. A substantial portion of the rhetoric opposing conscience protection makes it sound like those seeking it are aggressors of some sort, that their desire to opt out would somehow impose upon clients or patients. This proposed way of viewing the question is remarkable, and new.

Fourth, these high valuations of countervailing rights have not been presented as sufficient to defeat a well-pleaded and appealing religious freedom claim. On the contrary, it is more commonly said that the measure of conscience protection provided in PPACA is desirable, or "adequate." Thus, fifth, the PPACA episode is evidence of a shift in the meaning of religious freedom, as opposed to a set of markers about its effective scope.

III

Over the course of a generation ending at the year 2000, same-sex sexual conduct was practically decriminalized in the United States, as well as in many other English-speaking jurisdictions as well. Over the last decade, the law in these countries has moved rapidly from a stance of respect for sexual privacy, to where the political community affirms a favorable moral evaluation of same-sex acts and the orientation which they express. All discrimination by the state—in employment, housing, services—against homosexuals and lesbians has been made unlawful. Non-discrimination laws stretching into the private sector now often include "sexual orientation" alongside race, ethnicity, and gender as prohibited bases for decisions and actions. Legal recognition of same-sex relationships as marriages or as "civil unions" is common, and increasing.

British legal scholar Ian Leigh describes this "new orthodoxy" as a "fascinating reversal" of the celebrated Hart-Devlin debate over the legal enforcement of sexual morality. The trigger of that debate in the late 1950's was the Wolfendon Commission's recommendation to decriminalize homosexual conduct. Hart famously championed liberal principles against Devlin's arguments that society could justly enforce its shared morality, even with regard to private sexual acts.[23] Leigh argues persuasively that, today, "'homophobia' is the new homosexuality and sexual-orientation equality is the new shared morality." Public authorities have begun to treat "dissent from the new orthodoxy . . . as offensive to public opinion."[24]

One illustration of the developing sea-change was supplied by then British Prime Minister Tony Blair. Defending an Equality Law which effectively expressed Leigh's "new orthodoxy" and which made scant room for religious exemptions, Blair declared: "[t]here is no place in our society for discrimination. That is why I support the right of gay couples to adopt like any other couple. And that way there can be no exemptions for faith-based adoption agencies offering publicly funded services from regulations that prevent discrimination."

"By a strange irony," Leigh observes, "it is religious conservatives who are now out of step with the new morality and find themselves in need of the protection of liberal principles."[25] Religious freedom is chief among these principles. In this section of the chapter I offer, first, a brief survey of pertinent recent developments in the United States, the United Kingdom, Canada, and Australia. Then I provide an analysis of the emerging challenge which the "new orthodoxy" presents to religious freedom.

A. Recent Developments

Same-sex marriage has been legally recognized across Canada since 2005. In the run-up to enactment, the Canadian Supreme Court opined (at Parliament's request) that compulsion of religious officials or conscription of "sacred places" for same-sex weddings would violate the Charter of Rights.[26] Parliament thereafter included some express, but limited, conscience protections in the marriage law. Religious officials could lawfully refuse to perform same-sex marriages. Any religious group which upheld traditional marriage in its teaching was to be free of discrimination by any other Act of Parliament.[27]

The extent of this protected space was almost immediately tested by a lesbian couple who sought to use a Knights of Columbus (i.e., Catholic) hall for their wedding celebration. The provincial human rights tribunal upheld the Knights. The opinion was nonetheless very critical of the Knights' decision, and how much space dissenters from "marriage-equality" may safely occupy without legal penalty remains unsettled. The most perceptive analyst of religious freedom issues in Canada is close to the mark when he says that when the state decides in favor of same-sex marriage, religious groups upholding traditional marriage assume the status of "tolerated discriminator." To many of the dissenting groups, this looked like "pretty thin ice."[28]

In the spring of 2010 an independent Catholic School in Vancouver, British Columbia dismissed an openly lesbian teacher named Lisa Reimer.

The school authorities did not cite the integrity of their mission or the truths of Catholic faith as reasons for their action. They instead pointed the finger at outraged parents.[29] In other words, the school said that it acted under pressure from constituents, and not out of any principle of its own. Ms. Reimer declined to lodge a complaint with the provincial Human Rights Commission, even though the Human Rights Code applies to all publicly-funded schools (which, in Canada, includes Catholic schools).[30]

Australia famously possesses no national charter or bill of rights. A sizable movement to enact one crested in early 2010, short of the needed critical mass. For the foreseeable future, then, the several Australian states will be the theaters of conflict between the "new orthodoxy" about sexual orientation and religious freedom.

The earliest such conflict appears to be that of Jacqui Griffin. Sometime around 1995 she applied to the Sydney Catholic Education Office [CEO] for a teaching position. Ms. Griffin appears to have been academically qualified for the post. She was also a well-known lesbian activist. In fact, Griffin was a co-convener of the Gay and Lesbian Teachers and Students Association. The CEO rejected Ms. Griffin's application, stating (according to the hearing record) that she promoted views and causes "contrary to the teachings and values of the Catholic Church."[31] New South Wales' law prohibited discrimination in employment on grounds of "sexual preference," and religious schools in Australia, including those of the Catholic Church, are heavily subsidized by the government. Section three of the law granted an exception for religious organizations acting "in accordance with the doctrines, tenets, beliefs or teachings of a particular religion or creed," if the discrimination was made in "good faith in order to avoid injury to the religious susceptibilities of adherents of that religion or that creed."

The Human Rights and Equal Opportunity Commission hearing officer held in favor of Ms. Griffin. He found that, notwithstanding contrary claims by the Church's representatives, the "known or public stance of Ms. Griffin in relation to homosexuality does not conflict with the official teachings of the Catholic Church." Nor was her exclusion from employment "necessary to avoid injury to the susceptibilities of adherents of the [Church's] official teachings."[32] The CEO's action was therefore "not protected by the religious institutions exception" of the Act.[33]

The "Wesley Mission Case" arose under the same New South Wales Anti-Discrimination Act. Wesley Mission arranged foster care placements as an agent of the state. A homosexual couple applied to be foster parents, and were turned down because their relationship was contrary to the religious doctrines to which the Mission professed devotion. The hearing board upheld the couple's complaint in April 2008. The main basis for the holding seems to have been the tribunal's decision to treat the relevant "religion," not as anything distinctively Wesleyan, but as Christianity writ very large, within which there were (according to the Tribunal) several streams of theological opinion about homosexuality. Thus there was no one "doctrine" of "that religion" upon which the Mission could rely for the statutory exception. Late in 2009, however, an appeals panel reversed this ruling and remanded the case for new proceedings. The appellate ruling cited deficient interpretations of the terms "religion," "religious doctrine" and "religious adherents."

In 1988, the United Kingdom Parliament prohibited local governments in England from doing anything to "intentionally promote homosexuality" or to "promote the teaching in any [government-]maintained school of the acceptability of homosexuality as a pretended family relationship." This law was repealed in 2000. The Sexual Orientation Regulations of 2003 prohibited employment discrimination on grounds of "sexual orientation." The Equality Act of 2007 made it unlawful to discriminate on those grounds in the provision of goods or services, including family services such as adoptions. The 2010 Parliamentary extension of employment non-discrimination norms occasioned a lively debate about whether Catholic bishops risk prosecution if they do not ordain women and sexually active "gays" to the priesthood.

The Sexual Orientation Regulation of 2003 included an exception for "employment for purposes of an organized religion." The exception applied where the employer uses sexual orientation as a criterion "to comply with the doctrines of the religion," or "because of the nature of the employment and the context in which it is carried out, so as to avoid conflicting with the strongly held religious convictions of a significant number of the religion's followers." The exception was immediately attacked as invalid in court proceedings brought by some teachers unions. The Judgment of the High Court upheld the validity of the exception.

It was a hollow victory for religious freedom. In the course of litigation the unions secured a concession from the government, and then a ruling from the Court itself, limiting the statutory exception: it had no application to schools or to almost any other religious employers. The High Court determined that "[e]mployment for the purposes of organized religion clearly [is limited to] a job, such as a minister of religion, involving work for a church, synagogue, or mosque."[34] Even work for a synagogue or church or mosque itself was exempted only if either the faith's doctrines or the strongly held convictions of its members required that the position be limited to, say, heterosexuals. The effective scope of this exemption tracks very closely that found in American state laws mandating prescription contraceptive coverage, as it does the exemption for "religious employers" from the Health and Human Services' "contraception" mandate.

American criminal laws against same-sex sexual acts were very rarely enforced after around 1980. But it was not until 2003, in *Lawrence v. Texas*,[35] that the Supreme Court declared that such laws violate the Constitution. The *Lawrence* opinion was partly motivated by the Court's wider belief that different treatment of homosexuals and lesbians in any context was unjust: "When homosexual conduct is made criminal by the law of the State that declaration in and of itself is an invitation to subject homosexual persons to discrimination in the public and the private spheres."[36]

Within a few months Massachusetts' highest court relied upon *Lawrence* to make that state the first to recognize same-sex marriage.[37] Massachusetts' legislators subsequently legalized same-sex marriage in 2004, in response to this judicial compulsion. Since then, Connecticut and Iowa have recognized same-sex marriages by dint of judicial ruling, and Vermont and New Jersey did so (like Massachusetts) under judicial constraint. New Hampshire, New York, Maryland, Washington, and the District of Colombia followed suit. The Supreme Court is presently (in 2013) considering two same-sex "marriage" cases with potentially national implications.

Two recent American illustrations of the tension between the "new orthodoxy" and religious freedom involve Catholic social services. The cases are from Boston and the nation's capital, Washington, D.C. The Washington city council in late 2009 decided to legally recognize same-sex relationships as marriages. After fruitlessly seeking an accommodation with the city, the Catholic Archdiocese of Washington announced that its local social service organization—Catholic Charities—would no longer facilitate foster care. The Archdiocese also limited employee health care benefits to avoid coverage of same-sex "spouses."

In Boston the conflict centered upon Massachusetts' requirement—again, with no concession in favor of religious freedom—that state-licensed adoption agencies treat same-sex married couples like any other married couple when it comes to adoption services.[38] Massachusetts famously became the first state to legally recognize same-sex relationships as marriages in 2004. But even before then it had permitted same-sex couples to adopt children; marriage was not, that is, an essential predicate to the legal formation of families in same-sex households. Boston Catholic Charities had arranged its first "gay" adoption in 1997, in response to an earlier state administrative rule against discrimination on the basis of sexual orientation. By 2005 Catholic Charities had placed thirteen children with unmarried gay couples. Charities President J. Bryan Hehir, S.J., said that "if we could design the system ourselves we would not participate in adoptions to "gay" couples, but we can't." "We have to balance various goods," Hehir concluded.

The Massachusetts Catholic bishops had final authority over the conduct of Catholic social services. They issued a statement on Feb. 28, 2006 rejecting any "balancing" analysis. Absent an exemption from the legal requirement not to discriminate against "gay" couples, they concluded, Catholic Charities would have to withdraw from the adoption business. The state did not relent. Catholic Charities then abandoned adoptions after more than a century in the field, a field they entered in 1903 from concern that the state was consciously placing orphaned Catholic children in Protestant homes.

B. The Values at Stake

"An important tenet within the Church is a belief in the sanctity of marriage, together with the belief that the model for family life is provided by the Holy Family of Nazareth." Because of that belief, according to Justice Briggs in the *Catholic Care of Leeds* (UK) decision of March 17, 2010, Catholic Care's trustees refused to place children with same-sex couples.

The truth of such theological matters as marriage's "sanctity" and the unique merits of the "Holy Family" are by dint of constitutional stipulation beyond the competence of the state to judge. Public officials therefore cannot intelligibly weigh the importance of protecting these beliefs (just as such), over against the conviction that sexual-orientation discrimination in adoption is unjust. That latter belief might, of course, be mistaken. But the truth or falsity of it is not beyond the state's ken. Public authorities can nonetheless intelligently value assertions about, for example, "the Holy Family." They can do so by treating them as members of a class of beliefs to which respect is owed because a member of the community possesses the belief. Coupled with the assumed fact that some state action has placed a wedge between the belief and its possessor, public authority can rightly try to promote the good of harmony among any person's beliefs, choices, and conduct by relieving that person of the state-imposed burden.

This good we might call personal integrity. Its value can be enhanced by connection between a belief possessed and a greater-than-human-source of meaning and value. The good of personal integrity then acquires the added value of harmony with God, the gods, or some other divine principle. When this connection is made, public authority can promote two goods by making it easier rather than harder for persons in the community to be religious: a person's inner harmony and that same person's harmony with the higher power.

Of these two important values —personal integrity and the good of religion—we might say that, together, they make a prima facie case for "conscience protection." Over against many state justifications (such as administrative convenience or uniformity for its own sake) they might well be sufficient to justify conscience protection.

So far considered, belief in "the Holy Family" is indistinguishable from other member beliefs of the same class. The weakness of the *prima facie* or standing case is that any of these beliefs might be deeply mistaken, anti-social, or even pathological. The *prima facie* case can be pretty easily defeated by good extrinsic reasons, such as protecting an important component of public morality or forestalling injustice to specific individuals. So far considered, too, nothing in the *Leeds* defense implies or even suggests that Tony Blair was wrong about the gross injustice of sexual-orientation discrimination. The *prima facie* case by its own force has no tendency to belie assertions of that sort.

Interestingly, Catholic Care's lawyer "abjured" (the Court's word) any such basis as "respect [for] the beliefs of the Roman Catholic Church." "Wisely" so, said the Court. Counsel argued that Leeds Catholic Care was an indispensable performer: it was uniquely successful in placing "hard to place" children. For the children's sake, the court ought to grant the charity's prayer for relief.

This move is understandable enough. But its fragility is easy to see: the performance argument dissipates as soon as any competitor adoption agency catches up. This move also leaves the claim that Catholic Care would do a serious injustice to same-sex couples untouched. The performance standard's advantage lies elsewhere, in defeating that claim by claiming even greater injury to the kids.

In fact, the value of organizational ministries such as Leeds Catholic Care transcends the scientifically measurable results of their activities— the number of children placed in foster or adoptive homes, the number of homeless persons fed a decent meal, the gross output of a hospital's surgical rooms, or the standardized test scores of parochial school pupils. Religious providers are not generic institutions which happen to employ some people with peculiar private motivations for doing what they do. There is a great public good—that is, an invaluable service to the common good of the political society—precisely in the conspicuous presence of religion integrated into the ordinary affairs of society.

Boston's Catholic authorities did a better job articulating the grounds for an exemption than did their counterparts in Leeds. Like Leeds Catholic Care, Boston Catholic Charities was successful in placing difficult kids. The latter's defenders also referred to the good of religious witness (in effect, the twin pillars of the *prima facie* case). On several occasions, they also said that a Catholic institution could not "promote an agenda that it views as morally wrong."[39] But often enough Boston defenders pointed to the proper "moral development" and thus the genuine "best interests" of the adopted child. In the words of one authoritative Church teaching, the absence of "sexual complementarity" between the parents "creates obstacles to the normal [moral] development of children."

The main thought here is that a child placed with a "gay" couple can scarcely be expected to receive from his or her parents' sound example and moral advice about marriage as the union of male and female. When the child is later exposed to the proposal that the truth about marriage and sexual morality is deeply at odds with the parents' life together, that child is placed in an awful position. He or she is then faced with a choice between accepting the proposal and a profound repudiation of those who have loved and nurtured him. This raises the possibility that the Boston authorities sought to avoid complicity in injustice, more than they seek conscientious exemption, as is often the case with abortion-related exemptions.

This richer line of argument appeals mainly to morality, as it can be known to unaided human reason. This does not make the Boston Catholic Charities' claims true. If they are false, though, they are mistaken about what is reasonable and not only about what Catholic faith discloses. The advantage of this line of argument is that it engages Tony Blair's position. The point would be that no same-sex couple is wrongfully discriminated against if the only way to avoid that putative wrong is to do wrong to another person—here, the child. Even in a state which recognized same-sex marriage, the common good may be enriched by a plurality of social service providers. It does not have to be one-size-fits-all. There can be state-supported works which do not, for various good reasons, mimic the moral stance of the state.

Someone might object that this is the Boston defense's great weakness. This objector might say that this line of argument (about the moral hazard to children placed in same-sex households) runs headlong into a conclusive, contrary moral judgment by the state, namely, that marriage is not necessarily heterosexual. Same-sex marriage is good. The objection is misplaced. No doubt Massachusetts law settles that civil marriage is available to same-sex couples. Boston Catholic Charities did not dispute that fact. Its argument appealed rather to the truth about marriage and sexual morality and to what is genuinely in a child's "best interests." These claims are not necessarily incompatible with Massachusetts' law. The grounds for legally recognizing same-sex marriage in American jurisdictions have, in fact, been political norms about equality and autonomy for the adults involved. The deciding authorities in these jurisdictions have eschewed reliance upon claims about the nature or meaning of marriage itself. So, nothing in the legal recognition of same-sex marriage as such contradicts the proposition that Catholic Charities contributes to the common good of political society, precisely by taking the stand that it would take on sexual morality, chastity, and marriage while placing difficult children in loving heterosexual households.

Another objector might say that the case studies in this section show how unfortunately individualistic the prevailing conception of freedom of religion has become. This objector would mount claims on behalf of the "group" or the "institution" or the "collective," and try to craft a synthetic new meaning for "religious freedom."

This objection contains an important element of truth. But that element may be obscured by introducing the concept of "group." The operations of Catholic Charities or the Wesley Mission are best viewed, in my judgment, as a collaboration of so many individuals for a set purpose, mission, or for (if you like) a specific organizational common good. Whether they collaborate in healthcare, education, or social services, these individuals are united by their dedication not only to providing competent service, but to doing so with additional shared purposes, namely, to promote or otherwise witness to the truth (value, soundness) of the religion which animates their shared work.

Once we see thus far, it becomes apparent that when any member's conduct is reasonably judged by those in charge to be contrary to that set of purposes—like that of Lisa Reimer or Jacqui Griffin—then that person frustrates the collaboration. In doing so she treats the others involved in the work unfairly; she (in effect even if not by design) undermines their project and takes away from them the opportunity to do as they have covenanted to do.

CONCLUSION

The most urgent challenge to religious freedom in the United States is the challenge to conscience protection. The formidable novelty is that potential limits stem, not from administrative convenience or collective interests, but from claims about public morality, the demands of justice, and the rights of others. The high valuation of abortion access and sexual-orientation equality among powerful segments of American society is the critical force. For religious freedom to flourish, this force would have to be stymied somewhere short of Ian Leigh's "new orthodoxy." Anyone can see that resistance to sexual-orientation equality (less so, abortion) is already treated by many as if it were indistinguishable morally from racism as a sub-rational bias which harms other people or, at a minimum, invariably manifests an attitude of disrespect. Insofar as that comparison flourishes, conscience protection will suffer.

We can already see two arcs of development in the law of conscience protection under this sort of pressure. One is captured in Tony Blair's comments: there is a "public" "realm" whose precise boundaries may be disputed, but which includes (at least) any act or institution which receives public funds. In that realm there is one set of norms for all comers, all players, without exception. "No discrimination, by nobody. Full stop."

The second arc is found in the contraceptive mandates and some of the foreign laws: the realm of religious freedom is limited to the Church (or synagogue or mosque), its ministers of doctrine, and to the community's worship. These arcs converge upon the privatization of religion. Perhaps they are two expressions of the same impulse.

ENDNOTES

Chapter 1

1 John Finnis, *Fundamentals of Ethics* (Washington, D.C.: Georgetown University Press, 1983), 128.

2 John Gardner, *Offenses and Defenses: Selected Essays in the Philosophy of the Criminal Law* (Oxford: Oxford University Press, 2007), 204, 214.

3 Justice Kennedy addressed the ABA annual gathering on August 9, 2003.

4 Pope John Paul II, *Evangelium Vitae* (Boston : Pauline Books and Media, 1995), § 2266.

5 *See Exodus* 21:24, *Leviticus* 24:20, and *Deuteronomy* 19:21. Although found in and often thought to have originated with Scripture, the concept also appears prominently in other ancient sources, such as the Code of Hammurabi.

6 Gardner, *Offenses and Defenses*, 213.

7 H.L.A. Hart, "Prolegomenon to the Principles of Punishment," in *Punishment and Responsibility* (New York: Oxford University Press, 1982), 8.

8 Thomas Hobbes, *On the Citizen*, eds. Richard Tuck & Michael Silverthorne (New York: Cambridge University Press, 1998), 26–31.

9 Hart, *Punishment and Responsibility*, 22.

10 H.L.A. Hart, *The Concept of Law* (New York: Oxford University Press, 1994), 165.

11 Ibid.

12 Daniel Robinson, *Praise and Blame* (Princeton: Princeton University Press, 2002), 183.

13 John Locke, *Two Treatises on Government*, ed. Peter Laslett (New York: Cambridge Univ. Press, 1988), 271–76.

14 Robinson, *Praise and Blame*, 184.

15 Immanuel Kant, *The Metaphysical Elements Of Justice*, ed. John Ladd (Indianapolis: Bobbs-Merrill Co., Inc., 1965), 102; Immanuel Kant, *The Philosophy Of Law*, trans. William Hastie (Clifton: A. M. Kelley, 1887), 198.

16 H.L.A. Hart, "Murder and the Principles of Punishment," in *Punishment and Responsibility* (New York: Oxford University Press, 1982), 54, 75–76.

17 Rehabilitative goals fit within a system of punishment rooted in retributive commitments. My point is that they cannot morally justify *punishment*; indeed, the concept of "punishment" would be a misnomer. These goals should be seen instead as appropriate incidents of human care for those we have forcibly taken into our custody. One incident of any sentence of imprisonment is the state's

assumption of a paternalistic role concerning the offender, a role which would be wrong for the state to attempt apart from that custodial relationship. Prisoners cannot make many decisions for themselves. Their commercial options are those which the prison makes available to them. Their personal choices are limited by the exigencies of maintaining security in the prison. A prisoner with a drug habit may be obliged to seek treatment, both for his own good and for the sake of those living with him in prison. A man guilty of criminal assault may be filled with abnormal rage and required to attend anger-management sessions in jail, or perhaps even in lieu of jail.

18   This maxim is attributed to Benjamin Franklin, and was first used by the Supreme Court in 1895. *Coffin v. United States*, 156 U.S. 432. For a comprehensive treatment, Alexander Volokh, "Guilty Men," *Pennsylvania Law Review* 146, 173 (1997).

19   Judith W. Leavitt, *Typhoid Mary: Captive To The Public's Health* (Boston: Beacon Press, 1996).

20   Marie Gryphon, "It's a Crime?: Flaws in Federal Statutes That Punish Standard Business Practice," *Manhattan Institute*, December 2009, 12, http://www.manhattan-institute.org/html/cjr_12.htm.

21   Gerard V. Bradley, "Retribution and the Secondary Aims of Punishment," *American Journal of Jurisprudence* 44, (1999): 105.

22   John Finnis, *Natural Law and Natural Rights* (Oxford: Oxford University Press, 1980): 262.

23   One kind of apparent strict liability may be the punishment of the successful offender more than the unsuccessful attempter. This I think can be explained and justified only on the basis, not that the successful is punishable more severely, but rather that the unsuccessful attempter *need not be punished as much* — not because he deserves less punishment retributively, but because the ancillary aims of punishment, especially the reassuring of the law-abiding that they are not suckers, do not call for so much pursuit and reinforcement when the world-order itself, so to speak, has already subjected the offender to its order if not its "will."

Chapter 2

1   Thomas W. Church, Jr., "In Defense of Bargain Justice," *Law and Society Review* 13, (1979): 512.

2   I am speaking about the basic concept of plea bargaining—reduced sentence in return for pleading guilty. No doubt practices on the ground can be, and all too often are, abusive in various ways, not least by prosecutors' practice of so overcharging cases that defendants are practically coerced into accepting a plea offer. I do not here consider the question of *when* any defendant should plead guilty, save that it be *before* trial. It is likely the case that some defendants should plead early, perhaps even at arraignment. Others will rightly wait until certain pretrial motions, including suppression motions, are resolved before entering a guilty plea.

3   As I discuss in Part V.

4   For an account of how these ends may be integrated with retributive considerations

at sentencing, *see* Gerard V. Bradley, "Retribution and the Secondary Aims of Punishment," *American Journal of Jurisprudence* 44, (1999): 105.

5   John Finnis, *Fundamentals of Ethics* (Oxford: Clarendon Press, 1983), 128.

Chapter 3

1   Dan Markel, Jennifer M. Collins and Ethan J. Leib, *Privilege or Punish: Criminal Justice and the Challenge of Family Ties*, at (Oxford: Oxford University Press, 2009): xiii.

2   Ibid.

3   Ibid, xviii.

4   Ibid.

5   Ibid, xv.

6   Ibid.

7   Ibid, 150.

8   Ibid.

9   Ibid.

10   Ibid, 25.

11   Ibid, 25.

12   Ibid, xiii, 94.

13   Ibid, 25.

14   Ibid, 121 (emphasis in original).

15   Ibid.

16   Ibid, xiii.

17   Ibid, 212 n.78.

18   Ibid, 31.

19   *See* Federal Rules of Evidence, §404(b).

20   Markel et al., *Privilege or Punish,* 30.

21   Ibid, 25.

22   Ibid, 28.

23   Ibid, 151.

24   Ibid, 25.

25   This maxim is attributed to Benjamin Franklin. See Alexander Volokh, "Guilty Men," *Pennsylvania Law Review* 146, (1997): 181. The Supreme Court used related formulations as early as 1895. Coffin v. United States, 156 U.S. 432, 455–56 (1895).

26   Markel et al., *Privilege and Punish,* 28–29.

27   The presumption can be rebutted. Occasionally it is unjust to seek the conviction of a person who is provably guilty of a crime. The taxonomy of such occasions and their justification are beyond the scope of this chapter.

28   But this is not always so. One exception is when a civil plaintiff is denied the effective relief to which he is legally entitled by the need to preserve "state secrets," even if they constitute relevant, and perhaps dispositive, evidence in a civil suit.

29   John Finnis, *Aquinas: Moral, Political, and Legal Theory* (New York: Oxford University Press, 1998): 210–11.

30   Markel et al., *Privilege or Punish,* 94.
31   *Ibid,* 89.
32   *Ibid,* xviii.
33   *Ibid,* 95–96.
34   *Ibid,* xviii.
35   Peter Berkowitz, *Virtue and the Making of Modern Liberalism* (Princeton: Princeton University Press, 1999): 173–74.
36   John Rawls, "The Law of Peoples," *Critical Inquiry* 20, (1993): 36, 37.
37   Raz's leading work in this area is Joseph Raz, *The Morality of Freedom* (Oxford: Clarendon Press, 1986).
38   Ibid, 162.
39   *Planned Parenthood of Southeastern Pennsylvania v. Casey.* 505 U.S. 833, 851 (1992).
40   I am grateful to Peter Berkowitz for suggesting this way of mapping contemporary liberalism.
41   Markel et al., *Privilege or Punish,* 61.
42   Ibid, 87.
43   Ibid, 96.
44   Ibid, 89.
45   Joseph Raz, *The Morality of Freedom* (Oxford: Clarendon Press, 1986):162.
46   Markel et al., *Privilege or Punish,* 48.
47   Ibid, 84.
48   Ibid, 21. Feelings of "marginalization" are not necessarily bad if we believe that those who experience them can and will respond to such feelings by adopting more desirable behavior. A full discussion of whether that general principle applies to these particular issues is beyond the scope of this chapter.
49   Ibid, 84.
50   Ibid, 25. "[F]amily ties or status historically facilitate gender hierarchy[,] disrupt our egalitarian political commitments to treat similarly situated persons with equal concern[,] and discriminate against those without families recognized by the state."
51   Ibid, 21.
52   Ibid, 82.
53   The authors have previously contended that all consensual sexual activity should be decriminalized: "[W]e think that in situations where genuine and mature consent between the parties is possible, and where negative externalities can be eliminated, the criminal law should prescind from application." Jennifer M. Collins, Ethan J. Leib and Dan Markel, "Punishing Family Status," *Boston University Law Review* 88, (2008): 1391. Thus they argue against criminalizing incest and adultery. But their consent-driven analysis does not make sense of our criminal law about sex. The claim is also question-begging: its validity depends at least partly upon the truth about the family; if the family is oppressive, then forbidding mutually agreeable sex to *protect* the family is perverse for that reason. But what if the sexually chaste family is a great social and personal good?
54   The authors identify this position and describe it as an *ex ante* "prism" through

which one could see criminal law burdens as protecting and benefiting the "family as a social institution." To this they contrast an ex post "defendant-centered perspective," one that they link intimately to consent. Markel et al., *Privilege and Punish,* 75–79. The defendant-centered perspective emerges—unfortunately, in my view—as the dominant feature of their analysis.

55 I develop this line of thought more fully in Chapter Six.

56 I leave aside domestic violence and the extravagant neglect of parental duties to take care of children; these acts should remain the crimes that they presently are. The relevant questions have to do with their effective enforcement and appropriate punishment.

57 Markel et al., *Privilege and Punish,* 43.

58 Ibid, 149.

59 Ibid, 30.

60 Ibid, 38.

61 Ibid, 58.

Chapter 4

1 Parts IV and V of this chapter were developed in collaboration with Robert George and Patrick Lee.

2 Francis George, "Law and Culture in the United States," *American Journal of Jurisprudence* 48, (2003): 133.

3 Cufford Geertz, *The Interpretation of Cultures* (New York: Basic Books, 1973): 46.

4 Geertz, 91.

5 Ibid.

6 George, 135.

7 Ibid.

8 *Roe v. Wade,* 410 U.S. 113 (1973).

9 *Planned Parenthood v. Casey,* 505 U.S. 833, 860 (1992).

10 Ibid, 856.

11 George, 136–37.

12 *M.L.B. v. S.L.J.,* 519 U.S. 102, 116 (1996).

13 Joseph Raz, *The Morality of Freedom* (New York: Oxford University Press, 1986): 162.

14 Robert P. George, 'Same-sex Marriage' and 'Moral Neutrality,' in *Marriage and the Common Good* (South Bend: St. Augustine's Press, 2001): 93–94.

15 *Perry v. Schwarzenegger,* 704 F.Supp.2d 921, 992 (N.D.Cal. 2010).

16 *Goodridge v. Department of Public Health,* 798 N.E.2d 941, 961 (Mass. 2003).

Chapter 5

1 This chapter is a revised version of an essay which first appeared in volume 50 of *The South Texas Law Review* in 2008.

2 *Goodridge v. Department of Public Health,* 798 N.E.2d 941, 948 (Mass. 2003).

3   Lynn D. Wardle, "Multiply and Replenish: Considering Same-Sex Marriage in Light of State Interests in Marital Procreation," *Harvard Journal of Law and Public Policy* 24, (2001): 800–06.
4   *Goodridge*, 798 N.E.2d at 961–62.
5   *Baker v. State*, 744 A.2d 864, 869–70 (Vt. 1999).
6   *Goodridge*, 798 N.E.2d at 961.
7   *Baker*, 744 A.2d at 881.
8   Nancy K. Kubasek, et al., "Civil Union Statutes: A Shortcut to Legal Equality for Same-Sex Partners in a Landscape Littered with Defense of Marriage Acts," *University of Florida Journal of Law and Public Policy* 15, (2004): 249–50.
9   Nicholas Bala, "The Debates About Same-Sex Marriage in Canada and the United States: Controversy Over the Evolution of a Fundamental Social Institution," *Brigham Young University Journal of Public Law* 20, (2006): 198–99.
10   Ibid, 202–03.
11   Goodridge, 798 N.E.2d at 982.
12   Monte Neil Stewart, "Marriage Facts," *Harvard Journal of Law and Public Policy* 31, (2008): 335.
13   Ibid, 336.
14   Ibid, 346 and n.138.
15   Ibid, 343.
16   *Baker v. State*, 744 A.2d 864, 889 (Vt. 1999).
17   Ann Arbor, Mich., Code ch. 110, ' 9:87 (2001); Cambridge, Mass., Ordinance ' 2.119.020 (1992).
18   An Act Relating to Civil Unions, 2000 Vt. Acts & Resolves 72.
19   *Goodridge*, 798 N.E.2d at 982; *Baker*, 744 A.2d at 882.
20   *Baker*, 744 A.2d at 867.
21   Ibid, 867.
22   Ibid.
23   Vt. Stat. Ann. tit. 15, '1201(2) (2002).
24   *Baker*, 744 A.2d at 881.
25   Ibid.
26   Ibid, at 881–82.
27   Ibid, at 884.
28   *Lawrence v. Texas*, 539 U.S. 558, 605 (2003) (Scalia, J., dissenting).
29   Ibid.
30   *Romer v. Evans*, 517 U.S. 620, 644–46 (1996) (Scalia, J., dissenting).
31   See Chapter Six of this book.
32   *Goodridge*, 798 N.E.2d at 962.
33   Ibid, 962 n.24.
34   Ibid, 962.
35   Ibid, 962.
36   Ibid.
37   *Stanley v. Georgia*, 394 U.S. 557, 565 (1969).
38   *Lawrence v. Texas*, 539 U.S. 558, 578 (2003).

39   Ibid; *Stanley*, 394 U.S. at 565.
40   *Goodridge*, 798 N.E.2d at 964.
41   Tex. Fam. Code Ann. '153.002 (Vernon 2002).
42   *Hernandez v. Robles*, 855 N.E.2d 1, 32 (N.Y. 2006) (Kaye, C.J., dissenting).
43   *Hernandez*, 855 N.E.2d at 7. New York legally recognized same-sex "marriage" by action of its legislature in 2011.
44   *Goodridge*, 798 N.E.2d at 962.
45   Ibid, 1003 (Cordy, J., dissenting).
46   Ibid, 997.
47   Ibid, 998.
48   Ibid, 1000–02.
49   Ibid, 999–1000.
50   Ibid, 999–1000.
51   Ibid, 964.
52   Ibid, 963 (majority opinion).
53   Ibid, 962.
54   *Hernandez*, 855 N.E.2d at 7.
55   Ibid.
56   Ibid.
57   Ibid, 25 & n.13, 30.
58   Ibid, 31.
59   Ibid, 24–25.
60   Ibid, 30.
61   Ibid.
62   *Goodridge*, 798 N.E.2d at 995 (Cordy, J., dissenting).
63   Ibid, 963–64 (majority opinion). The argument against adoption by same-sex couples (and by that I mean two persons of the same gender who are sexually involved with each other) must rely upon precisely the moral hazard which arguments such as "optimal setting" are meant to bypass. Any child placed with a gay or lesbian couple can scarcely be expected to learn by word and by example from his parents the truth about marriage and about the immorality of non-marital sexual conduct. If and when the child is finally exposed to such true teaching, he is placed in the awful position of having to pay the price of repudiating those who nurtured and loved him, if he is to accept and embrace the truth.
64   *Planned Parenthood of Southeastern Pennsylvania v. Casey*, 505 U.S. 833 (1992).
65   Ibid, 851.
66   *Lawrence*, 539 U.S. at 574 (2003).
67   Ibid, 574 (majority opinion) (emphasis added).
68   Ibid.
69   *Casey*, 505 U.S. at 851.
70   Ibid.
71   Thomas Hobbes, *Leviathan* (Richard E. Flathman & David Johnston eds., W.W. Norton & Co. 1997), 72.
72   Ibid.
73   Ibid, 73.

Chapter 6

1   A longer version of this chapter is in volume 91 of *The Monist* in 2008.
2   *Lawrence v. Texas, 539 U.S. 558 (2003).*
3   Ibid, 574.
4   Ibid.
5   *Goodridge v. Department of Public Health*, 798 N.E. 2d 941, (Mass. 2003).
6   Ibid, 948.
7   Ibid, 969.
8   *Lewis*, 908 A. 2d 196, at 221 (2006).
9   The law's summary in part can be found in William Duncan, "Domestic Partnership Laws in the United States: A Review and Critique," *Brigham Young University Law Review*, (2001).
10   Such as the elderly sisters in *Burden and another v. United Kingdom*, ECHR (2006) 13378/05.
11   *In re Marriage Cases, 183 P. 3d. 384 (Cal. 2008).*
12   Vt. Stat. Ann. Title 15, section 1202.
13   Ibid, '1203.
14   *Maynard v. Hill*, 125 U.S. 190, 211 (1888).
15   *Griswold v. Connecticut*, 381 U.S. 479, 482 (1965).
16   Ibid, 486.
17   *Poe v. Ullman*, 367 U.S. 497 (1961).
18   Ibid, 545–46.
19   *Lawrence*, 539 U.S. at 568.
20   Ibid.
21   Ibid.
22   Ibid, 570.
23   Ibid. at 575.
24   Ibid. at 578.
25   Ibid, 585.
26   Ibid, 604.
27   Ibid, 604–05.
28   *Lewis v. Harris*, 908 A. 2d at 221.
29   Ibid.

Chapter 7

1   A similar treatment is Chapter Two of my book *Challenges to Religious Liberty in the Twenty-First Century* (Cambridge University Press: New York 2012)
2   *Van Orden v. Perry,* 545 U.S. 677, 727 (2005) (Stevens, J., dissenting).
3   I treat these doctrines in detail in Chapter Nine of my book: *Religious Liberty in the American Republic* (Washington, DC: Heritage Foundation, 2008).
4   *Van Orden v. Perry*, 545 U.S. at 728.
5   Ibid.

6   This important document is available in many places, including as an Appendix to the Court's opinions in *Everson v. Board of Education*, 330 U.S. 1 (1947).

7   *Muzzy v. Wilkins*, 1 Smith's (N.H.) 6 (1803).

8   Ibid. ("So sect and denomination are in this very paragraph [of the NH Constitution] used as equivalent to the three words, persuasion, sect and denomination.").

9   *Barnes v. Falmouth*, 6 Mass. 401(Mass. 1810) (the Court spoke of the "sect of Roman Catholics [who] are as fully entitled to the benefit of this clause [about Equal Protection of the law in the Mass. Constitution] as any society of Protestant Christians"); *Donahoe v. Richards*, 38 Me. 379, 406 (Me. 1854) (upholding the power of a local school board to expel a Catholic student who refused to read from the King James Bible (not for devotional purposes, the Court found, but as a reader). The *Donahue* court said: "[T]he authorities of the sect of which the plaintiff is a member, regard it as sinful to read in the version directed by the defendants . . .").

10 Very few of the founders were Catholic. Very few founders held that Catholicism could play the role that Protestantism played in a free society such as the one they were endeavoring to create. It would be almost as true for Justice Stevens to say, then, that the Establishment Clause "encompass[ed] the various sects of *Protestantism*," as it is true for him to so of "Christianity." Many of his sources say or suggest the "outsider" status of Catholics, and there is a vast trove of other sources available to the same effect. It is a bit of wonder how Stevens missed this point, or why he chose not to make it (if he did not miss it). Even so (again): never have I encountered an original source from the founding wherein Roman Catholicism was denied to be a "religion," even though an abundance of sources indicate that the founding generation thought that it was a very unappealing, and even perverted, religion.

11 *See* Gerard V. Bradley, "The No Religious Test Clause and the Constitution of Religious Liberty: A Machine That Has Gone of Itself," *Case Western Reserve Law Review* 37, (1987): 688–94, for citations in support of historical references see page 125 of the text

12 3 *Farrand's Records* at 227.

13 Ellsworth's proposal dovetailed with constitutional amendments offered during the First Congress (in both the House and the Senate), to insert the word "other" before "religious test." Neither proposal went anywhere.

14 IV *Elliot's Debates on the Federal Constitution* 215 (1901).

15 Ibid, 196.

16 *See* Gerard V. Bradley, *Church-State Relationships in America* (New York: Greenwood Press, 1987): 85–110.

17 *Van Orden v. Perry*, 545 U.S. 677, 727 (2005).

18 The incongruity into which Stevens fell would stand the founding on its head. By 1789 it was almost universally acknowledged that *everyone* was entitled to the free exercise of religion; that is, *no one at all* was to be forced to confess belief in a creed or to subscribe in some other way to a particular faith. Yet all the states maintained religious tests for office and most states limited public office to

professing Christians. Some excluded Catholics. Article VI was a remarkable display of liberality.

19   Art. LVI. Georgia Constitution of 1777, last modified June 29, 2011, http://georgiainfo.galileo.usg.edu/con1777.htm.

20   Art. XCI. Virginia Declaration of Rights, last modified June 29, 2011, http://www.gunstonhall.org/georgemason/human_rights/vdr_final.html.

21   Section 1 of the *Memorial and Remonstrance against Religious Assessments*.

22   *Barnes v. Falmouth*, 6 Mass. 401 (Mass. 1810).

23   *Van Orden v. Perry*, 545 U.S. 677, 728 (2005).

24   *People v. Ruggles*, 8 Johns 290 (NY 1811).

25   Ibid, 291.

26   *Van Orden v. Perry*, 545 U.S. 677, 729 (2005).

27   Ibid. It is a bit less of a "gotcha" point than Stevens seems to think it is. Justice Scalia has "confess[ed]" (his term) that "in a crunch I may prove to be a fainthearted originalist." Antonin Scalia, "Originalism: The Lesser Evil," *Cincinnati Law Review* 57, (1989): 849. Scalia wrote that he could "not imagine" himself given effect to a judgment imposing the punishment of "flogging," for example, even if he were not convinced that the punishment was contrary to the original understanding of the Constitution. No "confession" needed on this occasion. As the present paper shows, Stevens anti-Semitism charge is contradicted by the historical record.

28   Ibid.

29   J. Story, *Commentaries* 1868 (1970). An unattributed amalgam of Story's observations can be found in H. Rep. 124, dated March 27, 1854, on "Chaplains in the Army and Navy," 6: "At the time of the adoption of the constitution and the amendments, the universal sentiment was that Christianity should be encouraged, not any one sect. Any attempt to level and discard all religion, would have been viewed with universal indignation. The object was not to substitute Judaism or Mahomedanism or infidelity, but to prevent rivalry among sects to the exclusion of others. The result of the change above named is, that now there is not a single state that, as a State, supports the gospel."

30   Report, p. 3.

31   *Van Orden v. Perry*, 545 U.S. 677, 729 (2005).

32   *Philadelphia Mercury,* July 15, 1788, quoted in Strange at footnote 259.

33   Letter dated "August 1790," copy on file with the author.

34   An exception to this pattern is Jasper Adams' assertion (quoted by Stevens in *Van Orden v. Perry*, 545 U.S. 677, 728 (2005)) that the Clause "unquestionably" meant no "preference" by law to "one sect of Christians over every other." This testimony is either contrary to the great weight of the historical evidence, or it is the same mistake as that made by Stevens treating Propositions A and B as equivalent. Contrary to Stevens' suggestion, it is *not* the same testimony as that of Justice Story excerpted just below Adams' quote in Stevens's opinion.

35   This term for laws enforcing Sabbath restrictions came later, in the 1850's when Maine initiated a wave of renewed state laws about the Sabbath. The Maine law was reportedly (and for no reason I discovered) printed on blue paper, hence, "Blue Laws."

36 *Specht v. Commonwealth*, 8 Pa. 312 (Penn. 1848).

37 20th Congress, 2d Session, Jan. 19, 1829, p. 46.

38 *State v. Chandler*, 2 Harr. 553, 577–78 (Del. 1837).

39 *Barnes v. Falmouth,* 6 Mass. 401, 405 (Mass. 1810).

40 *People v. Ruggles*, 8 Johns 290 (NY 1811).

41 *Barnes v. Falmouth*, 6 Mass. 401, 405–06 (Mass. 1810).

42 Ibid.

43 Ibid.

44 *Terret v. Taylor*, 13 U.S. 43, 49 (1815).

45 *Holy Trinity Church v. United States,* 143 U.S. 457, 468 (1892).

46 Even now the vast majority of our state constitutions contain an explicit acknowl-edgment of "God Almighty," and express the people's "grateful[ness]" for God's blessings. *See, e.g.* AL Const. Of 1901, Preamble ("We, the people . . . invoking the favor and guidance of Almighty God, do ordain and establish the following Constitution . . ."); AK Constitution of 1959, Preamble ("We the people of Alaska, grateful to God and to those who founded our nation . . . do ordain and establish . . . "); AR Constitution of 1874 , Preamble ("We, the people of the State of Arkansas, grateful to Almighty God for the privilege of choosing our own form of government, for our civil and religious liberty, . . . do ordain and establish . . ."); CA Constitution, Preamble ("We, the People of the State of California, grateful to Almighty God for our freedom, . . . do establish this Constitution."); CO Constitution, Preamble ("We, the people of Colorado, with profound reverence for the Supreme Ruler of the Universe, . . . do ordain and establish this constitu-tion for the State of Colorado."); CT Constitution, Preamble ("The People of Connecticut acknowledging with gratitude, the good Providence of God, in hav-ing permitted them to enjoy a free government; . . . ").

47 *Donahoe v. Richards*, 38 Me. 379, 405 (Me. 1854).

48 Then Justice Rehnquist defended this alternative, largely on originalist grounds, in his dissent in the 1985 Alabama moment-of-silence case: *Wallace v. Jaffree*, 472 U.S. 38, 91–114 (1985). Justices Scalia and Thomas embraced it in the 1993, in *Lamb's Chapel v. Center Moriches Union Free School Dist.*, 508 U.S. 384 (1993). The present Chief Justice and Justice Alito have yet to make their positions entire-ly clear, though Alito's lower court opinions strongly suggest that he agrees with Thomas and Scalia. While Justice Kennedy has evinced considerable sympathy for (let's just call it) "public religion," he is *not* a "non-preferentialist." Maybe four votes on the present Court for the Incompetence Norm, and no more in the offing.

49 *Employment Division v. Smith, 494 U.S. 872 (1990).*

50 Ibid, 877.

51 *Church of the Lukumi Babalu Aye, Inc. v. Hialeah*, 508 U.S. 520 (1993).

52 *Cutter v. Wilkinson, 544 U.S. 709 (2005).*

53 Ibid, 719 (citing *Locke v. Davey).*

54 Ibid.

55 Ibid. (Citing *Walz).*

56 *Van Orden v. Perry*, 545 U.S. 677, 734 (2005). "We serve our constitutional man-date by expounding the meaning of constitutional provisions with one eye toward our Nation's history and the other fixed on its democratic aspirations." Ibid.

57   The money line connecting Stevens' proposal to what the founders wrought is his claim that the "evil of discriminating against atheists, polytheists[,] and believers in unconcerned deities, is in my view a direct descendant of the evil of discriminating among Christian sects." Ibid. (internal citation to Justice Scalia's opinion omitted).

Chapter 8

1   Reprinted from R. Garnett, A. Koppelman, ed., *First Amendment Stories* (Thomson Reuters New York, 2012)

2   At the heart of "modernism" is the affirmation of religious experience as the primordial stuff of religion; all the world's creeds, doctrines, and cultic practices are more or less adequate-but never definitive-human attempts to express and to memorialize our ineffable contact with the divine. "Modernism" thus implies the falsity of Catholicism's understanding of revelation as including the effective divine communication of propositional truths to humankind. The authoritative Catholic teachings on "Modernism" are *Pascendi Dominici Gregis* ("On the Doctrines of the Modernists") and *Lamentabili sane* ("Syllabus Condemning the Errors of the Modernists"), both issued in 1907. The last of the sixty-five proscribed Modernist propositions sums the matter up pretty well: "Modern Catholicism can be reconciled with true science only if it is transformed into a non-dogmatic Christianity; that is to say, into a broad and liberal Protestantism."

3   La Piana's Butler lectures were published shortly after their delivery in *Shane Quarterly*. They were made available in hardcover book form in 2002 as part of the title *Catholic Power v. American Freedom* (Amherst: Prometheus Books). In a brief and affectionate biographical introduction, Herbert Vetter reports (p. 8) that La Piana "was consulted on church-state issues by U.S. Supreme Court Justice Felix Frankfurter." Frankfurter's early November letter to La Piana is printed at p. 11.

4   La Piana's involvement in the writing of Blanshard's notorious and, to many, deeply anti-Catholic, book was far more extensive than Blanshard's acknowledgment suggested. In a letter to James O'Neill (who had inquired of La Piana about his work on Blanshard's book, but which inquiry La Piana directed Blanshard to answer), Blanshard wrote: "We spent together an afternoon (this was the first time I had the pleasure of meeting him) during which I read to him most of the chapters of my book. He called my attention on four or five of those statements which he judged to be either wrong or inaccurate and referred me to the official or authoritative sources (text-books of theology, of Canon Law and other works) in which I could find the authentic teaching and laws of the Church concerning the questions raised in my statements."

This account was false, as Blanshard told La Piana in a subsequent letter. "[W]hen I sent the original manuscript of Am. Freedom to the Princeton Library at their request, I stressed the part which you had played in examining the work, and said that you had suggested more changes than all other authorities combined.

Blanshard pointed out to La Piana that [the communication to Princeton] would apparently contradict your letter, for it indicates at least two careful readings by you." Letter of Jan. 31, 1951 in La Piana collection at Harvard. The "letter" of which Blanshard spoke was one in which La Piana dictated Blanshard's reply to O'Neill. It is also apparent from their correspondence that La Piana drafted Blanshard's published reply to O'Neill's unfavorable review of *American Freedon and Catholic Power* in the *Cornell Law Review*.

5 Frankfurter's early November letter to La Piana is printed in Herbert Vetter, *Catholic Power v. American Freedom* (Amherst: Prometheus Books, 2002): 11.

6 *Burstyn v. Wilson*, 343 U.S. 495 (1952) is the United States Supreme Court review of the New York decision.

7 *Burstyn v. Wilson*, 303 N.Y. 242, 255 (1951).

8 Ibid, 256.

9 "Spellman Urges 'Miracle' Boycott," *New York Times* (January 8, 1951): 1. The complete text of Spellman's statement is here, on the *Times'* front page.

10 By the time he and Frankfurter collaborated in *Burstyn,* La Piana was convinced that the Catholic Church was at its best when it had a powerful laity to oppose clericalism. In a letter dated November 6, 1948, Frankfurter consoled his friend about papal infallibility: "After all don't you think It's a bit of a comfort to have others relieve one of the responsibility of ultimate judgment. And they have had a long experience at it or, should I say, pretension to infallibility..."

11 A grateful Frankfurter wrote back just as playfully: "But for the fact that there are people who have far less kinship with His Satanic Majesty than you have (isn't that a fair description of your departure from the Faith?) I should have thought that the bug that hit you was divine punishment."

12 On February 4, 1952, to be exact. *Burstyn v. Wilson*, 342 U.S. 930 (1952).

13 Memorandum cover note in Frankfurter papers, HLS.

14 *Burstyn*, 343 U.S. 495.

15 Ibid, 505.

16 Ibid.

17 Ibid, 501.

18 Ibid, 504.

19 Frankfuter's concurrence contains substantial excerpts from La Piana's memoranda to him. There is no mention in it, though, of La Piana or of his published works. The only authors (among the many who have written about *The Miracle* case) who have mentioned the Frankfurter- La Piana connection are William Johnson, in his comprehensive: *Miracles and Sacrilege: Roberto Rossellini, the Church, and Film Censorship in Hollywood* (Toronto: University of Toronto Press, 2008), 328–33; and Andrew Driggs, in his Master's Thesis written at Brigham Young University. "In letters from La Piana, Frankfurter gleaned the information that he included in his memorandum to the Justices and which would make up a substantial portion of his concurring opinion." Driggs, *The Miracle: The Controversy and the Constitution* (1986), 125.

20 Ibid, 507–8 (citing Bosley Crowther, "The Strange Case of 'The Miracle'," *Atlantic Monthly*, (April 1951): 35.

21 Very modestly depicted, by the way. There is nothing prurient or even erotic in *The*

Miracle. No one who opposed its public exhibition suggested otherwise. As many of its defenders pointed out, *The Miracle* was passed by customers inspectors who were at least legally authorized to intercept "obscene" matter.

22 Crowther nonetheless went overboard in describing Magnani's performance as a "shattering *tour de force*" in his review the day after its opening in the December 13 issue of the *New York Times.* Bosley Crowther, "The Screen in Review," *New York Times,* Dec. 13, 1950, 59.

23 Rossellini is justly ranked among the best of Italy's post-war neo-realist directors. His *Open City* and *Paisan* are rightly considered to be neo-realist classics. *The Miracle* represents a break from this genre, though, especially from the neo-realists' emphasis upon social conditions over character development. Rossellini nevertheless relied largely upon non-professional actors for *The Miracle,* a reliance which was another earmark of neo-realism. Rossellini reaped an unexpected reward for doing so. In one scene, "Cosimino, who is Nanni's erstwhile suitor and companion 'village idiot', kicks all her worldly possessions off the church porch... to play this role, Rossellini found a local character who apparently had few inhibitions . . . his retarded-looking physiognomy itself is more 'real' than anything normally seen on the screen at that time . . . during the filming of this scene he went slightly beserk and could not be calmed down. Rossellini wisely kept shooting, . . ." Peter Brunette, *Roberto Rossellini* (New York: Oxford University Press, 1987), 95.

24 For a nativity story, the circumstances of *The Miracle's* birth are curiously murky. The initial push behind the movie was almost certainly Rossellini's wish to develop a star vehicle for Anna Magnani, who was by then (*The Miracle* was filmed in 1948) not only Rossellini's professional collaborator but also his lover. Rossellini's wish was not a case of neo-nepotism; Magnani was (according to one critic of Italian cinema) "the earth mother of Italian neo-realism; a brilliant actress as well as a force of nature." B. Dick, *Hal Wallis: Producer to the Stars,* 140–41. Magnani's breakout role had been at Rosselini's direction in his "Open City." Rosselini and Magnani completed filming *A Human Voice,* Rossellini's adaptation of Jean Cocteau's one-act play, just before shooting *The Miracle.* In *Voice,* Magnani appears alone on screen throughout the film, pleading by telephone with her lover who has abandoned her for another woman.

When Rossellini first described *The Miracle* plot to Magnani, he said it was based upon a Russian folktale. William Bruce Johnson, *Miracles & Sacrilege: Roberto Rossellini, the Church and Film Censorship in Hollywood* (Toronto: University of Toronto Press, 2008): 244. Rossellini later said that Fellini falsely told him it was a Russian story by an author he could not remember. Ibid, 420, n. 7. Rossellini later (in 1954 and in 1970) gave two more very different accounts of the story's origins. Ibid, 245. Peter Brunette, a leading authority on Italian cinema, reports that "one night, Fellini a close collaborator at the time, came up with an idea about a confused and somewhat disoriented goatherd...Convinced that Rossellini would find the story ridiculous, Fellini at first tried to pass it off as the work of a Russian short story writer. But when the director, who had become completely enamored with the idea, was becoming more and more frustrated at not being able to find the story so that he could buy the rights to it, Fellini finally admitted that he made the whole thing up, basing it loosely on a story he had heard many times during his childhood." Brunette, 92.

25 The need to interpret *The Miracle* starts with the opening scene. Here is my account of what is there depicted: "Saint Joseph" takes out what appears to be a bottle of wine. Nanni utters: "My lovely Saint Joseph." She drinks some wine. Then he does as well. She drinks some more. He gives her still more wine. In the English subtitles, Nanni is heard to say: "I'm all sweaty. Even my legs," she says, leaning back. She drinks some more and unbuttons her dress top, showing an undershirt. He touches her hair, leaning towards her. "Give me some more. I feel sick." She rubs her bosom area, as he gives her another long drink. She is visibly affected by the wine, and begins snacking on dirt and grass. She says: "I'd feel better not wearing anything." "My lovely Saint Joseph."

Most observers describe this scene as Nanni's "seduction" by the bearded stranger. Judge Froessel, in his majority opinion for the New York Court of Appeals, described Nanni as "intoxicated." *Burstyn v. Wilson*, 303 N.Y. 242, 257 (1951). On this understanding, the "seduction" is in truth a rape. Film historian Peter Brunnete proposes an almost opposite view of what is depicted. Brunette, 99–100. He sees throughout the scene what he calls Nanni's "ripe sexuality." Brunette maintains, too, that the English subtitles "do not give an accurate picture of just how sexually motivated is Nanni's attraction to 'Saint Joseph'. Her *'quanto sei bello'* ('you are so handsome') is translated once or twice, perhaps, but in fact she repeats it over and over, obsessively, during the course of her monologue . . . it is also clear that she consents because she has been sexually aroused herself. As she drinks more and more wine, she begins to perspire and says at one point, 'I have a fire burning inside me!'." Brunette, [99–100].

One important detail depicted seems to have escaped the notice of all these observers, perhaps partly because its meaning "depends," as Bosley Crowther might say, on one's "point of view." Near the end of the first scene Nanni says "I'm not well." Then the shot shows the view looking up from her prone position. The bearded stranger's shadow looms over her—an unmistakable reference to the Gospel of Luke, in which the angel Gabriel was sent to announce to Mary her favor. "The Holy Spirt will come upon you and the power of the Most High will overshadow you; hence, the holy offspring to be born will be called Son of God." Luke 1:35.

26 Bosley Crowther, "Short-Story Movie" *New York Times* (Dec. 17, 1950): X3.

27 The *New York Times* of January 13, 1951 carried the text of a cable from Rossellini to Spellman. The director wrote: "In *The Miracle* men are still without pity because they still have not come back to God, but God is already present in the faith, however, confused, of that poor, persecuted woman; and since God is wherever a human being suffers and is misunderstood, *The Miracle* occurs when at the birth of the child the poor, demented woman regains sanity in her maternal love." Frankfurter omitted the last line of Rossellini's cable: "They were my intentions and I hope that Your Eminence will deign himself to consider them with paternal benevolence. "Rossellini Appeals to Spellman on Film" *New York Times* (January 13, 1951): 10.

28 At oral argument before the Supreme Court, Burstyn's attorney Ephraim London

asserted (p. 4 of transcript) that all the professional actors were "devout Catholics," just as he had asserted in his petition for review. Frankfurter asserted in his concurrence that "all persons" with "significant positions in the production" "were Catholics." Burstyn, 343 U.S. at 515. But the main professionals involved were Magnani, Fellini, and Rossellini (who both produced and directed *The Miracle*). None could reasonably be described as "devout" in their Catholicism.

Rossellini, for example, "was never a practicing Catholic, but he always admired the ethical teachings of the Church and was fascinated by religious sentiment, which was too often ignored in the materialistic world he inhabited." Peter E. Bonandella, *The Films of Roberto Rossellini,* (Cambridge: Cambridge University Press,1993): 17. Peter Brunette called Rossellini a "religious atheist bourgeois revolutionary." Johnson, 280.

29   Ephraim London, Burstyn's Supreme Court attorney, is one exception. He squarely argued that even if *The Miracle* were sacrilegious, the Constitution precluded prior censorship of it.

30   *Burstyn*, 519.

31   Ibid.

32   *Zorach v. Clausen*, 343 U.S. 306, 313 (1952).

33   *Burstyn v. Wilson*, 278 App. Div. 253, 257 (N.Y. Ct. App. 1951).

34   Mrs. Looram reviewed films for the Legion of Decency from its inception in 1934 until1969.

35   Frank Walsh, *Sin and Censorship*, (New Haven: Yale University Press, 1996): 250.

36   Alan F Westin, *The Miracle Case*, (University: Published for the ICP by University of Alabama Press, 1961): 7.

37   *Forever Amber* was a risque Hollywood costume drama about a woman who slept her way to the top of Charles II's court. Otto Preminger directed it. *Amber* was one of the most expensively produced films of the era. Its protagonist's unrelenting promiscuity (among other grounds) caused the Legion of Decency to condemn the film. Cardinal Spellman denounced *Forever Amber,* too, and warned Catholics to stay away from it in a letter read at all Masses on October 22, 1947. "Spellman Scores 'Forever Amber'" *New York Times*, (October 23, 1947): 36. Other Catholic prelates joined the call to boycott. Bishop James Kearney of Rochester, New York, called *Amber* "a glorification of immorality and licentiousness" on October 27. "'Amber' Scored Up-State" *New York Times* (October 29, 1947): 31. Two days later the local police commissioner ordered the movie's exhibitor to immediately cease showing the film, even though it had been licensed by the state Board of Regents. The commissioner acted pursuant to a local ordinance expressly constituting him a film censor. But the state Supreme Court soon declared that provision to be invalid. *Monroe Amusements v. City of Rochester*, 190 Misc. 360 (1947). The court did not judge the film's content. Its decision rested solely upon the view that the state licensing law-the same as that involved in *The Miracle* case-pre-empted local censorship ordinances such as Rochester's.

The Catholic boycott of *Forever Amber* was nonetheless effective. The producers eventually made cuts substantial enough to relieve it of the Legion's condemnation; thus Burstyn's reference to Mrs. Looram.

38   Westin, 7.

39 The reason for grouping *The Miracle* with (as a matter of fact) Renoir's *A Day in the Country* and Pagnoil's *Jofroi* was purely commercial: none of them ran long enough to constitute a sufficient bill for paying customers. *The Miracle*, for example, is about forty minutes long.

40 "'Miracle' Banned By Regents' Board Court Fight Pends," *New York Times*, (February 17, 1951): 1.

41 "Vatican Views 'Miracle' Row," *New York Times* (February 11, 1951): 4.

42 Bosley Crowther, "The Screen in Review," *New York Times* (December 13, 1950): 59.

43 Walsh, 241.

44 Ibid.

45 Ibid. In reality the relationship was more complicated and less adversarial. According to one unusually perceptive recent student of the Catholic influence upon films: "The Catholic boycotts, the Production Code, and the success of a Catholic movie like "*Going My Way*" illustrate the depth of mutual involvement between two highly organized 20th century institutions: the American Catholic Church and the Hollywood movie industry in the years of the studio system and vertical integration of productions, distribution, and exhibition. Francis Couvares suggested something of th[is] relationship . . . when he wrote, 'the encounter of Church and movie industry was in some degree less a struggle than a mutual embrace, motivated by an urge on the part of both movie moguls and Catholic clerical and lay leaders to defend their institutional interest and achieve respectability and cultural authority in twentieth-century America.' The 'mutual embrace' that Hollywood and the Catholic Church effected during this period, through both organizations' uses of images and rhetoric, helped one another to 'achiever respectability and cultural authority' by giving each other the means to divine mainstream American in the process defining away the American that was historically suspicious of both institutions." Anne Marie Hanlon, "Mass Culture: Catholic Americanism at the Movies, 1930–1947" 2 (2007) (Master's thesis at the University of Maryland).

46 *Burstyn*, 343 U.S. at 532. The studios may have quietly chafed under the Code and the Legion's aegis, but there was money to be made by tacking with—rather than against—the winds of mainstream American culture. Producers shed few genuine tears for "art" sacrificed to the "sects." The really artistic element in Hollywood, on the other hand, largely shared Frankfurter's perspective (though these folks, too, wanted a paycheck which did not bounce). Elia Kazan's directed the movie adaptation of Tennessee William's *Streetcar Named Desire*. Warner Brothers made cuts in his completed film without his knowledge, much less his consent. Kazan's reaction was understandably bitter: "Warners just wanted a [code] seal. They didn't give a damn about the beauty or artistic value of the picture. To them it was just a piece of entertainment. It was business, not art. They wanted to get the entire family to see the picture. They didn't want anything that might keep *anyone* away. At the same time they wanted it to be dirty enough to pull people in. The whole business was rather an outrage." Quoted in Leonard J Leff & Jerold Simmons, *The dame in the kimono : Hollywood, censorship, and the production code from the 1920s to the 1960s*, (New York: Grove Weidenfeld, 1990): 182.

47   *Variety* reported in early 1951 that Hollywood was sitting this one out. "[I]t's because we don't want to get into an open battle with Cardinal Spellman any more than the *Times* does," and that "The MPAA itself would refuse a seal under its self-regulatory code if it were presented. The Production Code is specific in denying approval to a film which offends any religious group." "Crowther Rap Over 'Miracle' Stirs MPAA Bd." *Variety*, (February 28, 1951): 3. *The Miracle* would surely have been denied a Code seal, had Burstyn chosen to seek one. Not even the "cuts" which he dangled in front of Mrs. Looram could have saved it, because the problem with *The Miracle* was overall thematic content, not an isolated flash or bosom or a fleeting expletive.

48   James Skinner, *The Cross and the Cinema* (Westport: Praeger, 1993): 193–94.

49   Johnson, 249. Johnson mistakenly described December 12 as the *second* day of the trilogy's run.

50   Skinner, 98. Skinner assets that Masterson also gave the Police Commissioner a three-page memo of the Legion's objections.

51   McCaffrey was a prominent Catholic lawyer who rose through the ranks of the Catholic Veterans of Foreign Wars, and who was eventually named the National Commander in 1944. He also rose through the ranks of New York politics. He was named New York's First Deputy Commissioner of the Department of Water Supply, Gas and Electricity in 1946. In 1949, McCaffrey was appointed the License Commissioner of New York City.

52   In 1950, for example, McCaffrey suspended a theater's license after an "indecent" performance. Just before *Burstyn v. Wilson* was decided by the Supreme Court, McCaffrey threatened 1,200 newsdealers with arrest if they sold "Sunshine and Health" and "Sun" magazines because of those "nudist" publications indecent nude photos (for example, one of the magazines featured an attractive totally naked young woman on every one of its covers). Those publications filed suit, alleging that McCaffrey had strayed beyond his commissioner's ken. The state Supreme Court upheld McCaffrey's authority to protect public morals. *Sunshine Book Co. v. McCaffrey*, 8 Misc. 327 (1952).

53   Laura Wittern-Keller, *Freedom of the Screen,* (Lexington: University Press of Kentucky, 2008): 112.

54   Thomas M. Pryor, "'Censor' Aim Laid to Catholic Legion," *New York Times* (January 9, 1951): 28.

55   Wittern-Keller, 112.

56   McCaffrey told a *New York Times* reporter that he had received "no complaints concerning the film from any source" and that he had taken the action after viewing it and deciding that it was "blasphemous." Richard H. Parke, "Rossellini Film Is Halted by City; 'The Miracle' Held 'Blasphemous,'" *New York Times* (December 24, 1950): 1.

57   According to Andrew Driggs who personally interviewed Lillian Gerard and inspected her files, she was asked by Pathe to "handle the artistic affairs of the new theater. She was responsible for choosing the films that would play at the Paris and organizing the publicity" Andrew Driggs, *The Miracle: The Controversy and the Constitution*, (Master's Thesis, Brigham Young University, 1986): 125.

58 Richard H. Parke, "Rossellini Film Is Halted by City; 'The Miracle' Held 'Blasphemous,'" *New York Times*, (December 24, 1950): 1.

59 Westin at p. 5.

60 L. Gerard "'The Miracle' in Court," *American Film* 28 (July-August 1977) [hereafter "Gerard Memoir"].

61 *Variety* reported in late December that "Industryites were unanimous over the long Christmas weekend in promising support to the theater and to the film's distrib, [sic] Joseph Burstyn, in a full-scale legal fight." "Industryites Flock to Support of N.Y. Theatre in Ban of 'Miracle,'" *Variety*, (December 27, 1951): 4. They never came through. Less than two months later, Bosley Crowther called them out: "Why hasn't the American film industry shown any public interest in this case?" Bosley Crowther, "A Crucial Issue," *New York Times* (February 25, 1951): 89. The answer appears in note 47 to this chapter.

62 "Mayor Leaves Ban on Film to Court," *New York Times* (December 29, 1950): 36.

63 Thomas M. Pryor, "'Censor' Aim Laid to Catholic Legion," *New York Times* (January 9, 1951): 28.

64 "M'Caffrey, Warned of Injunction, Drops 'Miracle' Ban in 5 Minutes," *New York Times*, (December 30, 1950): 1.

65 *Burstyn v. McCaffrey*, 198 Misc. 884, 886 (1951).

66 "Spellman Urges 'Miracle' Boycott," *New York Times* (January 8, 1951): 1.

67 "Archdiocese Blasts 'The Miracle' Film, Calling It Insult to Faith of Millions Here" *New York Times* (Dec 31, 1950): 23.

68 Johnson says that Spellman relied for relevant information upon Masterson, Mrs. Looram or others. Johnson, 259. I do not doubt that Spellman had help drafting his January 7 remarks; the brief time between their perceived necessity (Steur's decision on January 5) and their delivery less than 48 hours later strongly suggests as much. But Spellman did not rely upon anyone for information about *The Miracle* because there is no such information in his remarks. All that Spellman said about the movie was that it involved the seduction of an idiot Italian woman. The rest of the Cardinal's remarks consisted of argument, opinion, and invective.

69 Auxiliary Bishop Joseph Flannelly (who had read the statement at the Saint Patrick's Cathedral Mass) said that the state Catholic Welfare Conference would seek strengthened censorship laws. Thomas M. Pryor, "'Censor' Aim Laid to Catholic Legion," *New York Times* (January 9, 1951): 28.

70 Sub-committee member Jacob Holtzman dissented from the "unanimous" decision, according to Driggs interview with Holtzman's "close friend" Ephraim London, in August of 1984. Holzman also viewed the film as part of the *en banc* proceeding. Presumably he dissented from that "unanimous" judgment as well. Driggs, 43, 86.

71 Douglas Dales, "'Miracle' Banned By Regents' Board Court Fight Pends," *New York Times* (February 17, 1951): 1.

72 *Burstyn v. Wilson*, 278 App. Div. 253 (1951).

73 *Burstyn v. Wilson*, 303 N.Y. 242 (1951).

74 Even though he had not seen the film.

75 Thomas C. Reeves, *America's Bishop: The Life and Times of Fulton J. Sheen*, (San Francisco: Encounter Books 2000): 251. Monsignor Broderick escorted Cardinal

Spellman to the pulpit of Saint Patrick's Cathedral on December 16, 1956 to deliver his censure of "Baby Doll."

76   Ibid.

77   Bosley Crowther, "The Strange Case of 'The Miracle,'" *Atlantic Monthly*, (April 1951): 36.

78   William Clancy & Eugene Green, *Time's covenant: the essays and sermons of William Clancy*, (Pittsburgh: University of Pittsburgh Press, 1987): viii.

79   Driggs, 47.

80   Walsh, 249–50.

81   *Mutual Film Corp. v. Industrial Comm. of Ohio*, 236 U.S. 230 (1915).

82   Ibid, 241.

83   *Burstyn*, 343 U.S. at 501.

84   Transcript of Supreme Court's Oral Argument for *Burstyn v. Wilson*, 17.

85   *Burstyn*, 343 U.S. at 501.

86   *Mutual Film*, 236 U.S. at 243–244.

87   Wendell Brown asserted at Oral Argument: "As the Court stated in the *Mutual Film* cases, while a motion picture may be a medium of thought, it is not the same thing as speech and writing, to which the First Amendment guarantees apply, and therefore are not similarly protected. But the Court went on to say that motion pictures are capable of evil, having the power which is greater because of their attractiveness, the manner of their exhibition, before mixed audiences of men and women, boys and girls and children, sitting together in the theater." Transcript of New York Court of Appeals' Oral Argument for *Burstyn v. Wilson*, 52–53.

88   *Burstyn*, 343 U.S. at 502.

89   Ibid.

90   "The Court knows from personal experience that the vibrant, vivid, graphic portrayal in a motion picture has an impact that the lecturing platform or the cold type of the written page or the still picture in a magazine does not. Add to that the setting in the which the movie is viewed, the darkened theater, the relaxed receptive audience, the complete concentration on the presentation, the company of a sizable or even vast audience, all simultaneously focusing on the screen, and also the vast number which the motion pictures reach, the wider and less selective audience made up of men and women together with teen-age boys, girls and children, and I think we have the difference in values in potential evil which this Court has said is the reasonable basis for legislative control and which requires differences in the application of constitutional guarantees." Transcript of New York Court of Appeals' Oral Argument for *Burstyn v. Wilson*, 54.

91   *Mutual Film*, 236 U.S. at 241–44.

92   *Burstyn*, 343 U.S. at 502.

93   Ibid, 505.

94   Clark quoted approvingly from the dissenting opinion of Judge Fuld of the New York Court of Appeals. Fuld claimed that *The Miracle* "makes no direct ...criticism of any religious dogma or principle. . . ." Ibid, 504. The Court may have again been misled by London, who asserted at argument that "[a]ccording to the Regents' interpretation of this picture it profanes the doctrine of the divine birth of Christ and indicates that he was actually illegitimate and not a divinely conceived being.

If that be true, and we say it is not, but if that be true that statement is entitled to the protection of the Constitution because the Constitution protects not only state-ments of religious belief but statements of religious disbelief." Transcript of Supreme Court's Oral Argument for *Burstyn v. Wilson*, 28.

95   *Burstyn*, 343 U.S. at 505 ("[T]he state has no legitimate interest in protecting any or all religions from views distasteful to them. . .").
96   *Winters v. New York*, 333 U.S. 507 (1948).
97   *Burstyn*, 343 U.S. at 501 (quoting *Winters*, 333 U.S. at 510).
98   *Burstyn*, 343 U.S. at 504–05 (footnotes omitted).
99   Ibid, 505.
100 Ibid, 526.
101 Ibid, 530.
102 Ibid, 530–31.
103 Ibid, 505–06.
104 *Freedman v. Maryland*, 380 U.S. 51 (1965).
105 The five decisions and the movies which they saved from the censors' bin are: *Gelling v. Texas, 343 U.S. 960 (1952) (Pinky*, a story of interracial friendship); *Superior Films v. Ohio*, (*LaRonde*) and *Commercial Pictures v. Regents of New York*, (*M*) 346 U.S. 587 (1954); *Holmby Productions v. Vaughn*, 350 U.S. 870 (1955) (*The Moon Is Blue*); *Times Film Corp. v. Chicago*, 355 U.S. 55 (1957) (*Game of Love*).
106 *Kingsley v. Regents of New York*, 360 U.S. 620 (1959).

Chapter 9

1   A slightly different version of this chapter appears in Allen Hertzke, ed., *The Future of Religious Freedom* (Oxford: Oxford, 2013).
2   Kent Greenawalt, "Coercion and Religious Exercises," in G. Bradley, ed., *Challenges to Religious Liberty in the Twenty-First Century*, (Cambridge: Cambridge University Press, 2011).
3   *People v. Ruggles*, 8 Johns. 290 (NY Sup. Ct. 1811).
4   *State v. Chandler*, 2 Del. 553, 577B78 (1837).
5   *Burstyn v. Wilson*, 343 U.S. 495 (1952).
6   John Witte. "Soul Wars: New Battles, New Norms" *The Review of Faith & International Affairs*, 5, no. 1 (2007): 13–19.
7   Sarah Claerhout & Jakob De Roover, "Conversion of the World: Proselytization in India and the Universalization of Christianity" in *Proselytization Revisited*, edited by Rosalind Hackett, (London: Equinox, 2010) 68.
8   *Church of Lukumi v. Hialeah*, 508 U.S. 520 (1993).
9   *Sherbert v. Verner*, 374 U.S. 398 (1963).
10   Gerard V. Bradley, "Beguiled: Free Exercise Exemptions and the Siren Song of Liberalism," *Hofstra Law Review* 20, (1991): 245–319.
11   *Employment Division v. Smith*, 494 U.S. 872 (1990).
12   *Church of Lukumi v. Hialeah*, 508 U.S. 520 (1993).
13   Bradley, "Beguiled: Free Exercise Exemptions and the Siren Song of Liberalism," 245–319.

14   Gerard V. Bradley, *Religious Liberty in the American Republic*, (Washington, DC: Heritage Foundation, 2008), 1–21.

15   *Employment Division v. Smith*, 494 U.S. 872, 890 (1990).

16   *Barnette v. West Virginia*, 319 U.S. 624 (1943).

17   *Wisconsin v. Yoder*, 406 U.S. 205 (1972).

18   18 U.S.C. 3597(b) 1994.

19   Sec. 728 of Title VII of Division C (Financial Services and General Government Appropriations Act) of the Consolidated Appropriations Act, 2010, Pub. L. No. 111–117.

20   Sec. 811 of Title VIII of Division C (Financial Services and General Government Appropriations Act) of the Consolidated Appropriations Act, 2010, Pub. L. No. 111–117.

21   Barack Obama, "Obama's Commencement Address at Notre Dame," *New York Times*, May 17 2009, http://www.nytimes.com/2009/05/17/us/politics/17text-obama.html.

22   I am grateful to Christopher Tollefsen for pointing out this conscience challenge.

23   Robert George, *Making Men Moral: Civil Liberties and Public Morality* (New York: Oxford University Press, 1993), 48–82.

24   Ian Leigh, "Homophobic Speech, Equality Denial, and Religious Expression," in *Extreme Speech and Democracy*, edited by Ivan Hare and James Weinstein, (New York: Oxford University Press, 2009), 375–76.

25   Leigh, 375–76.

26   Reference re; Same-Sex Marriage, (2004) 3 S.C.R. 698 (Can.).

27   Civil Marriage Act, SC 2005, ch. 33 ,'3, 3.1.

28   Iain Benson, "The Freedom of Conscience and Religion in Canada: Challenges and Opportunities," *Emory International Law Review*, 21, no 2 (2007): 146.

29   Robert Matas, "Catholic school denies firing lesbian teacher," *The Globe and Mail* (Toronto, Canada), April 29, 2010.

30   Jeff Lee, "Sexual orientation led to firing, teacher claims," *Vancouver Sun* (Vancouver, Canada), April 29, 2010.

31   Human Rights and Equal Opportunity Commission, *Report of Inquiry into a Complaint of Discrimination in Employment and Occupation*, HRC Report No. 6, 1998.

32   *Catholic Care (Diocese of Leeds) v. Charity Commission for England and Wales & Anor*, [2010] EWHC 520 (Ch) (17 March 2010), para. 16.

33   Ibid.

34   *R. (Amicus) v. Secretary of State for Trade and Industry* [2004] EWHC 860 (Queen's Bench Division) (Administrative Court) para. 104.

35   *Lawrence v. Texas*, 539 U.S. 558 (2003).

36   Ibid, 575.

37   *Goodridge v. Department of Public Health,* 798 N.E. 2d 941 (2003).

38   Daniel Avila, "Same-sex Adoption in Massachusetts, the Catholic Church, and the Good of Children," *Children's Legal Rights Journal* 27, no 3 (2007): 1B47.

39   Daniel Avila, "Same-sex Adoption in Massachusetts, the Catholic Church, and the Good of Children," *Children's Legal Rights Journal,* no 3 (2007): 13.